MW00442907

# We Have a
# No Crash
# Policy!

## A pilot's life of adventure, fun, and learning from experience

### ADAM L. ALPERT

AVIATION SUPPLIES & ACADEMICS
NEWCASTLE, WASHINGTON

*We Have a No Crash Policy!*
by Adam L. Alpert

Aviation Supplies & Academics, Inc.
7005 132nd Place SE
Newcastle, Washington 98059-3153
asa@asa2fly.com | asa2fly.com

© 2019 Aviation Supplies & Academics, Inc.

All Rights Reserved. No part of this publication may be reproduced, stored in a retrieval system, or transmitted in any form or by any means, electronic, mechanical, photocopy, recording, or otherwise, without the prior written permission of the copyright holder.

None of the material in this book supersedes any operational documents or procedures issued by the Federal Aviation Administration, aircraft and avionics manufacturers, flight schools, or the operators of aircraft.

**ASA-NO-CRASH**
ISBN 978-1-61954-858-9

Printed in the United States of America
2023   2022   2021   2020   2019        9   8   7   6   5   4   3   2   1

Cover art and watercolor paintings © Christina Lesperance

Photographs © Adam Alpert

Color version of the watercolors and some of the photographs featured in this book can be viewed on the **Reader Resources** page for this title by visiting **asa2fly.com/NO-CRASH**.

# Contents

# Dedication

Aviation, like all technical subjects, employs a special vocabulary of words, terminologies, and acronyms. There is also pilot-specific language used for communicating while flying, largely incomprehensible to those not trained and practiced. Taken together, the learning curve for anyone seeking even a vague understanding of the discipline seems insurmountably steep. Some aviators would have it no other way. Perpetuating the mystery is part of what makes the pilot persona appealing. There are others, though, like Captain Robert N. "Bob" Buck, Sr., author of *Weather Flying* and many other aviation books, who are only too happy to demystify the discipline in an effort to promote safety, utility, and better understanding.

*We Have a No Crash Policy!* is a personal memoir of flying stories from over forty years. It is also a meditation on a learning process made possible by people like Bob, and later his son Robert O. "Rob" Buck, an accomplished aviator in his own right, along with the many excellent instructors, mentors, and friends who helped me along the way. Their insight and generosity is what inspired me to write this book.

It is often said that adversity and error make for a great teacher, especially in hindsight. It has been, therefore, a guilty pleasure to write about missteps in planning, judgment, and all the things that went wrong. While bad decision-making in isolation can't be applauded, acknowledging mistakes, and the learning opportunities they present, suggests an interesting connection, especially for those open to questioning their own abilities.

While there are many ways to address novel and often complicated topics, I have found using relatable examples to be the most convincing. Many of the stories, therefore, stem from real life events. But the academic aspects should not be discounted. For every pilot who has inadvertently blundered into a strong, dangerous thunderstorm, there is, somewhere, a convective weather scientist standing by ready to deliver a postmortem on the convergence of events. Together they offer the best opportunity to learn and improve.

Mostly, though, aviation is about romance. What other technology reveals the magnificence and beauty of the earth as seen from above while simultaneously providing expedited transportation across vast distances to faraway exotic places where opportunity and adventure await? Just the joy of guiding a light aircraft to a perfect landing on an unimproved grass strip is worthy of mention. The mastery of amazing levitating machines, plying the skies in glorious flying ships, is a form of magic.

My father, Norman Alpert, fought in the Philippines as an Army Lieutenant during World War II. He contracted hepatitis there and barely survived the nearly three years of hospitalization that followed. He went on to earn a PhD in physiology from Columbia University and became a world-renowned expert in heart disease. In his spare time, he started a small life science company, BioTek Instruments, that over time blossomed into a multi-million-dollar enterprise, all while raising three kids with his loving wife Laurel in rural Chittenden County, Vermont.

Dad also was a romantic in the sense that he viewed science and technology as vehicles for achieving a more renaissance appreciation of the world. For Dad, the pursuit of knowledge and truth was paramount. The process, as opposed to the end result, was his focus. While fact-based guidance is key to flying, Dad's approach to continuous learning is worth considering. Given that there is no flying school that can address all contingencies, and all circumstances, it is up to the pilot to figure out the rest.

Dad liked to say "Onward and upward." Those three words have influenced my flying and other pursuits for as long as I can remember. Ever the optimist, he was propelled to move forward and do better.

I dedicate this book to my father; not just a survivor, but also a doer of great things, a truly inspirational role model. We should all be so fortunate to have someone like him in our lives.

# Acknowledgments

Writing a book and getting it published is a daunting task. Had I known the degree of difficulty prior to starting the project I never would have begun. So perhaps the notion ignorance is bliss deserves more consideration for those of us operating with less than unlimited willpower and drive. Likely more important to the cause, however, is the support and advice generously offered by others.

The story begins with Karen Jacques, BioTek's technical publications manager, who demonstrated much enthusiasm even while tirelessly editing the variably composed early trade journal articles that served as a practice forum for my writing of this book. It was also Karen who did the final review of the edited manuscript to make sure that my voice, with all it's blemishes, was not accidentally removed in the course of professional editing.

Blemishes aside, I am most grateful to my editor Ellen Bartlett who reappeared in my life after a forty-two year post-high school hiatus during which she worked for many prestigious newspapers including the Boston Globe. She applied much needed continuity to the writing, fixing all the grammar (and spelling) problems known to plague C+ students through the course of their grade school, high school, and even college English writing courses.

Fellow authors Ken Adelman and Stephen P. Kiernan deserve special mention. Knowing the challenges associated with a first book effort, they helped me identify likely publishers and then craft the perfect query letter for submission. You are reading these words largely because of Ken and Stephen's generous contribution.

Much credit goes to my reviewers F-16 fighter pilot Lt. Col. John "Wily" Rahill, TWA Boeing 747 Captain and fleet manager Hobie Tomlinson, and Falcon 900EX senior captain Paul Middlebrook. Collectively, they assured the concepts described were both valid and relevant, claims factually correct, while also providing practical insight into a broader range of career-linked flying experiences.

Captain Robert O. "Rob" Buck, also mentioned in the Dedication, was very kind to read early versions of the first several chapters. His honest critique and guidance to properly identify the good, bad, and ugly helped shape much of the subsequent writing.

I thank my very talented illustrator, Christina Lesperance, for her infinite patience puzzling through all those many unfamiliar aviation scenarios depicted in the beautiful watercolor drawings dawning each chapter. Fortitude, an idea discussed in this book, comes to mind when I think about Christina's contribution.

The star of the show, however, was my wife Gisela. Not only did she provide unending encouragement during the course of a project that seemed at times to be unending, she also lent herself to be the subject both in fact and as part of writing for many of the stories told. For this, she has my enduring gratitude.

# 1 | A Child's Dream

The three of us struggled to get the glider through the sliding door that led to the second-floor balcony at Eric Neunmann's house, in our Hyde Park, Chicago, neighborhood. Eric's parents had left for the day, assuring final assembly and testing could be completed undisturbed. This would be our first flight, and my younger brother Briar, the test pilot, age five, was willing but also apprehensive. Knowing he was the lightest of the three of us and therefore the obvious choice somehow wasn't reassuring. The one-story drop loomed large—the Grand Canyon, for all practical purposes. Fortunately, Briar had his big brother and friend there, to provide encouragement. Eric and I, being all of eight years old, were exceedingly confident.

The aircraft itself had been constructed out of discarded cardboard boxes, cut to size and taped together with packing tape. It was a delta wing design, tapered wings, narrow in front, expanding to a width of nearly eight feet at the back. Each wing had a tail, located at the wing tip, extending vertically about one-foot high. The small pilot's seat, also cardboard, was set on top, at the center point of the aircraft. Various creases running lengthwise provided rigidity, much like the creases in a conventional paper airplane, on which we had based our design.

The plan was simple. Eric and I would lift the aircraft onto the balcony railing. We would balance it, prior to flight, while the test pilot seated himself. When all was ready, Eric and I would provide the necessary forward propulsion—a shove—for takeoff.

Of course, looking back on this fateful day there is a temptation to ask the question: what could go wrong? The design team, consisting of Eric and me, had no formal schooling in aerodynamics, structures, or propulsion. Neither of us had worked on an aircraft of this size, let alone designed to carry people. Briar, the pilot, had no pilot training. Nor had he, at this point, ever been in an airplane. There had been no wind tunnel tests, or really any testing at all. The aircraft had no safety systems, not even a seat belt. To the extent that we did have experience with model aircraft, even the carefully-constructed balsawood toy planes we had flown prior to this mostly ended up crashed and broken, or caught in a tree. Yet, at the time, it all seemed reasonable—a reoccurring theme in many aircraft accidents, as it turns out.

The harsh reality is that accelerating from a fixed position to flying speed requires more than a shove by two eight-year-old boys. Rather than gliding gracefully to

*Adam and Briar, "the brothers," ages six and three-and-a-half.*

a soft landing on the lawn, the aircraft, with my brother on top, nosedived into the prickly bushes below, sprawling the branches in all directions. Eric and I ran downstairs to render whatever aid we could.

The intensity of the crying that greeted us ensured that we would not be the only ones at the scene for long. Neighbors from the adjoining units converged, along with others who had witnessed it all from the adjacent

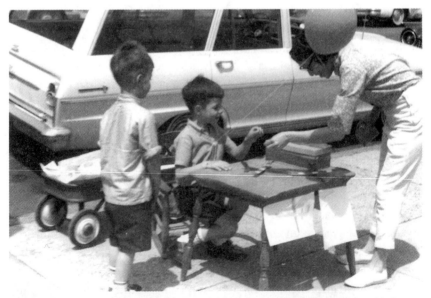

*Early entrepreneurs—the brothers establish a stand to sell home manufactured balsa model gliders.*

playground. It was a hard landing, for sure. Fortunately, the bushes had broken the fall. Briar emerged from the crumpled glider scratched, bruised, and furious, but otherwise okay.

Any possibility of a cover-up ended on our return home to Mom and Dad, my brother in need of antiseptic, multiple bandages, and vengeance. It became clear that someone would have to pay—me.

The exact nature of my punishment is a bit hazy after all these years, but it almost certainly was a record. I remember my mother being particularly upset, going so far as to restrict access to toy airplanes for a while. Much later in life, when I asked for a loan to attend flying school, she turned me flat down, saying she didn't want to finance the vehicle of my death. It also took many decades before Briar regained sufficient confidence to be willing to climb into one of my airplanes.

In the years following the cardboard glider adventure my enthusiasm for flying never waned. I built and flew hundreds of small model airplanes. Those flights were precarious for a different reason. Due to the lack of safe places for children to play in Chicago, much of the flying took place over busy city streets. The family's move to Vermont in the mid 1960s marked a huge improvement in flying safety, just due to the availability of open space and the absence of fast moving automobiles.

Vermont also brought about an even more exciting aviation development. Much to the consternation of my mother, my father, who had taken a few flying lessons during our time in Chicago, decided to go in on the purchase of a Cessna 172 airplane with several of his University of Vermont colleagues, in order to pursue his private pilot's license. I was delighted, of course, but my mother would have nothing to do with it. And she made it clear to my father that under no circumstances would the children be allowed to fly with him.

Buying an airplane wasn't the only thing Dad did that upset my mother. Soon after the plane, he surprised her with a giant St. Bernard named Ski Puppy—175 pounds with an enormous head exuding drool down to the floor. On winter days, the drool would freeze forming drool-cicles, perfect fun for the children who liked to invite the chronically damp dog into the house to play. Immediately upon

*Ski-Puppy.*

entering, the dog would shake, accelerating frozen drool into orbit around his mouth and nose until the drool, having melted and reached escape velocity, would fly off into space, onto Mom's white walls. I liked the dog almost as much as airplanes!

I was eleven when I abandoned airplanes briefly, to focus on rocketry. Amazingly enough, Estes, the model rocket company based in Colorado, sold not only rockets but also the chemical engines that made them go, all transportable via the US Postal Service. They were advertised as safe because the ignition system was based on an electric design—no fuses to light. So while Dad was busy as chairman of the Department of Physiology and Biophysics at the University of Vermont, and working on his pilot's license in his spare time, I was also busy dutifully building rockets, like NASA limited only by the budget: my allowance.

The rockets escaped detection for a long time. They didn't look like airplanes. To the unsophisticated eye all the kits appeared to contain was a collection of odd-sized cylinders, refreshingly innocent, likely sourced from a craft store. Further, I was careful to do the building secretly in my room, while conducting launches in the large open parade ground by our new home at Fort Ethan Allen, in the small Vermont city of Winooski. Whether my mother had any idea what was going on was unclear. I do recall her being delighted that I was playing outside instead of watching TV, my other favorite pastime.

I also have to acknowledge the benefit of attending private school—Overlake Day School. It was during science class that Mr. Robinson, who also was the school's principal, introduced me to the hobby of rocketry. He wasn't the best science teacher, and likely no more than an average principal, but he was inspirational and he served to further my aerospace ambitions in a big way.

Mr. Robinson had resources, as evidenced by the enormous model rocket inventory in the science lab. He had monster rockets like the Saturn V and Gemini spacecraft. He also had all the fancy engines, some of which had heavy boost and multi-stage capability, and he had no fear of using them. Plus, some of his rockets had cameras—Estes *Camroc*—capable of taking photographs at altitude, which was remarkable for the time in 1967. He taught me how money, the US Postal Service, and a catalog could deliver the latest in missile technology, or really anything for that matter. A year later, I was in seventh grade when I learned the school would be closing due to financial problems. I was pretty sure I knew where all that expensive tuition had gone. Priorities: Mr. Robinson was my hero.

The Estes company rocket engines were remarkably reliable, and clever, too. They came in the form of a high-density paper cylinder, about two-and-three-quarter inches long and a little less than three-quarters of an inch in diameter. Packed inside the lower part of the cylinder was a gunpowder-like propellant, leaving room in the upper part for a small delay charge and an ejection charge used to deploy a parachute. The idea was to return the rather pricey rocket safely back to earth for reuse.

After many successful launches I wanted to learn more about the engines, and how they worked. The instructions that came with the rockets contained certain recommended safety measures, emphasizing the importance of maintaining distance between the rocket and mission control (me). This made it very difficult to observe exactly what was going on. And once the rocket was at altitude, there was no way to see anything about the delay and ejection charge. I was determined to remedy that.

The first step in this experiment involved building a test stand to facilitate watching the working engine up close. I used available materials, including some of the packing provided by Estes for shipping the rockets and engines, to mount one of the more powerful engines to the shipping container—the box, provided by Estes—using Scotch tape. I then fastened the box to a small table, using multiple loops of kite string. The plan was to ignite the rocket engine, as specified by the manufacturer, almost exactly as had been done many times before on the parade grounds, just sans rocket, and in my bedroom.

It was a very exciting day. When I energized the igniter, I had no idea how loud the engine would be in the confines of my small room. And the stream of fire that shot out the nozzle must have been six feet long. Just long enough to reach the mattress pillow and set it on fire. Then came the delay burn. By this time, the room already had filled with smoke, but it was the ejection charge that sealed my fate. With the tape holding it now weakened, the engine let loose of the box, at high speed, and embedded itself in the wall, slightly above the tropical fish tank. Panic, an acknowledged danger in flying (and one discussed later in the book), followed, though I did manage to solve the burning pillow problem courtesy of a nearby open window. The damage to the sheet rock wall, and the smoke that permeated the house for days, that was a different matter.

The punishments I endured felt like overreactions, somewhat unwarranted, but they were opportunities for improvisation. With my fleet of airplanes and rockets grounded, I devised a skateboard-based aircraft using string. This flying machine had the novelty of being completely devoid of any motors or chemicals. By accelerating the skateboard in an arc, revolving around me, I was able to reach sufficient airspeed to attain lift. (During college physics classes, I learned that centripetal acceleration also was a factor.) While most kids were hell bent on riding their boards down some steep and scary stretch of road, I was fixated on endless twirling, revolution after revolution, watching the effect of board attitude controlled by the attached strings on its tendency to rise and/or fall, in due course. In fact, the skate board served as an excellent empirical introduction to angle of attack, and commensurate lifting forces—ideas that are discussed in subsequent chapters. Unfortunately, these experiments were not entirely error free. The boards and wheels in those days were heavy, easily 15 to 20 pounds, so to fly them required high energy. When the strings let go, as they did occasionally, the results were unpredictable. Happily, there were no injuries during my skateboard twirling period, and only a few dents in the cars in the lot, which were addressed by my father, with a combination of outstanding diplomatic skills and an accompanying open checkbook.

The model airplane flying eventually resumed and I was even allowed to go for a few rides with my father in the C-172 once he obtained his pilot's license. At the time, I thought the flights were great, but years later, and subsequent to completing my own flying license, I realized how difficult it

would be for the average untrained person to see the overall safety picture. Nothing terrible happened flying with my father over the years, beyond getting temporarily lost a few times and being yelled at by air traffic control for turning on the wrong taxiway, once or twice. I also remember arriving at an airport somewhere in need of fuel only to discover we had no more than $1.90 in cash (I supplied the 90 cents). Fuel was a lot cheaper in the '60s, but not that cheap. Still, away we flew, with the bare minimum of fuel needed to get home, well below the ideal reserve.

*Dr. Norman Alpert—onward and upward.*

The occasional missteps notwithstanding, I remember Dad as cautious and smart about his flying. Unfortunately, he suffered from a lack of currency (recency of experience) as a pilot, largely due to his demanding university job and Mom's lack of enthusiasm for the activity. Ironically, Mom thought less flying was a good idea, reducing his exposure to risk. But with flights too few and far between, it became increasingly difficult for my father to retain needed flying skills, and to remember all the rules and procedures for making our trips predictable and safe. Currency is a potential problem for any pilot, but none more so than someone with low hours. I knew nothing of this at the time, of course, and only wished for more flights, even with the occasional exciting moment.

When we moved from Winooski to Shelburne in 1969, Dad and his partners sold the airplane. Mother and I experienced opposite emotions. I was very sad. In hindsight, it was the right thing to do. Dad just wasn't flying enough to be safe. The loss of the C-172 did serve one purpose, however. It inspired resolve: I was going to find a way to fulfill my flying dreams, one way or another. To the extent there was any danger flying with my father, I would discover new ways to take it up a notch. From bumps, bruises, lacerations, and occasional near-death experiences, new aviation wisdom was born.

**Lessons learned:**

**Lesson 1:** Thinking you understand something is different from actually understanding it.

**Lesson 2:** Improvisation leads to unpredictable results.

# 2 | **The Rogallo Days**

**W**e had a ritual before afternoon flight practice, when the timing was right, of stopping by the milking parlor. The cows at Shelburne Farms estate, where my high school friend Robert lived, were Brown Swiss, a breed known for producing a rich delicious milk, made more so when fresh. Talk about farm to table: this was udder to cup, self-service. Risky? My scientist father had warned me repeatedly that drinking raw, unpasteurized milk was fraught with danger. The way we drank it, straight from the cow, put us at even greater risk of exposure to E. coli, Listeria, and multiple other nefarious bacteria. Curiously, the peril we faced launching ourselves off local cliffs, hills and mountains, attached to a variety of home-constructed gliders never came up in these conversations. My father left that to my mother.

The northwest sector of the farm was our preferred testing ground for new designs and assemblies. There, we could take advantage of the relatively steep relief, and because the hill faced west, toward the prevailing winds, conditions were favorable for foot-powered takeoffs. Unlike the Chicago days, these aircraft benefitted from "engineering" and came in kits manufactured by companies like Eipper Formance, which was known at the time for hang glider/kite designs. Our job was merely to assemble the various bits and pieces according to the plans provided.

The first aircraft was based on the work of a NASA scientist, Francis Rogallo. In 1948, he invented a flexible "parawing" as an alternative recovery system for the Mercury and Gemini space capsules.[1] The parawing, later known as a Rogallo wing, was delta shaped, formed by a rigid or semi-rigid frame with flexible fabric serving as lifting surface, much like a parachute, with the payload suspended below. But unlike most parachutes, the Rogallo wing offers significant efficiency advantages. In the form of a glider, the wing delivers good travel distances as a function of release height, also

---

[1] Rogallo, Gertrude Sugden and Francis Melvin Rogallo. Flexible kite. US Patent 2,546,078, filed November 23, 1948, and issued March 20, 1951.

known as lift over drag ratio (L/D). This is one of the reasons NASA originally saw promise in the idea.

Rogallo wings are also relatively easy to construct. In the case of the NASA application, the system used inflation to obtain rigidity. Other implementations, including ours, used poles and wires to obtain rigidity. All of this was well within the capabilities of a couple of high school students. Although Rogallo's design never saw its way into space, it was put to good use in the 1970s, in the proliferating sport of hang gliding. The word *hang*, of course, reflected the way the payload, or person in this case, connected to the wing. The typical hang glider featured a seat with a safety belt, suspended like a swing from the center point of the glider. For greater aerodynamic efficiency, there was a harness system that allowed the pilot to fly prone once airborne.

Our first kite from Eipper Formance came in one giant cardboard box. The loosely packed contents consisted of several long aluminum tubes, a few bags of hardware—nuts, bolts, brackets, etc.—and a large delta-shaped white Dracon sail with sleeves to accommodate the various tubes that formed the wing's delta shape. There was a smaller vertical aluminum tube, the king post, that mounted above the wing, and a triangular control bar below that, along with various wires, giving the craft its structure. It all seems primitive in hindsight, but at the time, I was enthralled by the complexity of the design.

I did most of the work of constructing the aircraft, but operating it was definitely a two or more person activity. Robert and I had limited ground transportation in the beginning, so just getting the kite to the launch site was a slog. After each flight, there was the chore of getting the glider back to the top of the hill, wrestling the awkward 100-pound craft by hand up a steep incline.

In addition to the instructions on how to build the glider, the kit manufacturer provided a five-page photocopied manual explaining the principles of flying.

I hadn't felt the need to read the manual in advance, but I did think to bring it for the first flight, in case there were any questions. In fairness, we weren't entirely naïve. Both of us had observed others engaged in the sport. And some of the flights we'd seen had been launched from high cliffs, not relatively gentle hills like ours. More to the point, we focused on the important things in our observations, e.g., launching, control while in flight, landing technique. I remember thinking to myself, "How hard can this flying thing be?"

Designing an aircraft that can be controlled, and then learning how to control it is much of what flying is about. This was one of the first challenges the Wright Brothers faced—it is still key to making even most advanced airliner or fighter aircraft safe and effective—and it applied to our simple Rogallo wing hang glider. But there is more than one way to do it. Conventional aircraft are equipped with some form of elevator, aileron, and rudder, operated by the pilot to alter pitch, roll, and yaw, respectively. Most hang gliders have none of those things. Hang glider pilots control their craft by shifting their own weight. It's an idea that originated in 19th century Germany, with Otto Lilienthal, a German pioneer of aviation who became known as the *flying man*. He was the first person to make well-documented, repeated, successful flights with unpowered aircraft.[2]

Unlike the flexible Rogallo wing, the wing of Lilienthal's early glider was rigid, modeled after the wing of a stork. But he employed the same weight-shifting technique. There were many advantages to doing it this way —simplicity being the main one. But there was one important disadvantage. To have "weight" you have to have gravity. Take gravity away, and there is no weight. There is also no control. Lilienthal died in 1896 flying one of his hang gliders. According to witnesses, he suddenly shifted his weight forward, causing the glider to dive. When he shifted back toward the rear of the glider to arrest the descent nothing happened. The glider continued its plummet, killing Lilienthal shortly after impact.

The explanation for Lilienthal's crash lay in his control strategy. The dive had rendered him weightless. Nothing happened when he shifted back toward the rear of the glider, because the forces normally in play due to gravity were absent. In freefall, there may be mass, but there is no weight. Without weight, there is no control, an inherent flaw in the hang glider design.

Weight dependent control is not limited to hang gliders. There are a number of helicopter manufacturers that employ similar schemes. Some helicopter designs, including Bell's iconic JetRanger and Robinson's R22 and R44, still rely on the effects of gravity to maintain control.

When flying helicopters, the issue is more about the blade system needing to be loaded (feeling the weight of the helicopter below). In cases where the blade system is accidentally or deliberately unloaded—when the pilot performs a rapid dive—loss of control can occur. This is due to the way

[2] "DLR baut das erste Serien-Flugzeug der Welt nach," Deutshches Zentrum für Luft- und Raumfahrt, February 11, 2016, https://www.dlr.de/dlr/desktopdefault.aspx/tabid-10280/385_read-16705/year-all/#/gallery/21944

the blades of the JetRanger and like kind are connected to the rest of the aircraft. The helicopter fuselage is suspended from the blade system, much like a ball suspended from a string. Subject the ball and string to a zero-G environment—freefall—and it is anyone's guess where the ball would end up. Under zero-G conditions in a helicopter, the blade trajectory is unpredictable. The blades could contact the fuselage, or even break off entirely (something called *mast bumping*) with disastrous results. Many crews and passengers have been lost in this way over the years.

Our early hang glider flights were short. After a running takeoff, we would almost immediately lose altitude, and inevitably settle back onto the ground. Part of the problem was the hill. It was steep, but not steep enough. The wind also played a role. The headwind made it easier to reach flying speed and provided some orographic lift—a kind of mechanical lifting caused by the rising terrain—but it also slowed our progress away from the hill. Without very precise piloting, most flights ended quickly, somewhere near the top of the hill. The answer: find steeper, bigger hills. Problem solved!

With the launching issue resolved, there was the matter of controlling the glider in flight. Independent of the concern about loss of gravity, controlling a glider by shifting weight is slow, so the pilot needs to plan ahead. There is also the problem of turbulence—chaotic wind gusts caused by terrain, thermals, and in rare cases, wave and its associated rotor, a kind of wind harmonic discussed in future chapters that is triggered by larger land features like mountains, often with tremendous energy.

Reflecting on the Rogallo days, it is a miracle we didn't die. Robert had many crashes, especially in the beginning. They usually started with an uncorrected pitch up, followed by a sudden dive left or right. In all cases abrupt ground impact followed. I was better at control. Most of my crashes were related to my inability to slow to running speed on landing. On one flight, I landed nose-first, colliding with the aluminum control bar at nearly full speed. That really hurt. A typical flying day concluded with multiple bruises, lacerations, and much repair needed. Fortunately, our injuries were minor, mostly because we didn't fly much higher than we were afraid to fall. It also helped to be young. But hang gliding is a notoriously dangerous sport. Over the course of the one to two years we flew them, we heard of many hang glider pilots who were lost or seriously injured. In our case, happily, it was mostly about having a good first-aid kit and a supply chain of materials to effect repairs.

Later in my life I had a second hang glider, a more conventional rigid wing like Lilienthal's. But hang gliding was unsatisfying, from a flying perspective. The time spent flying—compared to fixing and lugging the thing around—was just too short. It is interesting to note that over the course of the 2,000 glider flights Lilienthal conducted before his death, he only achieved five hours, total time, of flying.[3] I wanted to do better.

I never actually got sick from drinking raw milk from the cows, though my father remained convinced they presented a mortal danger. His view was that I was lucky, and perhaps he was right. Sometimes surviving errors in judgment is a path to better future outcomes, especially when there is acknowledgment of the error, and proper action taken.

Putting my hang gliding days behind me, uninjured, was a huge success. And I have been drinking pasteurized milk ever since.

## Lessons learned:

**Lesson 1:** Observing an activity remotely is not a certain path to success.

**Lesson 2:** Sometimes, parents are right.

---

[3] "From Lilienthal to the Wrights." Bernd Lukasch, Otto Lilienthal Museum, accessed January 8, 2012, http://www.lilienthal-museum.de/olma/ewright.htm

# 3 Sugarbush:
## A Glider Story

Flying conventional gliders was a big upgrade from the hang glider days. Not having to drag the aircraft up a hill to launch represented a huge improvement. Also gone was the constant need for a first-aid kit. But because gliders are "real" aircraft, regulated by the Federal Aviation Administration, there is a formal process to be followed to fly them including ground school, an FAA-authored written test, and a practical test given by the FAA or its designee.

There are number of soaring schools where this can be accomplished. The school I selected was the Sugarbush Air Service, located in the beautiful Mad River Valley near Warren, Vermont. Its owner and manager, John Macone, was a promoter, a character right out of *The Music Man*, except John's wares weren't instruments and sheet music. John was about creating amazing and sometimes perilous aviation adventures for an eclectic assortment of followers. I became a follower. Although truly scary things happened during my glider, and later airplane flying days at Sugarbush, my flying overall benefitted from having been schooled there. Few of us get to experience (and address) feelings of panic on such a regular basis.

When most people think of conventional gliders, they think of flying a motorless aircraft designed to descend slowly to the ground. But that would be selling the activity short. Not only are modern gliders very efficient, given the right conditions and weather they are capable of climbing above their launching altitude simply by using available air currents, also known as lift. It is under these conditions that a glider becomes a sailplane, and gliding becomes soaring, all courtesy of the energy in the atmosphere.

Gliders do need a bit of a push to get going. Instead of using foot power for a running start from a hilltop, gliders normally are towed by airplanes, or they are hauled aloft using ground based winches and in some cases automobiles. (Fast-forward to today, some are self-powered, known as motor-gliders.) Gliders have enclosed cockpits styled somewhat like airplanes. They look like airplanes, too, with wings, horizontal stabilizer, and vertical tail fin. But the key difference between the glider and the hang glider is the control system. Gliders, like airplanes, employ a three-axis system controlling separately for pitch (nose up or down), roll (left or right about the axis of the fuselage), and yaw (tail wagging left or right). The introduction of the three-axis system represented a big improvement in safety because control is accomplished aerodynamically independent of attitude and G-forces. Lilienthal might have lived to old age had his craft benefitted from these improvements.

Sugarbush Air Service used Cessna L-19 Bird Dog aircraft to tow their gliders aloft. The airplane had quite a legacy. It was originally used for forward observation in the Korean and Vietnam wars. Although the L-19 is a safe aircraft, wartime losses were high because the missions were mostly behind enemy lines, at low altitudes and relatively slow speeds—around 110 knots cruising speed. A shot from an assault rifle could bring one down.

The qualities that made the Bird Dog vulnerable in Vietnam, however, work to its advantage towing speed limited gliders. Problems with the L-19 extend mostly to keeping the airplane going straight while on the ground during landing or taking off in a crosswind. Ground loops (essentially a complete loss of directional control) in conventional gear (e.g., tail wheel) airplanes like the L-19 are more common than generally acknowledged, sometimes resulting in significant damage to the aircraft. Successful L-19 pilots learn very early that there is no such thing as too much rudder.

Fortunately, ground loops happen on the ground at relatively slow speeds. The greater danger, for the glider pilot, comes early in the tow, just after takeoff. Rope breaks and premature rope releases due to tow plane malfunctions are rare but they do occur. In most cases, the experience is startling, but manageable. In the event of a rope break at more than 500 feet above ground level (AGL), the right answer is to do a 180 and return to the airport, landing in the opposite direction. At 700 feet or higher, a normal landing pattern is possible. But when the rope breaks on a turbulent day, just after takeoff, when the glider is still low, possibly over trees, with no prospect of reaching an open field straight ahead, that's another story. I can confirm that making a 180-degree turn, after a rope break 250 AGL, is pretty exciting.

There is much debate in glider flying circles regarding the correct action when a rope breaks, or the tow plane engine quits, close to the ground. The training teaches a return to the airport providing the altitude above the ground is above 200 feet. Under ideal conditions a skilled pilot can make this work, but in turbulence and high winds the outcome is far from certain. Turning back to the airport risks loss of control, a classic stall spin accident. There was an accident at Sugarbush during my time there, in which a pilot elected to return to the airport after a rope break with insufficient altitude. While in the turn, the left wing contacted the ground, causing the aircraft to cartwheel across the runway. Both the pilot and her passenger were seriously injured. My own personal rule is to land straight ahead no matter what unless AGL altitude is equal to or greater than 300 feet.

"There is lift somewhere out there, it is just a question of where." Early in training, my instructor, Mike Ball, explained the Zen of soaring in terms of an intellectual and practical quest to identify sources of lift by studying variations in geography, atmospheric conditions, and sun energy. I found his approach unsatisfying, initially, with many (most) of my flights ending in a rapid descent back to the airport. My skills improved over time, but there was still much mystery to solve. Too often lift seemed out of reach while the sink was omnipresent. The key was monitoring altitude above the ground and not getting too low. Prudence demanded that a good field or airport be within safe gliding distance at all times.

The day of my glider practical test, the *checkride*, Mike had me perform all the likely maneuvers an examiner might request. These included everything from boxing the wake of the tow plane—essentially flying a square shaped pattern around the area of turbulent air created by the tow plane's propeller and airframe—to an emergency rope break at 250 feet followed by a 180-degree turn back to the airfield. Mike's preparation was thorough, and the checkride went well. What happened later that day, though, served as a reminder that testing well is one thing—mostly about knowing the right answer to any question asked. Expertise, experience, and judgment are something else.

As we walked back to the staging area to celebrate my success, Mike noted that the afternoon's wave was building. The shape of the lenticular cloud above suggested rising air in the lee of Sugarbush Mountain. If the sky's appearance was any indication, there would be an elevator waiting, capable of lifting a properly positioned ship thousands of feet skyward.

On a good soaring day, Mike was one to get his hands on an aircraft. Surveying the beckoning afternoon sky, it was no surprise when he suggested we forgo the champagne in favor of another flight. "You take the club's 1-26," he said. "I'll get the 1-34, and let's see if June will join us in her 1-26." I hadn't thought about another flight, but the euphoria of passing the checkride had not worn off, and there's no better way to celebrate a new rating than to use it. Further, with only 12 hours total flying time under my belt, this would be my first wave experience. How exciting was that!

June Moon was an instructor and avid aviation enthusiast. It took no effort to persuade her to join us. She was already at the staging area with her beautiful white Schweitzer ready for departure. "See you up there," she said as she strapped in.

Mike prepared his 1-34. In its time, the single-seat Schweitzer 1-34 was considered very high performance, meaning its L/D ratio was high and minimum sink rate low. Both convert into longer cross-country distances and greater endurance aloft.

The 1-34 had clean lines and was fully aerobatic. This was in stark contrast to the lower performance club 1-26 I was flying. And unlike June's ship, rebuilt from scratch and newly painted, my 1-26, 92U, while mechanically sound, showed the effects of time with its fading yellow paint and scratched canopy. But in wave flying, minimum sink rate matters more than cosmetics or gliding distance. When it came to getting the most climb rate out of the weather, the single-place club 1-26 was a star.

The tow planes lined up for connection to the cascade of waiting sailplanes. June had just taken off. Mike was next. The line person connected the tow rope to his ship and gave acknowledgment. Soon the 1-34 was rolling and off. Now it was my turn. I set the altimeter to zero, the custom for sailplanes restricted to the local airport, and completed the last phase of the checklist just in time to give the thumbs up to the wing runner, followed by a wag of the rudder to signal ready. With similar rudder acknowledgment from the tow plane I was on my way.

The 1-26 broke ground quickly and soon we were climbing at an incredible rate. Although the L-19 tow plane is powerful and the 1-26 light, the 2,000 feet per minute climb rate could only be explained by the weather, specifically, wave weather. Further, the climb rate was increasing, not typical with increasing altitude during the tow.

I'd arranged to be towed to 4,000 feet above ground level. Other pilots reported success entering the wave at lower altitudes, but I wanted more buffer. At 3,500 feet some puffy cumulus clouds appeared. No big deal, I mused as we passed 3,800, 3,900, finally reaching 4,000 feet. I pulled the release and peeled off to the right. The variometer, an instrument designed to indicate the rate of climb or descent, was pinned at 1,000 feet per minute up—indeed, just like an elevator. The mountain fell away far below. The small, single-person glider and I floated, seemingly motionless, with an indicated airspeed no greater than 45 knots.

Wave lift is arguably the most interesting of the three forms of lift available to sailplanes. Unlike ridge and thermal lift, wave imparts its lifting energy via a harmonic referred to as a standing wave because the rising (and descending) air tends to stay in the same place relative to the ground and the triggering obstruction. Much like the ripples in a river, downstream from a rock that is just below the water's surface, large undulating airwaves can be created by the impact of wind on a mountain ridge. But unlike ripples in water, mountain triggered wave can build high into the atmosphere, producing lift on the rising side that often reaches altitudes many times greater than the enabling land form. There can also be secondary and tertiary waves. Similar to the primary wave located just to the lee of the mountain, secondary and tertiary waves create lift many miles downwind.

In the afternoon sun, the thin layers of stratus to the west turned a brilliant yellow-orange hue. Similarly, there was colorful formation above, but unlike the clouds over the mountain these took on the form of the wave itself. It was like viewing an upside-down ocean, motionless, with swells larger than any sea.

Mike was putting the 1-34 through its paces, executing one inside loop after another, and June quickly joined in. I wanted to make it the Three Musketeers, but the combination of no parachute, no aerobatic training, and little sailplane experience in general caused prudence to prevail.

I decided instead to climb. I wanted to gauge the wave's maximum amplitude. The variometer read 600 feet per minute so, unlike the experience at the lower levels, the trip up was a bit slower. Still, Mike and June were soon left far behind as I climbed to 8,000 feet and beyond.

By the time I reached the wave's top, at a little less than 10,000 feet, I could barely see my friends below. Wisps of clouds, which had formed at all levels, partially obstructed the view. It was also getting darker, especially to the west where the setting sun had nearly disappeared behind a horizon of gray fog hovering over the mountain.

There is a moment, a sudden sense of concern, like a shiver. Nothing bad has happened yet, but the feeling intensifies quickly, from ominous to impending doom. What had been a scattered cloud layer below was consolidating, looking more broken every second, with the ground partially obscured. This was worrisome. Further, Mike and June's sailplanes, security blankets of a sort, had vanished. It was time to descend. The deployment of full spoilers and dive brakes produced a slow descent rate of 500 feet per minute. This was far slower than the 800 to 1,000 feet per minute I'd expected. The wave was still working and, if anything, getting stronger.

And there was a new problem. What holes there had been in the broken cloud layer were disappearing. In the forming undercast, there would be no way to determine the ship's orientation or location during the descent. I had no instrument training and the instrument panel in the 1-26 contained just a compass, altimeter, variometer (indicating vertical speed), and forward airspeed indicator. Penetrating the cloud would be a guess at best.

I pointed the nose toward one of the larger holes and hoped it would stay open long enough to get through. Below and to the west was a 4,000-foot mountain; there was a 3,000-foot ridge close by to the east. The prospect of descending through an opaque cloud deck between the two was becoming both more likely and increasingly unappealing.

At 6,000 feet it was clear the hole would be very small or gone by the time I reached it. We hadn't talked about flying in clouds in glider school. Still, there seemed to be three options: 1) remain aloft until the weather improved, 2) descend through the clouds in a spiral dive trying not to over-stress or overspeed the aircraft, or 3) spin the sailplane through the clouds and hope that the ceiling would be sufficiently high to allow for a recovery.

Given enough time, waiting for the weather to improve might have worked, but it was late afternoon and soon the grayness would turn into blackness. I didn't want to add the challenge of night to what was already a serious emergency.

The small footprint of the spiral dive and spin maneuvers assured a bet-ter chance of avoiding the mountain and ridgeline. But both had their pit-falls. The spiral dive solution meant monitoring both the compass, to gauge the rate of turn, and airspeed to avoid overstressing the aircraft. Even with full spoilers and dive brakes deployed, there was still the specter of a struc-tural breakup. The spin, basically a pilot-induced asymmetric aerodynamic stall, would be relatively gentle in comparison, but for this maneuver to work there would have to be enough distance between the ground and the ceiling to recover. And as the name suggests, there was the possibility of suffering from vertigo while turning rapidly through the cloud deck.

Approaching the undercast at 4,000 feet, I saw the last hole disappear. Given that the wave was still working I debated loitering in hopes of find-ing another hole. But the undercast was getting thicker. Waiting would just make the descent without visual reference longer.

Using a vague sense of my position relative to the last clear opening, I committed to the descent. Using full spoilers and dive brakes I began the spiral dive at a rate of one complete turn every 20 seconds. I wanted everything stabilized before entering the cloud. Airspeed was increasing, but slowly. The combination drag from the spoiler dive brake system was inhibiting acceleration.

Descending through 3,900 feet, 3,800, 3,700, puff, then total gray, as the ship entered the cloud layer. I froze the stick to produce a constant rate of turn and indicated airspeed just below red line. The altimeter read 3,500 feet, I was below the mountain. It was dark. At 3,000 feet it started to rain with large droplets onto the canopy. Still no sign of the ground. At 2,000 feet, I wondered whether my flying would come to a catastrophic end with only thirteen and a half hours total time.

Finally, at 1,800 feet above ground level, I broke out of the clouds, disoriented from the spiraling dive in the dark, but the ship was right side up, in one piece, and flying. And I could see the ground. I got my bearings. Amazingly, I was only a quarter mile from the airport. The emergency descent through the clouds had worked!

My landing was nowhere near perfect, but I was *down*. A small crowd approached 92U. Mike and June were there with disapproving looks. "You were very lucky," Mike scolded. "The examiner wants to talk to you."

At this point, so early in my flying career, I wasn't sure how licenses were revoked, but the end seemed inevitable. This will be some kind of record, I thought. How many people both obtain their private pilot's license and lose it in the same day?

The examiner was actually generous in his assessment of my wave adventure. After complimenting me for not getting myself killed, and warning me not to get caught on top again, he said the experience of seeing the weather go from good to bad so rapidly served as an excellent lesson. And so it did.

Reflecting on the conditions that day, I learned that visible moisture, and the unsettled weather often associated with it, can form spontaneously in one place. Mountain waves are excellent laboratories for the study of such phenomena because their inherent structure is relatively stable. The nature of the weather within therefore is determined by subtle changes in temperature, dew point, and other factors like the angle and intensity of the sun.

Happily, both the pilot and his license survived to see another day. This was early education, with many learning opportunities to come.

## Lessons learned:

**Lesson 1:** Passing the test is mostly about knowing the right answers to the questions. Flying safely requires recognizing the absence of knowledge and then taking the steps necessary to correct. All pilots experience scary puzzling events. Good pilots experience the same scary puzzling events no more than once—twice, worst case.

**Lesson 2:** Weather doesn't move, it forms as local conditions, such as air pressure, temperature, and humidity, change.

# 4 | Learning to Fly Airplanes

still have a soft spot for soaring. There is nothing quite like spiraling upwards in a thermal, sometimes in the company of a red-tailed hawk. Robert Buck, Sr., the accomplished aviator and author, once told me that "We fly gliders because of the weather, not in spite of it." He was right. There is a special satisfaction that comes from harnessing the atmosphere's boundless energy to achieve sustained flight. But there are limits, and utilitarian considerations. While it is possible to travel considerable distances in a glider, on air currents alone, the route is often circuitous, because of the often irregularly located sources of lift. There is also the inconvenience of occasionally landing off-field when there is no lift to be found. For travel from A to B, gliders have their limits. And when the weather is stormy, it is better to tell soaring stories in the hangar, *hangar flying*.

Airplanes are different primarily because there is a motor providing consistent energy, propulsion, "in spite of the weather." Travel from A to B really is from A to B, most of the time. The trips aren't just faster because the glider's zig-zag course is replaced with a straight line. Much of the speed improvement comes from the optimization of airframe and engine to favor speed over minimum sink rate. This is why most airplanes descend quickly as engine power is reduced. Not surprisingly, much training is devoted to learning what to do when the engine quits.

The practicalities of airplanes aside, my interest was more rooted in the romance of flying. The idea of being propelled skyward to exotic faraway places was exceedingly compelling. And the role of the captain, master of the machine, was intriguing. Once off the ground, the captain assumes final authority over everything necessary to assure a safe flight. And, yes, I was convinced that pretty girls would go for pilots, a suspect conclusion as it turns out.

Gliders and airplanes have much in common. Guidance of the aircraft is governed by similar control surfaces: ailerons, elevator, and rudder. The airplane is different from the glider in the effect engine power has on control, and the typically higher loading of lifting surfaces. A higher wing loading allows for faster airspeed. In exchange, the aircraft can feel, and be, more squirrelly, harder to control in some cases. At near aerodynamic stall—a slow speed, with a high angle of attack—an abrupt power change can cause a spectacular loss of control event. This is especially true of larger propeller driven aircraft with high wing loading and powerful engines. During World War II, many P-51 Mustangs were lost due to overly aggressive application of power on takeoff. P-factor and torque imparted by the motor to the fuselage overwhelmed every effort by the pilot, employing aileron, elevator and rudder, to control the plane. Pilots also had to deal with the phenomenon of gyroscopic precession, referred to in physics as angular momentum, caused by the massive, rapidly turning 450-pound propeller. Coupled with torque and P-factor, takeoffs in the P-51 could be very challenging indeed.

Early in my training, learning about recovering from a practice aerodynamic stall—normally a safe and predictable exercise—I scared the bejesus out of my instructor, Bob Glenn. Teaching flying can be exciting, right up there with dodging bullets in terms of adrenaline rush.

The scenario in play had us throttling back, slowing the airplane to the point where the wing would stop providing lift. The goal of the exercise: to recognize the onset of the stall, and then perform a controlled recovery, restoring the airplane to normal flight.

Recalling that fateful flight in the school's classic two-seat Cessna 150, a high wing monoplane training aircraft, a reasonable person might conclude that the student was trying to kill the instructor. At the point where the stall was imminent, I applied full power combined with application of right aileron to address a left roll. As the aircraft rolled more to the left, I felt my heart leaping into my throat. My reaction: add more right aileron. My aggressive attempt at control had us instantaneously upside down, in an accelerating spiral dive, the ground below rapidly approaching. Early instructor intervention occurred. Saved!

Reflecting on the event, a combination of P-factor and torque associated with the propeller accelerating clockwise, and insufficient rudder in the opposite direction (right), precipitated the left roll. Mostly, though, it was my enthusiasm for an extreme right aileron input without lowering the nose that sealed our fate, or would have, had Bob not intervened. Here we have the unfolding of a classic stall/spin/spiral dive accident. If not for the buffer of altitude, always employed when practicing stall recoveries with students, a crash almost certainly would have resulted. Bob and I lived to fly another day. Still, there was a mystery. How could this routine maneuver result in such a dramatic loss of control?

The scientific answer is rooted in the nature of the three axis control system that replaced Lilienthal's weight shifting scheme, as well as the concept of angle of attack and lift capacity. The abrupt right aileron input, the left wing control surface itself being deflected downward, angle of attack in the vicinity increasing dramatically, caused the left wing to stop flying. Hence the spin entry. Lift capacity is the key. Given a specific wing design, airspeed, and loading, there is always a maximum lift capacity. Exceed the lift capacity available and the wing will stop flying. In the case of the correction for the roll left, my application of right aileron effectively increased the load on the left wing, asking it to lift more than it could given the relatively slow airspeed. Rather than lifting the wing back up to level flight, it ceased flying altogether.

Perhaps more interesting than the aerodynamics in play is the emotional component. When the airplane flipped over, the initial feeling was astonishment, followed by abject terror. Both reactions are a window into the emotions experienced by pilots when all hope is lost.

Removing reckless flying and catastrophic mechanical failure from the list of probable causes, most accident chains start out innocently with the pilot believing that there is nothing wrong with the plan. Only at the very end, when the airplane is trapped in a level 4 thunderstorm, or on the verge of fuel starvation, or stuck with ceilings and visibilities deteriorated below forecast, or beyond the pilot's or airplane's capabilities, does reality set in. In the last few minutes of the flight, consumed with feelings of despair and puzzlement, the pilot ultimately succumbs to fate.

Bob actually went on to fly Aérospatiale Lama helicopters in support of mountain and ambulance missions in Norway, and then served as a police detective in Anchorage, not always the safest occupation, but perhaps less stressful than teaching student airplane pilots.

There were many scary moments training to fly airplanes at Sugarbush, some more life threatening than others. The most memorable occurred during one of my early solo flights. (The solo is a milestone in the training during which a student pilot is permitted to fly the airplane alone when sanctioned by the instructor, but without an instructor on-board.) On this particular summer day, the skies were clear, winds down the runway a steady 15 knots. It was a perfect flying day. The takeoff, in Sugarbush Air Service's C-150 N2930S, was textbook, and the climb out well-rehearsed, only with a better than typical rate of climb due to the absence of the instructor. Suddenly there was a loud bang, followed by a noticeable loss of power. The airplane shook violently, as motor oil streamed down the pilot's side door. Bad! Then panic set in.

Until this flight, strangely, I had never experienced true panic in my life. It's a terrible feeling. Worse is the side effect of incapacitation, the loss of ability to think clearly and take appropriate action for some period of time. In this case—my first solo and my first engine failure—it seemed like eternity. In reality, the delay was likely short, probably 10 seconds. Still, 10 seconds is a long time when in two or three minutes the airplane is going to be on the ground somewhere.

In a fog, I ran through the emergency checklist procedures in a clumsy attempt at restoring normal power. With oil streaming aft in copious quantities, this was really about hoping against hope. No success! To the extent there was good news, the engine was still running, barely. And, because the airplane had climbed faster, due to its sans-instructor lower gross weight, it was at a higher than usual altitude. The airport was also a little closer, due to the brisk headwinds in the direction of takeoff. I performed an immediate 180-degree turn hoping to get blown back to the airport with enough altitude to land (or crash) somewhere on the field.

There has been much discussion in aviation circles over the years about the merit (or lack thereof) of "turning back." Unlike gliders, airplanes without power experience a relatively high rate of descent, so to make the maneuver work starting altitudes have to be high, 1,500 feet or more above the ground. There is also the danger of loss of control during the turn, caused by poor aileron/rudder coordination, wind shear, steep bank angle, and a host of other factors. Having logged about fifteen hours of total airplane experience at the time of the incident, I knew little of this. Although we had talked about stall/spin accidents during glider training, most of the focus had been on avoiding them. In the case of both junior glider and junior airplane pilots, maintaining proper airspeed and staying in the traffic pattern serves as  an excellent defense against spins and other unforeseen dangers. Most of the time all is well. But when something surprising happens, like engine failure, followed by an improvisational, perhaps incorrect action initiated by the pilot, all bets are off.

Ignorance must be bliss, because both the student and airplane made it safely back to the airport. Having the benefit of a partially working engine, the turn had worked with a more or less normal traffic pattern and landing to follow. Not all are so lucky. Shortly after my adventure, a Taylorcraft pilot attempting a steep uncoordinated turn to Sugarbush's south runway lost control and augured-in. He lived to fly another day, but only after an obligatory trip to the hospital. In the case of the Taylorcraft, the story was mostly about flying technique. No prior emergency had transpired. Still, poorly executed maneuvers near the ground can have very bad outcomes.

The cause of the engine failure in the C-150 I was flying did not remain a mystery for long. The airplane's O-200 engine had received incorrect spares during a recent repair. Whether it was rings with the wrong tolerance, an incorrectly sized seal, or some other cause, I had clearly suffered from another Sugarbush Air Service improvisation; the degree of malfeasance unclear. Knowing virtually nothing about engines, I was left to accept John Macone's explanation. Macone, also the field mechanic, said that sometimes parts borrowed from engines of similar type are not always the same. "They looked the same", he said, a mea culpa of a sort.

How quickly anger, disappointment, worry, and fear can be replaced by a sense of accomplishment. John and the others showered me with accolades for the save. Everything had worked out. It helped to be young—twenty-year-olds enjoy a certain sense of invulnerability.

Far more troubling was the seeming normalcy of the event. No one was particularly surprised (or concerned). It wasn't the first time one of Macone's airplanes had had a problem. Not until many years later did I realized how foolish I had been. It would have been better if I had dismissed the praise, and demanded a little more from Sugarbush's maintenance department. Still, it was the panic experience that left the lasting impression. Awful as it was, debilitating, this first encounter with panic would serve me well.

My training wasn't the only source of excitement at Sugarbush Air Service. I recall a student mistakenly landing on a taxiway after being cleared for one of the runways at Burlington International Airport about 26 nautical miles north of Sugarbush. The taxiways at BTV are at least 50-feet wide, compared to the 35-foot wide runway at Sugarbush. The student exclaimed that the taxiway was the most pavement he had ever seen. Fortunately, there were no vehicles or other aircraft on the taxiway. It probably helped that everyone involved, including the controllers, were students—lots of empathy. When it comes to complying with the rules, student pilots are given a lot of leeway, the consequences of unintentional violations largely falling on the shoulders of the instructor. (So if a violation of the Federal Aviation Regulations is in your future, it would be a good idea to get that sort of thing out of the way during the student pilot phase of your training.) In the case of the taxiway incident, I recall the instructor getting at least one scolding telephone call from the tower. I am not quite sure what happened after that.

The controllers at Burlington committed occasional violations of their own. My favorite involved the "misuse" of the Automatic Terminal Information Service (ATIS) system. The ATIS, available at all terminal (tower-controlled) facilities, transmits a recording on a unique frequency that pilots use to ascertain weather, runway(s) in use, closed or inoperative facilities, and other information pertinent to operating at the airport and in the surrounding airspace. The pilot typically acknowledges receipt of the information by saying the phonetic letter associated with the message when calling "approach" and prior to entering the airport's airspace; e.g., "have information Bravo." This tells the controller the pilot has the right version of the ATIS and is familiar with all the information needed to operate safely to and from the facility. On the day of the ATIS incident, I was making a short flight from Sugarbush to Burlington to practice touch-and-go landings. To my surprise there was an advertisement for an Old Town canoe "for sale, used" tagged on to the end of the recording. At the time, I thought "how creative." Unfortunately, creativity and improvisation are not always rewarded in aviation. The controller advertising the canoe got in a lot of trouble.

I completed my private pilot rating in 1976, for a total cost of $742.94. That is approximately $3,231 in today's dollars—a bargain compared to the expense of doing the same thing now at a modern flight school.[1]

While not quite apples to apples, the cost of recurring annual training for flying our (my chief pilot and I) Citation Jet 4 (CJ4) is about $10,000, and both of us are already type rated in the airplane. Larger jets cost much more. This is just to show how complex and expensive flight training has become since the Sugarbush days. Why so? While it is theoretically possible to complete primary flight training by demonstrating the traditional skills associated with basic navigation (dead reckoning and by visual ground reference), radio communication, and basic airmanship ability, even the most basic accreditation, limiting flying to daytime in good weather in light single-engine aircraft now requires competence in automated flight management systems (FMS), engine graphic monitor systems (EGMs), advanced autopilots, and in some cases even ballistic recovery systems (BRS)—a giant parachute for saving the day when all else fails. This is not to mention dealing with an increasingly congested and complicated airspace and mastering the many new federal aviation regulations that have been promulgated since 1976. Everything has to be learned and demonstrated.

---

[1] 2017, at the time of writing.

Some aspects of flying have gotten easier, and better, as the technology has improved. In my experience, aviation weather forecasts are about 85 percent accurate in a time span of 24 hours. Still, terminal aerodrome forecasts (TAFs), the weather predicted for individual airports, generally go no farther than 30 hours. This may be due to the influence of trial lawyers looking for opportunities to find fault with forecasts, or a rapid reduction in accuracy three, four, or more days out. More likely, the shorter forecast horizon is an acknowledgment that most flights are shorter than 24 hours. No need for the longer forecasts.

The delivery of the forecasts is over the top. Even light training aircraft like the C-150 have a full menu of weather products in the cockpit, and in near real time. But the bigger menu means more to learn and understand, and the rating challenge gets harder. Training addresses these and other aspects of the ever-expanding discipline, much more for the pilot to master than in my day. I had spent 28.4 hours in an airplane and 58.4 hours total time, including in gliders, when I took the private pilot practical test. Today, the typical number is 60 to 70 hours in category (e.g., airplanes); 100 hours is not unusual, although the FAA requires a minimum of only 40 hours by regulation, less in the case of special schools.[2]

Shortly after achieving my private pilot's license, I was invited to accompany Bob, my ever-resilient primary training instructor, for a "commercial" flight from Sugarbush to Barnes Municipal Airport in Massachusetts. Our mission was to collect the FAA Designated Balloon Examiner, who would test Tom Watson for a practical balloon rating at Sugarbush Airport (FAA Identifier 0B7). Yes, this was Thomas J. Watson Jr., of IBM fame.

The novelty for me was threefold: 1) the weather in Massachusetts was terrible, with low ceilings and visibilities, and rain. Except for my one glider dalliance with bad weather, and practicing instruments under the hood in the C-150, I had never flown real instrument flight rules (IFR) weather. 2) The airplane was a Cessna Turbo 210 Centurion, max gross takeoff weight (MGTOW) of 4,000 pounds, completely unfamiliar to me, and very different in character from the C-150, which is about 1,700 pounds max gross takeoff weight. And 3) in hindsight, there were probably some legal problems with this plan. A brand new pilot with only a private license, manipulating the controls of a high-powered retractable-gear airplane on a commercial flight. In fact, it wasn't clear that Macone's operation had the necessary permission

---

[2] Code of Federal Regulations, Title 14, Part 141: Pilot Schools.

to conduct a commercial flight. Needless to say, I didn't question my commercial and instrument rated instructor. I just happily reported for duty.

The retractable landing gear T-210 is a magnificent aircraft. Gone were the struts bracing the wings; a carry through spar provided all the structural support necessary. It had a huge control yoke that would do justice to a 747, along with six seats. It was sleek, and spacious inside, compared with the airplanes and gliders that had been my experience to date. The single 310 hp (231 kW) TSIO-520-R Continental engine came with turbocharger—that was special, too. This exhaust-powered device supplied a steady flow of compressed air to the engine intake that when combined with the injected fuel served to make the engine perform as if it were operating below 10,000 feet, even when the airplane was twice as high. (I had heard that everything in terms of high maintenance costs reverts to the turbo charger so there are many procedures in place to avoid blowing the thing up. No matter what, I wasn't going to do that.)

The airplane's cruising speed of about 190 knots true at altitude is fast for a single-engine airplane. This compared to the C-150's 100 to 105 knots. The T-210 had another interesting characteristic. While I was not the shortest pilot ever, at 5'8", it did take cranking the vertical chair adjustment all the way for me to see over the glare shield and out the window. This was mostly due to the massive instrument cluster in the panel, including a radarscope, and other technology I had never seen before.

The mission itself went fine. Yes, there was a lot of shouting from the right seat about staying on course down the localizer while shooting the Instrument Landing System (ILS) runway 20. Bob was passionate about instruction. Moreover, he didn't want to die. Real instrument flying represented a completely new challenge and this T-210 experience was just a taste. There was a lot more information to integrate, more instruments to operate, and a new vocabulary to learn. For much of the flight, there was no visual reference, just gray out the windscreen. The actual flying was about interpreting the instrument information in just the right way, and then responding with the proper control inputs. Flying more modern airplanes also means being able to program the various flight management system (FMS) computers properly to facilitate automatic navigation, including departure, arrival, and approach procedures—usually the biggest challenge to safely operating aircraft in today's environment. In short, instrument flying is hard.

We dutifully picked up the balloon examiner, his crash helmet already donned, and returned to Sugarbush, arriving later that morning. I don't recall the exact details of my own activities after depositing the balloon examiner at 0B7 where the weather was considerably better than in Barnes. My logbook says I did a solo-trip to Montpelier in the C-150 followed by a dual-trip in Macone's PA-24 Comanche, with Bob; Montreal and back. This was another "complex" airplane I had never flown before. What I do remember is that on my return to Sugarbush, there was a commotion near the terminal building. The IBM founder and chief executive's balloon envelope lay in tatters with the basket crushed. The CEO himself was standing with blood running down his face and cheek. Same for the examiner, except he also appeared to be limping. (Crash helmets have their limits.)

What had happened? Well, Watson reported he had made a "minor" miscalculation descending near the West Ridge, Lincoln Gap area, part of the Appalachian Mountain cascade in Vermont. With the downward momentum of the balloon increasing, even the full power of the balloon's burner couldn't produce enough hot air, and therefore buoyancy, to arrest the descent. The crash came next.

There were many narrow escapes during my time training at Sugarbush. Watson's adventure would not be any different but for the epilogue. With paperwork completed and in order, the still bloodied and injured balloon examiner dutifully wrote out a temporary license granting the IBM CEO the privilege of being a private pilot rated in balloon aircraft. All the privileges were now in force: flying solo in balloon aircraft, including bringing passengers, providing they were not paying. What could go wrong? Only at Sugarbush does a crash landing resulting in the destruction of the aircraft serve to meet the minimum practical test standards set forth by the FAA. Yet, that was the airport's charm, a guilty pleasure.

## Lesson learned:

**Lesson 1:** Angels watch over all student pilots.

# 5 | Tailwheel Mysteries

It was a beautiful crisp summer morning at Sugarbush with clear skies and light winds. Dew had formed on the grass by the hard surface runway where we were practicing our landings. On our second landing John Macone let me operate the controls of the PA-18 Supercub unaided. I was still working on my private pilot license, and had fewer than 28 hours total flying time, so no one was more surprised than I was at the satisfying outcome. The airplane touched down gently on the turf surface, tracking straight as it gradually decelerated and came to a stop.

We taxied back to the grass runway's threshold for what I thought would be another instructor and pilot circuit around the pattern. Instead, Macone undid his safety belt and climbed out, signaling that it was time for me to do this one solo. One might assume I'd feel some apprehension, having had only two takeoffs and landings in an unfamiliar ship, but this was Sugarbush where "everything will probably be okay" was the mantra. So off I went, on my first solo flight in the Supercub.

The PA-18 is a fabric-covered airplane. Its fuselage and tail structure are made of chrome-molybdenum tubular steel while its wings (ribs and spars) were an aluminum-based design. N1081A, the airplane I was flying that day, was outfitted with a 95-horsepower Continental C-90 engine, the smallest in the model line. This was a stick (as opposed to yoke) controlled airplane with three-axis control via aileron, elevator, and rudder. Unlike the Cessna 150s from my training past, the Cub had no flaps.

The biggest novelty for me, though, was the Super Cub's landing gear. Viewed as old-fashioned today, the Cub is equipped with what the FAA refers to as a conventional landing gear "undercarriage" system, with the main wheels located forward of the center of gravity, and a small tail wheel in the back. When stopped or taxiing slowly on the ground, the airplane sits tail low with its nose pointed upward—hence its nickname, taildragger. The planes I had flown previously had a tricycle landing gear "undercarriage" arrangement, with the two main wheels aft of the center of gravity, and a smaller wheel under the nose to facilitate steering while on the ground.

Beyond noting the difference in the airplane's attitude and appearance, I had never considered—and nor was I informed—that conventional design airplanes, taildraggers, would have characteristics that demanded special handling by the pilot. I had no idea, for example, that the line between maintaining control and losing control during takeoffs and landings could be very thin. Yet there I was, accelerating down the grass runway, blissfully assuming my past experience with tricycle landing gear-equipped airplanes applied. This coupled with the morning's success bolstered confidence.

The Cub accelerated quickly; with no instructor in the back it was lighter. It also veered markedly left during the ground roll, but because flying speeds are only about 45 mph in the Cub, the airplane was airborne before the arcing trajectory led to hitting something on the ground. And once in the air, if anything, the Cub felt more docile than other airplanes I'd flown.

Sugarbush has a left-hand pattern to runway 22, the southwest facing runway. After reaching an altitude of about 800 feet above the runway I started the left turn for the crosswind leg, which I'd follow shortly afterward with another left turn for the downwind leg—the leg in the airport pattern that has the airplane traveling in the opposite direction for landing.

The Cub is a simple airplane. There are no flaps, so the checklist is short, amounting to applying carb heat (to prevent carburetor ice caused by the Venturi effect), throttling back, and trimming as necessary to eliminate any undue control forces. Typically, we would turn toward the base leg at about 800 feet and then on to final approach at no lower than 500 feet while maintaining speed of at least 80 mph. (To the school's credit, maintaining adequate airspeed and establishing a stable final approach was a focus of both glider and airplane training.) Only on final would the student slowly bleed off the speed, with ground contact occurring close to a full aerodynamic stall. Ideally, the three wheels would touch the ground at the same time—a three point landing.

The approach was going well, but with late morning a 12 to 15 knot wind had come from the southeast. There's a wind sock midfield and to the east of the runway, so it is easy to gauge wind direction and speed. I had dealt with wind in the tricycle gear airplanes, a challenge on stormier days but not worrisome with velocities in this range. Once on the ground the idea is to correct steering as necessary with rudder and nose gear along with some windward aileron induced banking to keep the airplane going straight.

I'd demonstrated a willingness to take on challenges as a Sugarbush student pilot, but I must admit that I had some concern. The other landings had gone well, but what I wasn't entirely sure of was why. It's a natural tendency of students in any challenging discipline to wonder, "Can I do that again?" The answer, of course, is revealed in the result.

As the airplane touched the ground there was a sudden jerk to the left—not like the takeoff, with its pronounced yet slower and steadier left-turning event (and then the airplane was flying before anything happened).

My first thought was "holy crap"—a not untypical reaction to a startling, unpredicted, potentially dangerous, flying-related event. I applied right opposite rudder pedal in an effort to counter the excursion to the left. I even got a bit of right heel brake, but it was all too late. The airplane was sideways and moving fast, now pointed perpendicular to both the grass and hard surface runways. And it was happening with the pilot participating mostly as a scenic observer on the way to the crash.

And then, amazingly, mercifully, it was over. My first solo Super Cub landing adventure ended quickly, with the nose of the airplane pointed in the opposite direction to the approach, engine idling at zero thrust. Chastened, I looked around. To my surprise, there was no surge of rescue forces approaching the aircraft, dispatched to extricate me from the wreck.

Pilot, heal thyself. Happily, both captain and airplane were undamaged, saved by the forgiving design of the airplane, a very wet grass surface, and luck—discussion reserved for the roasting that evening, celebrating another day of Sugarbush adventures. Under Macone's management, there was always an event triggering the popping of a champagne cork.

The question—what happened that day to cause such a dramatic loss of control—was not answered for some time. Macone, always calm and collected, a consummate charmer, simply said, "I am going to have you do landings until you get it right. So, get to it." And off I went for another try. The next landing went well, as did several subsequent landings. Still, I wondered.

Much of the answer lies in the nature of the conventional landing gear set up. Unlike tricycle gear airplanes, with a nose wheel, taildraggers don't naturally track straight while rolling on the ground. Imagine the challenge for a trucker trying to back an 18-wheeler along a straight line. The task is manageable when approached slowly. By making lots of little adjustments, the driver can steer the trailer precisely, tracking the road, straight or otherwise. But what if the goal were to do the same thing at flying speeds of 40 to 50 mph. Harder? That's the challenge taildragger pilots face when landing and taking off.

Conventional landing gear airplanes aren't trucks. Still, the same physics are in play. Like the taildragger, trailer trucks have a natural tendency to deviate right or left when in reverse. The only way to avoid jack-knifing is to apply constant correction. So it is for the taildragger, whether taking off or landing, except instead of a steering wheel, the pilot uses the rudder and in some circumstances brakes, to make the corrections. Tracking instability is what both an 18-wheeler in reverse and a tailwheel airplane have in common. Taildragger tracking actually improves with increased airspeed, at least in the hands of a competent pilot, because the airplane's control surfaces, especially the rudder, are more effective at higher airspeeds.

There are a range of airspeeds in taildragger flying that are slower than what's needed to fly (or assure good control), but fast enough to cause a lot of damage in the case of a loss of control event. For the Super Cub, this no man's land extends from about 15 to 35 knots, normally encountered about midway through takeoff and, on landing, just after touchdown. It's a period of transition during which the tail is coming off the ground or landing on it. Many degrees of freedom, lots of things going on at the same time. The problem is exaggerated on a windy day, especially when the wind has a perpendicular component. Crosswinds, even small ones, are the bane of taildragger pilots, and the leading cause of loss of control events. During takeoffs and landings, the pilot wants the airplane to go straight, but the crosswind wants the airplane to weathervane. The end result can be a ground loop, a rapid excursion left or right, usually followed by the nose and tail swapping ends. This is exactly what happened during my first solo landing attempt in the Cub. Like any loss of control event, ground loops are potentially dangerous, and can be expensive. I was lucky. I was landing on grass and the grass was wet. As the tail whipped around, the airplane slid sideways, avoiding stressing the landing gear to the point of failure and/or driving the right wing into ground. The Cub, and pilot, came to a stop, upright, no worse for wear. Wooooo!

Ignorance is bliss? Unknown to me at the time, loss of control in tailwheel airplanes is a real issue. Fortunately, there are techniques the pilot can employ to address this. To start, just having the airplane pointed straight, in the direction of travel, for both takeoffs and landings, is a big advantage. In my case, because I had corrected in the air for drift cause by the developing crosswind, my touchdown was just a little bit crooked, thereby triggering the chain of events. Once on the ground, I was right in applying opposite rudder, counteracting the effect of the wind, but I was late. Even when I finally got on the rudder, I didn't use enough. *Note to file:* the key to saving the day is to apply all the opposite rudder available. Push the pedal to the floor! Worry not about flooring it, there will be opportunity to reduce. The same cannot be said for putting in too little rudder when more is what is really needed.

In some cases, opposite brake can be helpful, but because the main wheels extend close to the center line of the fuselage and have little leverage against the wind pushing at the opposite side of the fuselage and tail fin, braking to stay straight should be viewed as a last resort. And in takeoff, using the brake for directional control can make things worse, slowing the acceleration of the aircraft, and lengthening the no man's land period. Of course, my application of the brake was hopelessly late, and most likely counterproductive because the airplane's center of mass was already well to the right of the right braking wheel's direction of travel. Before there was ABS braking, cars could experience this in slippery conditions. In the event of a fishtail, locking the brakes, especially those controlling the front wheels, would aggravate the situation, causing the car to slide sideways or even reverse direction—a bootleg turn.

High on the list of useful techniques during takeoff is banking into the crosswind by applying aileron and opposite rudder. If done properly close to flying speed, the downwind wing will fly first causing the weight of the airplane to shift from both main wheels to the upwind wheel. Shortly thereafter, the airplane will be flying at a slight angle in the general direction of the crosswind. Upwind refers to the side of the airplane pushed by the wind, causing a weathervane effect. Downwind is the other side of the plane. Landing works the same way, with the upwind wheel touching the ground first, while in a shallow bank, followed by the downwind wheel and opposite rudder as needed to counteract the crosswind. Had I known about the aileron and opposite rudder technique, also known as cross-controlling, I might have avoided the embarrassing episode entirely. But I doubt I would have understood the underlying aerodynamics or physics in play. Not many new pilots do.

All of this begs the question: why taildraggers? Why adopt a design that has so many challenges. Tricycle gear airplanes have been around for a long time. They are easier to take off and land, fly equally as well, and generally offer better visibility out the windscreen while on the ground. There must be more to it than just a bunch of type-As trying to prove something.

The answer is utility. To understand this, it is important to remember that in the early days of aviation, the 1920s through the 1940s, there were very few airports. Those that existed were more like open fields, especially when compared to a modern jetport with its acres of pavement and reinforced concrete.

What unimproved surfaces there were, were often much unimproved. In some places, like Alaska, airports today are much the same—riverbeds and glaciers more than hard surface runways. Airplanes landing on such surfaces required a robust undercarriage, and a way to protect the engine and propeller system from damage caused by inadvertent contact with an irregular and often contaminated runway surface. Airplane engineers of the time were aware of the controllability advantages of the tricycle gear arrangement, but designing a nose strut and wheel elements that could withstand rough surfaces presented a true structural engineering challenge. The narrow profile of the fuselage's nose, with its lack of resistance to torsional loads, made it difficult to apply the stiffening and bracing needed to cope with the stresses associated with taking off or landing on a rough surface. This, coupled with the nose wheel being the tip of the spear, the first support element of the aircraft to experience the effects of rough terrain during taxi, takeoff, and landing, further contributed to the design's vulnerability.

Tricycle gear airplanes are also much more vulnerable to inadvertent prop strikes. The same level attitude that provides the pilot with good visibility when taxiing, taking off, and landing makes it much more likely that the engine or propeller could experience damage, because the rotating propeller tips are closer to the ground compared to those on tailwheel airplanes. Assuming the right combination of irregularity, contamination, and ground speed, a prop nick, strike, or worse can occur. Not good!

The issue is not just academic. Several years after the Cub adventure, I had a close call while operating a tricycle gear Cessna 182 on an improved taxiway at Rochester International Airport. Approaching the tiedown/parking area I cut a corner. As the nose wheel and right wheel went over the lip onto the unimproved surface, the nose strut compressed, causing the propeller to contact the gravel. Although the engine was just idling, the impact kicked up a huge cloud of dust and debris. Fortunately, the damage amounted to no more than a few nicks to the prop's leading edge, easily fixed. I would have expected much worse. As it turns out, tricycle gear airplanes do not make the best off-road vehicles.

So, for pilots wanting to expand their range of airport options, tail draggers offer a real solution, but also demand special handling, proper technique, proficiency, and experience. High on the list is a commitment to flying the airplane (operating the aerodynamic control surfaces) consciously, at all times the airplane is in motion.

Mike Ball taught me this early in my glider flying. He stressed that gliders become airborne at slower speeds than the tow aircraft, meaning the tow plane could be on its takeoff roll, gaining speed but still on the ground, while the glider is already in the air. The tow plane tracks straight on the runway; it is up to the glider pilot to follow suit. Proper use of stick and rudder from the beginning to the end of the tow is a must.

The same applies to taildraggers, the goal generally is just to get the airplane to track straight. A combination of rudder, ailerons, elevator, and proper application of power gets the job done. But there are subtleties beyond cross-controlling, opposite rudder, and ailerons positioned to bank toward the crosswind, especially during landing, when most of the loss of control accidents happen.

In the case of landing directly into the wind, mostly the goal is as previously described, keep the airplane flying straight. At the point where the airplane reaches the runway, at a height of 20 to 50 feet, the pilot begins the flare, pitching up while also decreasing engine thrust. If done properly, the airplane gently descends toward the surface, and, before it reaches maximum lift capacity of the wing (aerodynamic stall), the wheels contact the runway.

Some schools teach a full stall technique, the idea being to touch down at the slowest possible speed over the ground, the point of aerodynamic stall. There are two problems with this technique: first, it can be difficult to gauge exact height above the runway, especially when flying low. (There is a big difference between loosing lift at 1 to 2 feet off the runway and 10 to 20 feet.) Also, thermals induced by the asphalt surface, when hot, could cause the airplane to balloon upward just at the point where all lift is exhausted. A full stall landing risks hitting hard; once lift ceases, the airplane becomes a falling object. Second, there is greater potential for a loss of control event to occur. As the airspeed decreases, control surface effectiveness also decreases. In a tricycle gear airplane, assuming survival from the impact, loss of control is less of an issue because once on the ground the airplane tends to track straight, or it can be made to do so by steering with the nose wheel. Not so with a tailwheel airplane. At the point where the controls produce the least effect, the airplane is at its most vulnerable to the effects of side gusts. Touch down, especially in a full stall configuration, is also the moment when visibility is the worst. Landing our Stearman biplane using a full stall technique means, basically, giving up all forward visibility at the very moment it is needed to keep going straight. In exchange for achieving a lower energy touchdown, avoiding a bounce should the main wheels contact the ground first, advocates of the full stall accept the risk of loss of control due to poor visibility and/or lack of control surface effectiveness, not to mention possible damage to the small, less robust tail wheel in the back. Similar to the weakness of the nose wheel design operating on rough terrain, touching down at the high angle characteristic of a full stall landing can cause the tail wheel in some airplanes to hit the ground first. If the hit is hard enough, both the wheel and assembly may be damaged, or worse.

There have been many taildragger landing accidents linked to poor visual reference and/or loss of control surface effectiveness. Curiously, though, the full stall landing technique is often taught first to aspiring taildragger pilots. The rationale is that the corresponding slower ground speed at touchdown reduces risk of exposure to no man's land—15 to 35 knots. It is almost as if the instructors assume the students are going to lose control and crash anyway. Their job is to reduce the damage.

In contrast, wheel landings tend to facilitate a more deterministic outcome. The airplane is flown all the way down, at a speed above aerodynamic stall, with the main wheels contacting the ground first. If done properly, control effectiveness and visibility are preserved at touchdown and for much of the rollout.

Now, imagine there is a crosswind in play. Here the vector of wind velocity perpendicular to the runway direction, also known as the crosswind component, is most important. For example, if the wind direction is from 45 degrees to the right of the runway direction and the velocity is 15 knots, the crosswind component equals 7½ knots. There are graphs and tables available to calculate the crosswind component precisely, but as a general rule once the wind velocity reaches around 30 knots caution is warranted even if the blow is straight down the runway. The worry is that high winds also tend to be gusty and variable. Even a small shift in wind direction can produce a crosswind component that is high, perhaps in excess of what was demonstrated or certified by the manufacturer of the airplane.

We experienced an extreme example of this on one of our trans-Atlantic flights in the CJ3 fanjet. On approach to Reykjavik, a deep low developed suddenly over the airport with winds as high as 90 knots out of the south. Although the landing runway was oriented in a southerly direction, it was clear that once on the ground maintaining directional control could be challenging. A wind shift as small as 15 degrees to either side would produce a crosswind component in excess of the airplane's 20 knot demonstrated capacity. A memorable experience for sure. More on that in Chapter 17.

## Wheel landings vs. full stall landings in a crosswind

Happily, on many days the winds are in the light to moderate range, with the crosswind component well below the maximum demonstrated by the airplane manufacturer. Still, to conduct landings safely, proper technique is key. Best practice begins on approach, with the airplane tracking over the ground in alignment with the runway. To counteract the crosswind component, the pilot crabs the airplane by pointing its nose in the direction of the wind as far as needed to counter the crosswind effects. There are formulas for figuring out the exact number of degrees but after a little practice most pilots know instinctively how much to crank in.

As the airplane nears the runway threshold and the flare begins, a transition takes place. The crab is discontinued as the pilot establishes a small (appropriate) bank in the direction of the crosswind, with a small amount of opposite rudder to keep the airplane going straight relative to the direction of the runway. This positions the airplane in a way that insures the upwind main wheel contacts the surface first. Upon contact, and while maintaining directional control with the rudder, the pilot allows the airplane to level naturally, the downwind main wheel contacting the surface next, followed by the tailwheel. Airspeed is above stall through the period when the downwind main landing gear wheel contacts the surface. Ideally, the airplane never enters no-man's land until both main wheels are on the ground, direction of travel aligned with the runway.

The merits of wheel landings are most apparent in crosswind conditions. There are two reasons for this:

1) The physics in play. As the upwind wheel touches the ground first, some of the kinetic energy of the aircraft, a function of speed and vertical descent, is transferred into a torsional force along the longitudinal axis of the aircraft, running in a straight line from the nose of the fuselage to the tail. The downwind wing, still flying, acts like a cushion, effectively damping the torsional force, making the downwind wheel's contact with the ground gentler and more controlled. This upwind wing-low wheel landing technique has the added benefit of discouraging a bounce. With a significant portion of the descent-related kinetic energy dissipated by the damping effect of the downwind wing, less energy is available to effect torque about

the lateral axis, a line from wing tip to wing tip. It is torque about this axis that, if severe enough, can cause a conventional gear airplane to suddenly pitch-up, perhaps going airborne unexpectedly. In the case of a true full stall, landing lift capacity on both wings is gone or nearly gone. Hence much less dampening effect. Further, due to the lack of control effectiveness, the airplane is much more likely to contact the ground in an unpredictable way, perhaps with both main wheels touching at the same time. Should this happen, all the remaining descent-related kinetic energy will translate into increased pitch attitude, sharpening the wing's angle of attack. To the extent there is any flying speed left, the airplane may become airborne again briefly before falling back to the ground. Most likely, it will be the main wheels that remain airborne, while airplane's tailwheel is driven hard into the ground.

2) The bigger issue is that by establishing the ground roll with good control surface effectiveness, the pilot simplifies the landing. With the touch down and ground roll segment of the landing occurring while good control is present, needed corrections for gusts can be made robustly. What remains then is to maintain the already-established good tracking through the more dangerous no-man's land airspeed period to taxi. Mostly, this is about being on the rudder and continuing to hold some banking aileron as the airplane slows. In contrast, the full stall technique has the pilot doing everything necessary (kicking out the crab, touching down, correcting for unexpected crosswind gusts, adapting from level flight to a tail low/nose high sight picture) nearly simultaneously, and at a time when control surface effectiveness is minimal. At the point where the airplane finally makes contact with the ground it had better be going straight or bad things are likely to happen.

## Full stall landing merits

Truth in advertising: there is one important negative to consider when adopting a wheel landing philosophy. Landing distances, ground rolls, likely will be a little longer because the total kinetic energies in play are greater. Still, under most circumstances, this is a small price to pay for avoiding the risk of hitting something, wrecking the main/tail wheel landing gear, and/or bending the wing. In the event that securing a minimum ground roll is necessary, it's time for a determination of risk and personal flying skills. In the hands of an expert, a low energy approach and landing can be a thing of beauty. If you need to land on a riverbed in Alaska with raging water all around, the benefits of touching down close to or at a stall are many. For most of us, however, routine flying where runways are long and crosswinds/turbulence are the biggest hazard, maintaining good control authority to the end matters most.

It is interesting to note that some modern-day aircraft manufacturers like Cub Crafters, cornering the short runway market with products like the X-Cub, have designed their airplanes to provide very high lift capacity at very low (e.g., 45 mph) approach/landing speeds. While the idea has merit in calm winds or winds that align with the runway orientation, the same rules for effective control apply to less optimized crosswind affected runways. The lower the airspeed, the harder it is to counter a large crosswind component. Still, to the extent the design's stall speed approaches zero, crosswind priority decreases because every landing is by definition going to be close to or 100% into "the wind!"

Full stall and wheel landing advocates have been agreeing to disagree since the invention of the first "conventional landing gear" aircraft. Most pilots who have mastered both techniques know that neither applies to all situations. More useful to the cause is general agreement that early, aggressive, and correct application of rudder to address excursions from the desired course can save the day. A rare case of détente in aviation.

## Lessons learned:

**Lesson 1:** Early, aggressive, and correct application of rudder to address excursions from the desired course can make up for a multitude of sins. (More is more.)

**Lesson 2:** Maintaining robust control surface effectiveness from takeoff to landing is a prerequisite to success.

**Lesson 3:** Aerodynamic dampening effect associated with wheel landings and the up-wind, wing-low technique can significantly reduce the chances of a bounce.

# 6 | Girlfriends and Airplanes

Relationships are often defined by shared experiences. So it was with Loretta and me. When the tower asked if we wanted to declare an emergency, the look of alarm on my date's face suggested that our future together might require more than a safe landing.

It was to be a routine ferry mission. A Cessna 182 Skylane, N15AP, was being returned to service following an annual inspection and needed to be relocated from Burlington, Vermont, to Warren/Sugarbush Airport. Like many new pilots seeking flight time, I had made known my interest in ferrying airplanes to my Sugarbush pilot friends, along with local maintenance shops in the area. The pay was terrible, but ferrying gave me an opportunity to fly a lot of different models. In the case of the Sugarbush patrons, some of whom seemed to add an airplane to their stable on a monthly basis, there was the bonus thrill of being the first to vet the newly acquired specimen. And, more to the point, my logbook totals were increasing rapidly.

Burlington weather that day was visual flight rules (VFR) with a high thin overcast layer. It was windy, 20020G30KT, sustained winds of 20 knots from the south, gusting to 30, but the winds were optimally aligned both for Burlington's runway 19 and Sugarbush's runway 22. I knew it might be little bumpy, but I was relieved that the low visibilities and ceilings characteristic of many prior ferrying runs would not be a factor. Conducting the mission in daylight was also a big plus.

Loretta and I had been dating for a couple of months. She wasn't particularly happy about flying, but she wasn't afraid of it. She was a rock singer and frequently toured by air. With her striking good looks and deep sexy voice, Loretta covered artists like Janis Joplin and Stevie Nicks, and performed her own original material to adoring crowds. No, in Loretta's view flying's biggest risk was *bad service*. It hadn't been easy persuading her to join me for the short flight to Sugarbush. I ultimately appealed to her sensuous palate by promising dinner at Chez Henri, an exclusive French restaurant near the landing site. Loretta craved their specialty, "Chocolate... Chocolate... Chocolate Cake."

My experience with ferry flying had taught me to invest adequate time performing the pre-flight. In addition to the standard checks, like oil quantity, fuel integrity, control surface security, I usually asked to have the engine cowls opened or removed for an inspection of connections and to look for leaks, especially in areas where components have been repaired or replaced. It is not always easy. Having just reassembled the airplane, some shops would balk at the request because unlike older designs, modern airplanes tend to discourage easy viewing of critical components, like the engine. The C-182P engine, for example, is cowled up in a way that makes tools mandatory for seeing anything beyond the oil level. During one such pre-flight I discovered the airplane's controls had been rigged in reverse. The shop insisted they were correct until the mechanic sat in the airplane and operated the controls himself. When it comes to unfamiliar airplanes and/or post maintenance missions it is wise to presume that somewhere, something wrong is just waiting to kill you.

Happily, N15AP checked out fine. We were ready to go. Respecting Loretta's limited interest in airplanes, I resisted the temptation to discuss the high-wing four-place single's performance or flying characteristics as part of the passenger briefing. Instead, I focused on the practical things passengers should know, including the function of the door, seat, and safety belt/shoulder harness. We talked about the doors in particular because in the C-182P there is a locking lever instead of the door handle characteristic of earlier vintages and many other Cessna models. The lever recesses into the armrest, so to open the door the lever must first be pulled up, out of the arm rest, then slightly past 90 degrees to release the latch. The system is simple and works well, but it is not intuitive.

Buckled in and ready to go, I brought N15AP's Continental O-470 engine to life. With 230 horsepower available, the engine produces a throaty sound, even at idle. This, coupled with controls that in terms of magnificence would be fitting for any airliner, makes the C-182 feel like a big airplane.

As expected, the runway in use was 19. Winds also were as expected, although at sustained levels a little higher than forecast. We taxied to the runway and did our run-up. All was normal, and Loretta even seemed mildly enthusiastic. I wasn't sure if it was the prospect of a romantic dinner with a pilot, complete with delicious dessert, or our impending flight, but in the spirit that arguing with success is often ill advised, I didn't seek to ascertain.

Run-up complete, I called the tower and received clearance for takeoff. The initial ground roll was short, largely due to the winds. Winds above were even stronger and dramatically slowed our progress over the ground during the climb. Reaching 85 knots, at a height of 700 feet, we still had runway below us. Accelerating to climb/cruise airspeed, we continued southbound. Our clearance was to continue along the runway heading to 2,000 mean sea level (MSL) feet before turning southeast, bound for Sugarbush.

Any anxieties I'd had earlier dissipated as we climbed through 1,500 feet. The air was remarkably smooth given the winds and, better yet, Loretta was having a good time. Her interest in the surrounding sights suggested that any apprehension she'd had about little airplanes was now in the past. I was flying with a rock star, and a happy one at that.

The good times were short-lived, however. The initial sign of trouble was a small vibration, a tremor. Engine instruments showed green and the airplane was climbing as expected, so I wasn't ready to conclude we had a problem. The explosive *BANG* and fiery eruption from under the engine cowling certainly changed my mind.

Loretta immediately recognized the situation as dire. She grabbed my shoulder and screamed over and over, "What's happening?!" Also caught in the moment, I screamed back, "Let me go, I have to fly the airplane!" Along with some other less than loving words. Freeing myself from her grip, and after what seemed like an endless spell of panic, as I came to learn typical of anyone faced with an in-air engine explosion, I collected my wits and focused on the matter at hand.

The windscreen was covered in oil, but the fire appeared to have self-extinguished. The vibration had stopped, too, consistent with the airplane's seized propeller and silent engine. I lowered the nose to maintain airspeed and started an aggressive right turn back to the airport. We were at about 1,800 feet MSL (1,500 feet AGL). My plan was to complete the 180-degree turn in the hope that the winds would be sufficient to blow us back to Burlington. Remarkably, I also remembered to cut the mixture and kill the fuel, an act that was somewhat disorienting due to the floor-mounted position of the valve.

I cleared my throat while simultaneously pushing the airplane's radio talk switch; the coughing sound alone an indication that not all was well. "Tower, it's 15AP, the Skylane, we have had a catastrophic engine failure, will be returning to Burlington, will attempt to make runway 01." The tower's response was dutiful, but not particularly helpful. "15AP, would you like to declare an emergency?" There was also something about wanting to know the number of souls on board, "when you have time."

Since we were going to be on the ground in about 90 seconds, I wasn't sure by what measure of available time they were imagining. Still, I managed to convey our enthusiasm for declaring (an emergency) and the passenger manifest. "There are two of us, and we are on fire, please send the equipment."

Although the fire appeared to be out, I suffered no guilt over the transmission. Smoke continued to emit from under the engine cowl. Where there is smoke there is fire, a reasonable application of poetic license given the circumstances. And at this point a crash-and-burn-free landing was by no means assured.

With the ground rushing up, I was working hard to finish the turn with enough altitude left to level the ship. I really didn't want to be that statistic where everyone dies because the pilot decided to turn back without enough altitude. Of course, the alternate decision to land straight ahead with a failed engine off-airport has its own risks. If the airplane disintegrates on landing, any fire in play will accelerate, and no emergency services will be immediately available to put it out.

Although the peek-a-boo picture through the oil-smeared windscreen made targeting the runway difficult, I was confident we would at least hit the airport. The strong south wind was indeed pushing us closer, but this presented its own challenge. The slightly higher approach airspeed needed to safely conduct a dead stick landing, combined with a 30-knot tailwind, meant touchdown ground speeds would be very fast. Assuming we made the runway, it might not be possible to stop the airplane in time to avoid going off the end. Disaster!

Loretta was still demonstrably terrified, but no longer incapacitated. Panic takes many forms, and for some people the recovery time to regain coherent function is lengthy. I was relieved because in the event the landing was less than ideal, Loretta might be on her own exiting the airplane to escape a possible fire.

I asked Loretta to crack her door to prevent possible jamming in case of a crash. Our discussion about operating the door lever turned out to be prophetic; she engaged the door lever and the suction from the outside airflow did the rest. I briefed her on what to do after landing: unbuckle, open the door, exit, and run, away from the airplane as quickly as possible.

"Cleared to land," was the tower's last transmission. It was time to change the focus from just making the airport to achieving something more graceful, like landing safely on one of the runways.

By now the forward windscreen was completely opaque, so my ability to judge runway height and distance was limited to a peripheral view out the left side. It was something of an improbable success but somehow we managed to achieve close to level flight while lurching forward in the general direction of runway 01. To the extent there was any good news, we were definitely going to make the airport. Unfortunately, we were still flying fast and high relative to our chosen runway.

I deployed the electrically operated flaps to 40 degrees in an attempt to slow the airplane. Up to this point I had elected to keep the airplane clean for maximum glide. The deceleration was dramatic, largely because our airspeed was substantially faster than what was allowed for the requested flap setting (a credit to Cessna engineers, the flaps remained attached to the airplane). Unfortunately, although we were slowing, the deceleration was not enough. The airplane crossed the painted runway numbers at about 200 feet. Too high! In a last-ditch effort to get down, I cranked in a slip to the right resulting in a more rapid descent and—a most welcome side effect— better visibility out the left side window.

Anticipating a less-than perfect landing, I asked (well, more like commanded) Loretta to cinch her belt tight. There was no discussion. At this point we were largely in sync, at least in terms of the goal of the mission. The airplane touched down smoothly on runway 01, and not as far from the threshold as anticipated given the erratic approach and glide angle. Still, with substantial wind on the tail, our speed over the concrete was dramatic.

As we whizzed by taxiway Bravo, about half way down the approximately 4,000-foot runway, I could see the parade of fire trucks perched and ready. The airplane was slowing but the tires were screeching and squealing. Easy on the brakes. The last thing we needed was a blowout resulting in loss of control. Finally, after crossing the intersecting runway 33, the airplane came to a stop with about 50 feet to spare. Switches off, we were down!

What happened next was no less dramatic. Sticking to our plan we threw off our harnesses, shoved open the doors, and leapt out of the airplane, Loretta dashing off to the right and me to the left, as the fire crew aimed their full regalia of high pressure nozzles at the smoldering aircraft. In seconds, fire retardant spewed everywhere and made short order of any fire that remained. We were down and safe, all was well. At least, that's what I thought...

I circled around the back of the airplane and ran toward Loretta who was crumpled on the grass next to the runway. Although physically unhurt, she was far from unscathed. Drenched in retardant from head to toe, her foamy white face said it all. Apparently an overly enthusiastic retardant gun operator had knocked her flat as she ran away from the airplane.

Despite all attempts to comfort Loretta, and wipe away the sticky foam, my expressions of concern and the successful outcome of our emergency landing did not carry the day. Loretta was miserable, and the car ride back to Sugarbush that afternoon was painfully silent.

Loretta and I never did have our dinner at Chez Henri. There were a few phone calls, mostly initiated by me, but no more dates. Regrettably, it seemed our dramatic flying adventure punctuated the end of our relationship.

The C-182, on the other hand, lived to fly another day following the replacement of its badly mangled and charred engine. Root cause for the failure was determined to be a missing intake tube gasket. Cylinder one was running lean to the point where ultimately detonation punched a hole in the piston. The resulting debris did the rest.

Detecting the absence of an intake tube gasket demands an ultra-ambitious preflight. Nonetheless, the C-182 experience has prompted me to look for missing parts in difficult to reach places with more enthusiasm. As for damsels in distress, I fear I won no accolades for a dramatic rescue. While our culture tends to teach from an early age that great romance will follow scary adventure and derring-do, I'm inclined to believe that romantic endings generally come from preventing distress in the first place.

## Lessons learned:

**Lesson 1:** Attempting a low-altitude 180-degree reversal to facilitate return to the airport is a bold and risky move. Given that my outcome was good, and the victors write the history, the decision in this case was clearly a good one. The reality, however, is that things could have ended very badly, and for a whole host of reasons including loss of control in the turn, failure to achieve level flight prior to reaching the runway, or just hitting something with high energy within the airport environment. Keep in mind that due to oil contamination, visibility out the windscreen was poor. There was also a honking tail wind that could easily have triggered a runway excursion event. It is amazing how many things there are to hit at the airport.

This was my second experience with engine failure, and again, fortunately, everything worked out. Both the airplane and its occupants lived to fly another day. Still, it may have been wise to at least consider that a straight-ahead, off-field landing into the wind might have been the better choice. The landing would have been survivable, perhaps even injury free. And with ground speeds as low as 25 knots at the end, it is possible the airframe would have survived too.

**Lesson 2:** The seemingly endless spell of panic that followed the bang was in fact likely relatively brief. After all, the entire episode unfolded in about a minute and a half. More interesting, though, is that I recognized the feeling, which I'd first experienced in the Cessna 150, and remembering that served to somewhat decrease my total panic time. Can it be that familiarity with the feeling of panic makes it easier to get back on track? While I am not encouraging the courting of real emergencies as a way to improve panic recovery time, it does appear that more exposure may improve performance. Refraction times do indeed seem to be affected positively by the frequency of occurrence.

**Lesson 3:** If at all possible, fly aircraft with a history that is known to you and is exemplary. Do you want to have to be the best pilot you have been ever in your whole life to survive when the engine quits? Yes, training helps improve one's chances, but it would have been safer never to have had the emergency in the first place. The quality of aircraft and their mechanics varies. Limit your flying only to those that are competently maintained under a zero-defect policy by a mechanic who is personally motivated not to kill you.

**Lesson 4:** Girlfriends really don't like being scared to death. No amount of rescuing will overcome that.

# 7 Instrument Flying: A Room Without a View

Success can be defined in many ways. For me, it meant having the money to buy bottled beer after many a twenty-five-cent draft. This was owing to my new tenure as a junior software engineer at the Hayward Tyler Pump Company, my first real job after graduating from college.

The work was fun and challenging, designing software to perform finite element structural analysis on the company's many N-Stamp designs. "N" stands for nuclear, and the purpose of the software was to predict how large pumping systems behave when subjected to earthquake conditions. All nuclear power plant systems must meet strict regulations to assure proper function under a number of abnormal circumstances, e.g., earthquakes, where the concern is the development of some form of destructive resonance leading to failure. It was during my time at the Pump Co. that the Three Mile Island nuclear facility in Pennsylvania experienced a partial meltdown. That was quite a fire drill for those at home involved with the tertiary cooling system, which was built by us. Fortunately, the automatic back-up system continued to function, preventing a total meltdown of the reactor—this despite the best efforts of the operators to turn it and our pumps off.

Going from a work-study night job in college paying $2.50 an hour to $6 an hour meant more than just bottled beer. I now had the means to pursue flying—without my mother's help. Even more exciting, Hayward Tyler Pump Co. had a sister company in Kitchener, Ontario, about 50 miles west of Toronto. Burlington to Kitchener is at least 10 hours by car. With stops in New York or Philadelphia on commercial airlines, door to door flying times weren't much better. By single-engine Cessna, on most days, the trip could be done in 2 hours and 40 minutes, faster on the way back due to prevailing winds.

*The author (right) explaining the seismic analysis numerical methods used to qualify one of Hayward Tyler's centrifugal pumps for nuclear-class applications.*

So, with draft mission parameters in hand and much determination, I made the pitch to my manager that the company fly to Canada privately. The flights would be conducted in a four-place Cessna 182 rented by the company. Naturally, I would captain. As many as three passengers could go. We would navigate the trips VFR, meaning that the weather had to be nice, because, at the time, I was only certified to fly under Part 91 visual flight rules. The flights also had to occur in daylight, because Canada doesn't allow VFR at night.

*The Hayward Tyler flight department days.*

In hindsight, this was a brazen idea. Unknown to the company, my entire airplane experience amounted to just 90 hours of logged flying time, and much less in type, e.g., C-182. The Burlington to Kitchener routing spanned more than 300 nautical miles. That's a long way to expect perfect weather to last, all the time, especially in the winter. And much of the route was over rough and isolated terrain with little or no radar coverage. Go down there, and it could be a long time before rescue. It also didn't help that most of the trips needed to be scheduled weeks, or even a month, in advance to accommodate our Canadian colleagues. Predicting a perfect day weeks ahead of time is hard to do, as it turns out. Still, the time saving advantage was compelling. And with two or three passengers, the cost of Cessna 182 plus me (my salary) was only a little more than flying commercial. So off we went: Hayward Tyler Pump Co. now had its own flight department!

Flying the border route to Kitchener enjoyed the added novelty of being an international flight. This was before 9/11, so immigration was much less of a hassle than it is today. The pilot would file a VFR flight plan with US or Canada flight service organizations, depending on direction; the filing would document pilot, passengers, aircraft, time en route, and routing/altitude particulars. A note to "Ad Cus" (advise customs) in the Remarks section was helpful, although in most cases I would phone the immigration people and provide the ETA and other information, just in case. Although city of Kitchener itself is unremarkable, I loved the Customs ladies there. In their mid-sixties, dressed patriotically in formal Canadian immigration uniforms, prim and proper, they would greet us politely, in the most perfect British Broadcasting Corporation accents: "Welcome to Kitchener, your passport, please." Charming! These women could just as easily have been in Churchill's situation room during the Battle of Britain moving the model ships and warplanes about on a giant strategic map.

The biggest challenge, of course, was weather. Being restricted to clear, good visibility days, also required being extremely lucky picking the day. Both the origin and destination weather would have to be clear or nearly clear, with only scattered clouds and visibilities greater than three miles. In the event of less than ideal ceilings and visibilities en route, there had to be a way to navigate safely below or to climb to the top of the cloud deck, in the clear, without entering a cloud. Same for the way down. Thunderstorms or freezing rain in the forecast meant an absolute no-go.

What is remarkable, a miracle really, is that for the first year and a half, travel-day weather was perfect. On many days the skies were clear with unlimited visibilities. The blessing from the weather gods didn't just apply to the Canada trips. From Portland, Maine, to Rochester, New York, Philadelphia, Pennsylvania, to Bedford, Massachusets, all the many and varied trips we took during this period enjoyed fabulous, clear, calm skies. Even during the winter months, not one trip cancelled.

Tempting fate? It did not escape the captain that the dispatch reliability, the percentage of flights that depart as planned, had been remarkable. More challenging was meeting the growing expectations of management. Reliability had been better than airlines at a similar cost, with half the travel time, and no lost luggage. Enthusiasm! We were taking so many trips at one point that I was having trouble keeping up with my engineering duties. While a happy problem, I knew our good luck couldn't last forever. Now about 35 trips into the project, it seemed prudent to upgrade capabilities, and secure an instrument rating for that inevitable bad weather day. So, hat in hand, I made my case. Not just to my manager, or his. I had to make the case for training money in the boardroom, with all present including the CEO, Dennis Chalmers.

Dennis had never accompanied me as a passenger, but he was aware of the project and clearly understood the merit of what we were doing. After all, it is hard to argue with success, or the savings in time, to which he could attest, having made the drive to Kitchener personally. Still, Dennis was a ferociously bottom line guy. I recall him throwing a checkbook across the room at my boss, Norm Schrieb, because he had failed to complete the necessary engineering documentation for the release of the month's high-revenue pump system shipment. "Ship it" was the company motto, resulting in tense moments toward the end of the month for those responsible for assuring quality. Dennis did, however, have an analytical side. He recognized the huge advantage of flying privately, given the terrible airline service between Burlington and Toronto. Further, being a Canadian by birth, he knew northern weather could be bad. After a number of budget reviews, demand rationalizations, and advocacies from the frequent flyers, the instrument rating project was approved. The budget: $1,000.

Most of the time, the weather is good, as evidenced by the early HTPC flying experience. But forecasted ceilings and visibilities don't have to be all that terrible to increase uncertainty to the point where it becomes imprudent to go VFR. Marginal VFR, for example—three to five miles visibility, and 1,000- to 3,000-foot ceilings—can be very challenging. Imagine mountains in the way, shrouded by cloud cover, valley routings the only option. And what if that three to five miles becomes one to two miles, or one mile, prior to arriving at the destination. That's a big problem. The advantage of Cat 1 instrument rating, the most typical, is that a crew can navigate with visibilities down to a half-mile and with 200-foot ceilings, much worse than the weather that happens 95 percent of the days at most airports. With Cat 3B, assuming the right equipment and currency, a crew can tackle a thick fog, 200-meters visibility, all the way to the ground. In places like Zurich, Switzerland, this category of instrument landing is more the rule than exception, especially during winter months and in the morning.

Being both instrument rated and having an instrument-certified aircraft greatly increases the options. Assuming good aircraft maintenance and pilot proficiency, IFR flown trips enjoy a very high dispatch reliability. They are safe, and normally stress free. A private/corporate aircraft operating in the weather has further advantages, including the flexibility to operate under Federal Aviation Regulations Part 91, more flexible than the much stricter Part 121 or 135 rules typical of airline and on-demand charter operations.

Still, small airplane Part 91 Cat 1 pilots do have to be more careful due to limitations on aircraft performance and the more liberal guidelines. For example, although permitted, it may not be a good idea to take off in a single-engine airplane, in zero-zero weather, with the nearest VFR weather airport 100 nautical miles away. For Part 121 and 135 operators nothing is left to the imagination. Generally speaking, zero-zero departures are forbidden.

Learning instrument flying at its most basic level requires mastering three skill sets:

1) The pilot must be able to operate the aircraft without reference to outside visual cues, and by sole reference to the instruments. This includes mastering procedures that are necessary to safely navigate a course or routing, along with arrival and departure, and precision and non-precision approaches to the airport.

2) The pilot must understand a complex set of regulations that govern instrument flying, including rules governing pilot qualification, suitable weather, and required equipment.

3) The pilot must have a good grasp of meteorology that is germane to flying. This includes knowledge of the underlying mechanics of weather, different types of systems and fronts, and the nature and effect of various modifying factors, including the influence of mountains, seas, lakes, and other earth/air features, basically the earth-air interface. Weather services publish information in various formats, codes, a language that must be learned for quick assimilation of what's important to the flying mission at hand. Weather also affects airplane performance, especially lift and propulsion, critical information when departing heavy on a hot day, or topping a mountain with ice accumulating on the wing.

Captain Robert Buck's book *Weather Flying*, the best exploration of the subject ever written, explains how weather is flown, leaving how it is made to the academics. Instrument flying is taught much in the same way, with emphasis on things practical, a necessity due to the breadth and complexity of the subject. But there is a price to be paid for pragmatism, especially with the encroachment of clever automation and an increasingly complex system.

My early memories of flying solely by instruments are mostly about mastering a juggling act, managing many largely autonomous single-function instruments in an effort to construct the total picture, us with respect to the outside world. There wasn't much time for anything else. It felt as if every flight verged on a near death experience, unless aided, or allowed to jettison the vision-obstructing hood meant to simulate real time IFR conditions. Consider that information from attitude indicator, airspeed indicator, vertical speed indicator, altimeter, directional gyro, and engine rpm gauge, each indicator located in a different place on the instrument panel, all of the information needed simultaneously to paint a minimal picture, just enough situational awareness to keep the airplane straight and level, or perhaps conduct a coordinated turn. Imagine more complex maneuvers like a climbing or descending turn, or guiding the aircraft to the runway on a stormy night. All this while communicating with ATC in a compressed shorthand of WilCo(s), squawks, and clearance acknowledgments. So much information to assimilate and integrate. The jobs of a pilot are many!

I struggled with this in my early instrument training. They call it the *scan*, surveying all the instruments in quick succession with comprehension of meaning feeling always just a bit late, no time to catch up. The bandwidth needed to gain accurate insight into the aircraft's role in the world was daunting. We had a scenario in which a ground-based non-directional beacon (NDB) located three to four miles from the airport was our sole radio source for navigating to the runway. Might as well been an AM radio pop music station, it had the same frequency range and precision. No matter how many times I tried to find the airport, I failed. I was miles off course, in some cases. Small comfort, but much later in my flying while conducting a similar approach during my first jet type rating simulator experience I saw the airport disappear behind me, the runway threshold whizzing by at 120 knots. I prayed that scenario wouldn't be on the test.

One novelty, somewhat reassuring, is that unlike the private pilot rating process, student instrument pilots are never left to their own devices. There are no solos, so the worst that can happen is an ongoing risk of bruised ego, characterized by loss of control events, failed navigation, a host of instrument landing procedure programing errors, and incredibly awkward and ill-conceived radio transmissions. I did eventually get better.

Curiously, in some ways the job has gotten harder since the steam gauge days (various instruments scattered about the panel) when I was learning. Modern integrated systems from companies like Garmin, Collins, and Honeywell have served to greatly automate flying, but with that comes an increased programming and monitoring burden on the pilot. Much mystery surrounds the way the magical flight management systems (FMS) work, with intimate knowledge of function dispensed largely on a need to know basis. The setups also can be challenging in the sense that it is very easy to make a mistake entering commands or organizing the configuration. And the new modern autopilots, while very powerful, sometimes deliver puzzling results. Monitoring is very important.

Fast forward to the near present, on one of our flights to the busy San Jose International Airport, I accidentally switched the navigation source, normally tuned to the ILS, to RNAV, also known as GPS. In the case of a precision ILS approach, the Citation Jet 3's Collins system is designed to support hybrid sourcing strategy, where guidance begins with satellite and then automatically switches to the more precise ground station-based ILS to obtain lateral and vertical guidance. But because of my error both sources were now set to deliver GPS guidance. As a result, when we crossed the point in space where the switch from GPS guidance to ILS guidance would normally occur, nothing happened. The computer had dutifully switched sources but because they were both GPS, the ILS intercept failed. Exciting! Fortunately, the weather was pretty good and the airport largely in sight. This gave us the time we needed to diagnose the problem without having to go around. So much drama, all caused by an accidental push of one soft key on the primary flight display.

There is also a lot more heads-down behavior in the cockpit with these systems. Entering route changes into the FMS, changing frequencies, etc. With two pilots this is less of a problem, but as a single pilot (SP) the need to interface with the computer so much of the time can lower the margin of safety. This is especially true when mixing it up with VFR traffic in high-density airspace—lots of targets.

The other downside comes not from the equipment, but from the way the airspace is organized. This is especially true in terminal areas like New York, Miami, Dallas, San Francisco, and LA with their high traffic densities. With the advent of precision GPS transitions, arrivals, approaches, and departures, compound navigation profiles have become practical, and from ATC's point of view desirable, because more traffic can be supported without increasing the burden on controllers. A challenge for pilots, however, because the procedures are often much more complex, more difficult to program, monitor, and modify once commenced.

The airspace has been complicated for a long time, but these procedures are unique. They are characterized by numerous waypoints, many incorporating curvilinear courses in-between, combined with rapidly unfolding and varied descent or climb profiles. Speed restrictions are sometimes incorporated. More concerning, some arrival and departure procedures are so byzantine that it isn't practical to fly them without help from the computer—a weak spot in the system because if the programming is wrong there is no good manual recovery option for the pilots.

Most of the time it all works, though sometimes even the best intentions go unrewarded. We were flying Songi Two Hotel departure procedure out of Zurich, departing from runway 34. The procedure is relatively simple compared to some, having just a couple of curved segments, one altitude restriction, and one speed restriction. Still, I managed to mess it up by cutting a corner passing the first waypoint after takeoff. Ironically, the mistake occurred transitioning from hand flying to FMS control. Rather than following the charted course, I had the computer going direct to the next waypoint, thereby missing the first waypoint by about a quarter of a mile. There was never a safety issue, but that didn't stop the Federal Office of Civil Aviation (the Swiss FAA) from sending us a summons. Their issue was noise abatement, and in our case the small shortcut took the airplane over a noise sensitive area. Fortunately, ours was a first-time offense and with a little lawyering the problem went away.

Europe is the worst, at least when it comes to airspace complexity. Almost any trip has the airplane in New York City—like Class B airspace all the way. The problem is in part traffic density, and in part confined geography—Europe has a lot of airplanes and very little room. There are also sovereignty issues, especially when it comes to noise abatement, the instinct being to put the noise on top of someone else's country. Culture plays a role, too. Europeans have become accustomed to increasing degrees of regulation, and it is clearly present in their aviation system. VFR is highly restricted in most countries. Even on a nice day, flying anywhere far requires an instrument flight plan. Enforcement is intense, especially now that the new mode S transponders are required on all aircraft operating in positive control airspace, where most of the flying is done. These devices tattle on the pilots in real time, making it easy for governing bodies to identify the "guilty" parties. Compounding the issue, radio communication is often hampered by the wide variety of thick accents along with occasional non-standard, sometimes non-English, radio transmissions. Flying in Europe is a tiring day.

Happily, most of the US is not nearly as restrictive. There are still many parts of the country with airspace that is completely free of restriction (at least up to 18,000 feet). Still, the European model is gradually being adopted with more NYC-style airspaces cropping up, along with a proliferation of both permanent and temporary flight restrictions. Worrisome! General aviation advocacy groups are fighting back, but their efforts likely amount to, at best, a holding action. With the lines drawn, it is and always will be, up to the well-intentioned controller and talented, well-trained, resourceful, instrument pilot to make the system work.

Instrument flying has gotten a lot easier in one way. Weather forecasting is much better, and weather reporting is now almost in real time. The terminal aerodrome forecasts (TAFs) are about 85 percent accurate, even out to 30 hours, the maximum forecast period. Voyage times are a lot less than that. More germane to actual flying, forecast information, along with the aviation routine weather reports (METARs) and next generation weather radar (NEXRAD), is available in the cockpit. Knowing that even short-term forecasts are largely probability statements, being in a position to observe changes in weather along the route of intended travel is a huge advantage. This is especially so when bad weather, like thunderstorms, is forecast for all or a portion of the flight route. The ability to see the storms as they form gives the pilot options for avoidance, such as deviations to the right or left of the original route. In the case of destination weather, a good aerodrome forecast gone bad revealed in a timely way is not the end of the world. Usually, there are plenty of good alternates and plenty of time (and fuel reserve) to reach them, if the decision to divert is made early.

There are, however, limits to these technologies, and traps await the unwary. Returning from Oshkosh, Wisconsin, (the AirVenture event) on our way to White Plains, in Westchester County, New York, one stormy evening the airplane experienced a failure of its primary *on-board* radar. This is the system that paints storms (intensity of precipitation, really) accurately and precisely in real time, with both horizontal and vertical scans incorporated into the picture. (There is a strong correlation between heavy precipitation and severe turbulence, especially in electrical storms.) We were flying a Cessna 525. It's the smallest in the line of Citation Jet turbofan models, but has plenty of pep. The airplane's maximum cruise altitude is 41,000 feet, allowing it to top most build-ups while affording the crew enough of a vantage point to steer around anything higher. The reality, however, is that all missions, however high or fast, have to end in a descent, often with much weather along the way. So it was with our arrival into White Plains.

Admission: NEXRAD, the near real-time, ground-station-generated, telemetry-based weather tool that is available in most cockpits really should only be used as a strategic tool, a way to miss storms entirely by altering course from many miles away. The system's precision and timeliness should not be relied on to find a safe way through a densely packed line. At a minimum, the pilot needs onboard Doppler radar for that. With NEXRAD, the display can be more than 12 minutes old, plenty of time for an existing storm to recycle or a new one to be born. Further, the resolution of the ground-based radar representations is limited. Each square pixel represents, at best, a two square kilometer area. Too big! At the outer limits of NEXRAD's range, the resolution is much worse. And the elevation depicted (height where precipitation was detected), is variable because the ground station's radar beam projects upward at an angle of 0.5 percent. Nearer the station the precipitation will be depicted at a lower altitude; the farther away the higher the altitude (e.g., 50,500 feet at 124 NM from the station). There can also be a "cone of silence" over the station where absolutely no data is generated. Composite analysis smooths out these effects to some extent, but it isn't really possible to conduct a thorough assessment of the storm's entire profile, not in the way that onboard radar can. In particular, not having the vertical information makes it difficult to determine the best altitude to fly. Needless to say, picking one's way through the abyss, solely dependent on this technology, can be very exciting.

Yet, that is what we decided to do on our way home from Oshkosh. I recall thinking that the best way to penetrate the line would be to try to guess the movement of the bad (heavy precipitation) areas on the display. Yes, the information was old. My hope was that the trending would offer insight into where not to go. This was definitely a good idea on paper. Too bad it didn't work. Ironically, NEXRAD's trending (extrapolation really) caused us to enter where the weather ended up being the roughest. The relatively clear areas, away from the depicted movement, were a trap. Unbeknownst to us, brand new and strong storms were firing up there. It is wise to remember that "weather doesn't move, it forms, evolves, as conditions change."

The passengers in the back, most of them pilots returning from aviation Mecca, were terrified, experiencing their first real encounter with a level 3 or 4 thunderstorm, in a jet no less. Funny observations and nervous joking turned to silence, the constant lightning and severe turbulence dampening the mood. Those of us flying were terrified, too. The deafening sound of the storm, thunder combined with rain pelting the fuselage, was unrelenting.

Big storm rain or hail noise should not be underestimated. Heavy rain alone in the cockpit has acoustics similar to a freight train. Loud! The noise cancelling headsets help, but they are certainly not foolproof. Black boxes play back all too frequent "Can you say that again," or, "I don't understand" exchanges between the captain and the first officer before that really bad event happens. A bigger problem, turbulence, can make it challenging to program the FMS or even make a heading/altitude change, steady hands being in short supply. Severe turbulence can lead to a loss of control and/ or structural failure. Fortunately, hail wasn't an issue in our case, but it certainly could have been. There are many examples of airplanes being destroyed (leading edge surfaces pounded in) due to hail. This all contributes to the creeping chaos that is so typical of inadvertent thunderstorm encounters.

We survived this cumulonimbus adventure feeling lucky to be in one piece, with damage limited to minor erosion of the radar dome paint. Years later, Steve Berson, one of the pilots observing from the cabin, told me he'd thought there was no way out and we were all going to die. And his assessment wasn't without merit. There were many ways we could have lost the ship. Anything from dual engine flameouts to catastrophic structural failure was on the table. Scary! If you survive your errors in judgement, and also have the ability to recognize them, you will be a better and safer pilot. To the point, I never made that mistake again. No need, there were always new ones lurking.

Accomplishing the instrument rating represented a big upgrade in utility and safety. Weather that would have stopped us in our tracks under visual flight rules became more of a footnote, the discussion turning to how to properly prepare and plan; to fuel reserves, alternates, proper charting, and so on. This is, however, a cautionary tale. The first Pump Co. trip scheduled after achieving my instrument rating had to be cancelled. The 40 hours of dual training, a very tough written test, followed by a practical test in the airplane that was both technically challenging and extremely comprehensive—i.e., long—just wasn't enough to overcome the Kitchener forecast of low ceilings and visibilities (fog). Rescheduling the next day wasn't the answer, either. This time, being winter, it was ice in the clouds that stopped us. Amazingly, it took four attempts before the weather cooperated and the trip was a go.

The irony of the situation was not lost on me, or my Pump Co. colleagues. We had flown VFR for years without ever seeing a cloud, not one mission cancelled. Now, with all these IFR capabilities at our disposal, we were stuck, several scheduled flights all a no-go. How could this happen?

The answer is very simple: while it is true that the vast majority of weather days are good, certainly good enough to fly IFR in a small airplane, the few bad days are often very bad—terrible, really. Any forecast with a deep low pressure system, ice, a line of big thunderstorms, very low visibilities over a large area, or high winds (aloft or at the destination) demands pause. Bigger and better equipment increases the options, but the same general rules apply. Freezing rain, for example, will bring down a large fancy turbofan aircraft just as fast as it will a piston twin or single, under some circumstances.

After those initial setbacks, the Pump Co.'s flight department redeemed itself with a long series of IFR flights, all safely conducted in IFR weather, and completely on schedule. Reliability delayed but not denied? Perhaps the proper mantra for this thing we call modern aviation.

## Lessons learned:

**Lesson 1:** There are a lot of very nice flying weather days, but the few bad ones can be really bad.

**Lesson 2:** Present day automation doesn't necessarily make the job easier. Our time is one in which the pinnacles of complexity and capability have been reached. At best, throughput is enhanced, but in exchange the burden imparted to the crew grows, and is worrisome. The future foretells something different. Likely beginning with sport aviation, then Part 23 normal category, AI technology will help the pilot communicate with and program the various devices. Later it will make suggestions as to strategy and tactics. This is a new world in which the copilot may be a computer.

**Lesson 3:** European airspace sucks! If you have to fly there, carry a big checkbook to handle the exorbitant fees, speak clearly and simply, confirm everything requested by ATC, read the small print on the charts (twice), make sure that the little airplane on the moving map is following the charted course, and have a good aviation attorney standing by.

**Lesson 4:** Ground-based weather systems, especially radar systems, are not timely or precise enough to penetrate a line of thunderstorms.

**Lesson 5:** Be cautious, especially when flying near deep low pressure systems, thunderstorms, freezing rain, wide areas of very low visibility, and high winds.

# 8 | Training Experience Risk

In aviation, there is a rating, a certificate, for everything. Not all are pilot ratings, involving certification to fly something, either. There is a rating for the dispatcher—the person who determines the flight planning, weather information, loading, fuel requirements, and a bunch of paperwork needed to comply with the regulations. Flight engineers, the person typically seated sideways in the cockpit, have a special rating, too. A disappearing breed, they have enjoyed a long and celebrated history, keeping cantankerous engines and other systems running, all before more reliable designs and automation made their function redundant. There is a parachute rigger rating for those interested in packing chutes. Curiously, there is no rating for the person who actually uses the parachute and jumps out of the airplane—perhaps a commentary on the skillset required for each activity.

My fantasy rating has always been airships, including blimps and rigid dirigible style designs, like the Hindenburg only using helium, of course, instead of hydrogen. How can one resist the opportunity to captain a giant sky yacht? So far that fantasy hasn't been fulfilled, but I've done the preparation work, including reading the Navy's K-Class type training course, largely written by the manufacturer, Goodyear, and studying the FAA Practical Test Standards. Interestingly, during World War II, the Navy training course was classified, so there are many references to the Espionage Act. Just losing the blimp manual during that time was punishable by a fine of $10,000 and two years in prison.

Now that the secrets are out, anyone, in theory, can become a blimp pilot. Unfortunately, there are no blimp/dirigible schools so, in practice, the ambition is exceedingly difficult to fulfill. One could buy a blimp, of course, but even for those willing to incur the expense, there would be the challenge of finding an instructor and ultimately an examiner. The statistics are telling. Blimp pilot numbers are so low the FAA doesn't bother reporting them in their annually published Civil Airmen Statistics. According to the

Washington Post, there are only 128 people qualified to fly airships in the US and one designated examiner.[1]

Fortunately, there are many other pilot ratings to pursue, most obtainable either by enrolling in an FAA-approved school or through private instruction from a certified flight instructor. Training aircraft are available, as well, usually on a rental basis. There are two- and four-year aviation degrees available, Perdue University and Embry-Riddle Aeronautical University being two sources. These schools provide flight training along with a formal curriculum to prepare the undergraduate for a well-rounded career in aviation, with courses in disciplines like finance, marketing, and engineering, to name a few. There are many options for the aspiring pilot.

Given the number of options, selecting a path forward can feel daunting. On top of that, there is a large financial component to the decision. Flying school is expensive. It is also important to select a provider based on a determination of the curriculum needed. If the goal is to fly for an airline company or fractional, the more formal, comprehensive, and concentrated university experience may be the right answer. Airlines typically will not consider an applicant who doesn't hold a four-year degree in something.

Getting a job as an airline pilot doesn't necessarily mean that only pilots need apply. Many airlines, especially in Europe, prefer college graduates with no flying experience. Not having been contaminated, it is, presumably, easier to teach them how to fly the company way. (The airlines better hope there are no flaws in the training, the fear being that the graduating trainees may all make the same mistake some day.)

Big schools are not the only way to go. There are Part 141 schools that focus 100 percent on teaching flying, and freelance instructors who teach with their own aircraft or a rental. These smaller operations can be good for somebody who is primarily interested in recreational flying, or for business travel unrelated to the flying itself. They also can provide a more intimate and customized training, which is especially helpful for students who like to proceed at their own pace or have other commitments.

All of these options can yield a good training experience, but do they guarantee a good safe pilot at the end? It depends. The schools play a part, but these days predicting a graduate's safety record is much more about assessing the pilot's character, curiosity, judgment, emotional intelligence, analytical intelligence, reflective abilities, ability to analyze risk, and risk

---

[1] Andrew Van Dam, "The blimp industry is changing, right over our noses," *Washington Post*, June 9, 2018

tolerance. The risk equation, in particular, is interesting because predicting the likelihood of a pilot-induced (pilot error) accident requires both knowing the individual's tolerance for risk and ability to analyze risk. For example, a pilot with a low tolerance for risk and no ability to analyze risk is probably just as likely to have a problem as the pilot with high risk tolerance. Being unaware of the risks or unable to analyze them makes it difficult or impossible to ascertain whether the trip can be conducted safely.

Schools try to train students to avoid high risk scenarios by teaching by rote—don't fly into level 4 thunderstorms, don't go below minimums on the approach, don't run out of gas. Pay-for-service charter and airline operations teach through a complex set of standard operating procedures (SOPs) and governance rules. The better operations add scenario-based training into the mix. These strategies have merit, but they are not foolproof. The crash of the Asiana Boeing 777, Flight 214, at San Francisco International Airport is a case in point. There were four highly qualified, well-trained pilots on that flight. All systems were functioning normally, and it was a clear sunny day. Yet the airplane hit a seawall prior to reaching the runway 28. How could this happen? The NTSB concluded that the entire approach had been mismanaged, with the final incorrect action causing an undetected disengagement of the auto throttle, leading to loss of airspeed. By the time the error was recognized and power added manually, it was too late. Deteriorated speed and altitude made the crash inevitable. More telling was the role that training played in fostering the accident. Asiana pilots were taught to always use the FMS and autopilot system when making approaches. Even on a nice day, hand flying was never part of the Asiana approach and landing SOP. Why didn't at least one of the pilots recognize the looming risk associated with a deteriorating airspeed and then take action, like disconnecting the autopilot and adding power? The report states that Asiana pilots rarely practiced hand flying and were nowhere near proficient at it. There was no one in the cockpit with hand flying experience beyond the very little taught in simulator school.

After the deaths of three passengers, injury of 187, and total loss of the aircraft, Asiana changed its training procedures to include more hand flying both in school and in the air. The change certainly addresses one problem. Unfortunately, there are likely others looming for them. Routinized uniform curriculums have made flying safer than it ever has been. Still, applying rehearsed response actions to real world flying challenges does not guarantee a good outcome 100 percent of the time. The human being in charge must be able to synthesize the right answer, instigate the right outcome, even when the training and systems fail to do so. This is especially so when flying alone or on an unfamiliar route, in unpredicted weather or with a mechanical failure. Assuming a great technical foundation, can experience and judgement be taught in a way that effectively mitigates for flying's risk and danger? Is it possible somehow to impart a minimal wisdom before those wings are pinned on? The old aviation saying, "Good judgment comes from experience, and experience comes from bad judgment," reflects the conventional thinking that flying safely equals the sum of poor decisions, errors in judgment, and just plain bad luck. Certainly, trial and error can improve safety longer term, but it also has to be acknowledged that there is still exposure to danger. In most cases, things work out. The pilot learns from the experience and next time he or she does better. Occasionally the outcome is bad. Sometimes a look back at the pilot's history reveals a missed opportunity to learn. More often, though, an unfamiliar set of circumstances unfolded, leaving the pilot unable to cope. The feeling expressed at the very end: puzzlement.

Something like this happened to me while flying a business trip with several colleagues from Burlington, Vermont, destination Portland, Maine. The travel distance is short, about 132 nautical miles, and well within the single-engine Bonanza V35's full fuel range. Shortly after takeoff I noticed fuel slowly porting out the fuel caps on both the left and right sides. (Located very near the wing's leading edge, a low-pressure area when flying, the Bonanza caps are finicky, notoriously difficult to seal.) Not knowing the rate of fuel loss, I decided to land at Sugarbush to close the caps and get more fuel. It was daytime, and the weather was good. And, of course, I was very familiar with the airport.

With caps closed and tanks full, I took off for Portland, now about 30 minutes away. Unfortunately, my efforts made no difference on the right side. Fuel was still porting out. Damn it! While not a gusher, it was apparent that something was wrong with the right cap. Rather than land again at Sugarbush, I decided to press on to Maine where there would be maintenance. The left tank cap was working and the quantity of fuel carried in that tank was well beyond what was needed for the distance. There was no risk of fuel starvation even assuming a complete loss of fuel out the right side. Messy blue stain on the wing from fuel dye, yes. Increased danger/risk, no. At least that is what I determined at the time.

The remainder of the trip to Portland was uneventful. I landed, taxied over to maintenance, and then drove off to the previously scheduled meeting. When I returned that evening, the cap problem was reportedly fixed, and the airplane refueled. The weather had deteriorated, though; rainy with ceilings at both airports around 1,200 feet, visibilities 3 miles. No problem, both the pilot and aircraft were IFR certified. Although winter, temperatures aloft were relatively warm, and no ice was forecasted. The mission profile was well within our capabilities.

We departed Portland at around 4:30 p.m. December days are short in New England so by the time we reached altitude it was dark. Not really expecting a problem, I pointed the cockpit flashlight out the window to confirm the leak had been fixed. To my surprise fuel was porting out the right side, and in copious amounts; much more than before. So much for quality maintenance, I muttered to myself. As before, the short distance to our destination, well within the range of the airplane with the fuel contained in the left tank, suggested nothing worse than low mileage, so we continued home where maintenance there would presumably do a better job.

As we approached Burlington, the weather improved a bit. They were calling for broken 3,000-foot ceilings, visibility five miles. Flying IFR in the dark does up the risk somewhat, especially in the case of an engine failure. There are advantages, however. Generally, the distinctly patterned and illuminated airport environment is easier to see at night, easily distinguishable from its amorphous surroundings. Such was the case this night.

The active runway was 15, but the winds, while light had shifted to the north, making the northwest facing runway, runway 33, more desirable. We were told by the controller to wait for two F-16s on final approach in the opposite direction. Shortly after the F-16s landed we were cleared for the visual approach to 33.

The approach itself was uneventful. Winds were perfect, 330 degrees, and, although the runway was wet, at 8,500 feet in length there was no landing distance issue to consider. Cleared to land several miles out and with the lights defining the runway end and borders plainly visible, I lowered the landing gear and set the flaps to maximum. Some larger runways have center lights, but Burlington's 33 has none, so it does appear from the cockpit that the airplane is descending into a giant black rectangular hole. Unfortunately, the only recourse is to ignore the illusion. Most general aviation airplane landing lights aren't powerful enough to reveal the runway itself until right on top of it.

As the airplane neared the runway, I glanced at the right wing. Now painted in the ambient light of the airport it was apparent that things had gotten worse. The fuel leak had become a gusher. No problem, soon we would be safely on the ground, all defects made good in the morning.

I reduced power to slow the airplane in preparation for the flare. Now that we were close to the threshold, the runway numbers were partially visible, although the surface beyond remained mostly a void. Aligning with the white lights ahead and those peripherally in view, I initiated the flare. Then, just at the expected moment of touchdown, there was a deafening BANG. At the same time, the entire airplane shook violently. Touchdown followed shortly after, but the short, intense bang, though unaccompanied by fire and explosion, was just terrifying. The shudder, more prolonged, had me convinced that the airplane was coming apart.

To my amazement, we tracked straight on the runway with no indication of damage. We were shaken for sure, but still in one piece. What had happened?

After slowing to taxi speed and exiting the runway, I called ground control to inform them of our experience. I said, "It felt like we hit a 4x4 on the runway." Ground acknowledged our report and said they would check the runway for debris. While taxiing back to the ramp, we got another call from ground control requesting that "the Captain" call the tower. I stopped the airplane on the taxiway, WilCo-ed the request, and then dutifully wrote down the number prior to proceeding to parking.

Opening the door of the airplane, we could see something was seriously wrong with the right cap, filler port, or both. There was fuel everywhere. Because the Bonanza has only one passenger door, and it is located on the right side, everyone had to step through a blue puddle of reeking fuel to exit. The airplane itself appeared to be undamaged.

What about the call to the tower? Usually, a request like this means something bad has happened—with the pilot undoubtedly the guilty party.

Miracle of miracles, it turned out the pilot was innocent. The tower chief, who answered the phone himself, sheepishly admitted that the Cab crew had forgotten to lower the arresting cable after the F-16s landed. There was no 4x4, but there was a 1¼ inch diameter cable strung across the runway, perhaps 8 inches above the surface at its lowest point.

Burlington, also an Air Guard Base, uses a BAK 12 arresting system that can be raised and lowered under Tower control. Basically, it consists of a wire, held taut, that engages the emergency tail hook of an F-16 or other military aircraft in the event of brake failure after landing. On this particular night, the system was engaged, which is SOP when F-16s are landing or taking off. Normally the cable at the end of the runway is the one raised, and so it was, at least from the point of view of the F-16s landing on runway 15. Not so for us, the traffic landing on Runway 33. By both forgetting to lower the barrier after the F-16s landed, and switching runways, the Tower had placed a barrier in the middle of the runway touchdown zone. Yikes!

I confirmed with ATC that everyone was okay, with no apparent damage to aircraft. My operational assumption was that the main wheels had grazed the cable. Eventually, I told the passengers what had happened. I elected not to share my own doubts about the series of decisions made during the trip.

It's pure speculation, wondering whether the cable could have snagged the Bonanza's landing gear. If it had, the relatively light aircraft no doubt would have experienced serious damage, perhaps even failure of undercarriage or other related structural components. Loss of control, gear failure, or worse, were real possibilities. The wild card, of course, was the AVGAS pooled on airplane's right wing, standing at the ready to spark a spectacular fire. Knowing the primary exit is located on the right side completes the picture. Disaster would have been the likely outcome.

There are a number of lessons to be learned from this experience, including whether it is ever a good idea to fly with a fuel leak. The more interesting conversation, however, is about pilot decision-making and ways to make it better. There is an acknowledgement that good judgment is difficult to teach, but what about good decision-making? Is there a systematic way to teach, and to learn, how to make better decisions?

In the case of the Portland trip, the decisions seemed prudent at the time. The initial problem, fuel leaking from both the left and right tank was recognized as an existential threat—fuel exhaustion—hence the impromptu landing at Sugarbush. With the airplane refueled, departed from Sugarbush, and on the way to Portland, a quick visual inspection revealed that the left tank problem had been fixed, but the right tank problem remained. The decision to continue was made knowing that 1) there would be sufficient fuel to reach the destination, and 2) competent maintenance would be available in Portland. Then, on the return, subsequent inspection revealed that maintenance had failed to correct the leak on the right side. Whatever happened in Portland, had only served to make the problem worse. The decision: *carry on*, just as before.

Reasonable persons may disagree about the right path forward, but independent of the choice, there was something new going on, something not internalized by the pilot as a potential treat. The new thing was a big leak instead of a small one. That meant risk of fire, a red alert. The prudent choices, at this point, would have been to return to Portland or continue on to Burlington, but in any case, it was time to leverage all resources, definitely informing ATC that something was wrong.

Assuming destination Burlington, the Bonanza likely would have received priority, even over the F-16s. At the very least, Tower personnel would have been on a higher state of alertness. The arresting system mistake might never have happened, the error prevented because of a heightened sense of awareness and urgency. Further, in the worst case, with everything unfolding as before, the airport's emergency teams would have been ready, on stand-by, quickly available to fight any fire.

I never made the error again, but with training could the error have been avoided in the first place? I think the answer is yes, if it is also true that pilots can be taught to identify risk, in isolation and as a series of prospective branching decisions—a decision tree, where most or all of the branches are identified, including those with bad outcomes. This is not so much about guaranteeing the safety of every flight. That is impossible to do. The idea here is, as best as possible, to come to an understanding of relative risk, both in advance of the flight and ongoing.

In the case of the Bonanza flight, there was a failure on the part of the pilot to recognize the risk of fire while en route or on landing. The mistake occurred after takeoff. Perhaps a more imaginative or paranoid pilot would have worried about the cap not working before leaving Portland, but that is probably too much to ask. After all, maintenance declared the problem fixed. How best to address?

Prospective risk management is a tool that can help. The inputs to the problem are relatively simple: 1) pilot capability skill set and currency, 2) weather, 3) aircraft performance, capability, and loading, 4) aircraft reliability and maintenance, and 5) the airspace environment in play. Understanding these five things on a dynamic basis, along with the mission profile, is enough to ascertain a good assessment of the flight's risk from beginning to end, and it's all entirely teachable.

A simple example: we routinely fly our Citation Jet 3 (CJ3) from Burlington, Vermont, to Boca Raton, Florida. The normal routing distance is about 1,200 nautical miles and the airplane has full fuel legs equal to about 1,800 NM. Given the following conditions, what would be the prospective risk?

1) Weather in Burlington is good, but from South Carolina and for the remainder of the route the weather is bad; stormy with low ceilings and visibilities. It is windy, too, with headwinds as high as 80 knots all the way down. Also, the trip would be conducted at night.

2) The payload includes six passengers and luggage, so fuel loading will have to be reduced from full fuel, 4,800 lbs, to 4,200 lbs. The six-hundred-pound reduction is equal to 30 minutes less endurance and perhaps 200 NM less range.

3) Boca Raton's best approaches are GPS based (RNAV) so ceilings there will have to be higher than 300 feet. The forecast has the weather at Boca and the surrounding area with ceilings 300 to 500 feet, visibility 2 miles.

4) Everything is functioning in the airplane, but the alternate airport, West Palm, has a Notice to Airmen (NOTAM) posted indicating that the ILS to runway 10 left, the only approach able to deliver the airplane to 200 feet above the ground, is broken.

There likely would be other factors, including traffic flow control/congestion at the destination, and the experience of the crew, but for this example the four inputs listed are sufficient to make the point.

How to assess the risk? The first step would be to identify conditions that diverge from ideal. In this case there are four: 1) adverse winds and bad weather at the destination, 2) night conditions, 3) less than maximum fuel hence less than maximum range/less than maximum endurance, and 4) an alternate lacking a precision landing system to guide the aircraft to a safe landing under worst case weather conditions.

The next step would be to ascertain if any of the less than ideal conditions suggest something really scary is likely to happen. An obvious possibility would be fuel exhaustion due to adverse winds and a lower fuel inventory made necessary by the number of passengers on board. While the weather isn't forecasted to go below the approach minimums at either the destination or alternate airport in this example, what if the forecast is wrong, and in the wrong way? Would there be enough gas to get to another airport with better weather?

Here is where it gets interesting, step 3. This is where the identified risk is either accepted, mitigated, or rejected as unacceptable. All three pathways must be considered, both in terms of prudence and the merit (importance) of the mission flown. For example, if flying the mission as originally planned commanded a high degree of merit, it may be okay to accept a higher risk profile in some cases. The military operates this way all the time. In the case of civilian flying, mission merit rarely reaches a level sufficient to justify exposing crew and passengers to danger, but there are, of course, shades of gray.

I recall a trip from Burlington to Palm Springs in a CE-525, the original Citation Jet. The CE-525 is really slow by jet standards, with a maximum speed of about 350 knots true. On this particular winter day the winds were bad, really bad—120 knots on the nose sometimes. With two fuel stops, it took us almost 13 hours to reach the destination. We were a crew of two, and both of us were tired. Indicative of fatigue, the last landing of the day (by then night) was not exactly smooth. Under Part 91 there is no crew rest requirement, so our long day was legal. Was it prudent? In hindsight, I would have had us rest up overnight somewhere along the way, but the meeting was important, and key events were scheduled prior to any next-day arrival time. And everyone on board wanted to be done with traveling for a while, so all were motivated to tough it out to the end. We consciously elected to accept the risk of flying in a state of some fatigue in exchange for arriving at the destination on time—proof by example, a risk versus reward decision.

My answer to the Boca trip problem would be to ensure there always will be enough fuel to land somewhere safely, no matter what. One way to do this would be to stop north of South Carolina and refuel as a contingency. Then, if Florida weather failed to cooperate, worst case, the plan would be to return to somewhere north. So, with a fuel stop built into the plan as a backup, off we would go. Most likely we would follow the plan as proposed, with the fuel stop, but what if both winds and weather shaped up to be more favorable while underway? Has the risk equation really changed? The answer is perhaps, but the pilot would need to be very careful not to fall into the trap where everything works, up to the point where it doesn't.

Are the better than expected ceilings and visibility revealed by an updated METAR received while en route a genuine improvement reflective of something fundamental like a front moving faster or slower than expected? If not, beware. The improvement may be temporary, caused by something local and unsustainable. Key to learning a good decision-making process is being able to differentiate between fundamental cause and effect events, and others that may seem happy in nature but difficult to explain. Be wary of the latter.

This idea is important, especially when trying to gauge risk in a dynamic environment. As you are flying along, the world is constantly changing. Most of the time, the changes are inconsequential, presenting minor challenges. But what about outside-of-the-box events, a fuel leak, or something more insidious like a generator failure? The CJ3 has a dual generator system, plus a battery to power all systems. Normally, the airplane operates with all three sources of power in the loop. Should one generator fail, the other is completely capable of running the airplane's electrical system and charging the battery. What about a dual generator failure, what happens then? I actually had a chance to practice this in the simulator while at school. Very exciting! I can testify that a dual generator failure is a real emergency. Like many jets, the CJ3 is a highly electric airplane, so with no generators working flying becomes a race against time. In the case of this airplane, assuming maximum conservation, the time to total electrical failure is less than 30 minutes, after which options diminish significantly with little or no avionics available, gear extension a one-way manual blow down process, and no flaps or spoilers. There better be a nice weather airport with a long runway somewhere, ready and waiting.

In real life, I have had a generator failure only once flying the Citation Jet series. We immediately aborted, and diverted to the New York Cessna Service Center in Newburgh. Thinking about the Boca mission, assuming forecasted weather or worse, I would do something similar, perhaps attempting Orlando (where there is also a Cessna Service Center), but only if I were 100 percent confident the weather there would cooperate. Otherwise, the answer would be to make a complete 180 and head north. Then, worst case, should the other generator fail, an emergency VFR landing could be safely conducted on Piedmont Triad's (Greensboro, North Carolina) very long 9,000-feet runway. They have a Cessna Service Center, too.

The final answer to the question, no matter what the scenario, is less important than the thought process. This is about the ability to ferret out branches of the decision-making tree that end with both desirable and less than desirable results. Whether the pilot elects to follow a path with one or more of the possible outcomes potentially bad, making that decision is less important than having the ability to make the analysis. Accurately assessing and comparing the risks identified with the rewards delivered is what leads to prudent and effective flying, a skillset ideally mastered at a very early stage.

## Lessons learned:

**Lesson 1:** Decision-making skills can be taught; judgment, not so much.

**Lesson 2:** Risk analysis can improve safety, provided the analysis is accurate and the pilot's decision-making process always rates any prospective serious danger higher than the merit of conducting the mission as originally planned.

**Lesson 3:** Pilots consciously electing to fly dangerous missions using a risk analysis decision-making process are more likely to succeed than pilots who don't. This is because rehearsing the scary branches of the tree in advance of the flight increases the probability that events likely to lead to a bad outcome will be recognized and addressed early.

**Lesson 4:** Fuel leaks are a serious threat (fuel exhaustion, fuel imbalance, and fire).

**Lesson 5:** The autopilot is a valuable tool, but it is not a substitute for demonstrated hand flying ability.

# 9 | Tug Driver

How many bad days begin with no indication of trouble? Curiously, in aviation, they all seem to start that way. And, yet, to the extent that there is trouble brewing, innocence and a sense of wellbeing are almost always the precursor. So it was for me, number two for runway 4 at Sugarbush, flying the tow plane, following a glider that failed to find lift after taking one of the first tows of the day. Early morning soaring can be challenging, because the sun's rays are weaker, slow to kick off the thermals that gliders need to stay aloft. It was also a busy day, nearly a dozen gliders already waiting for a tow, lined up on the grass to the left of the hard surface runway. We were flying the tows closer to the airport, making our descents faster and steeper, and the patterns much tighter, all to keep the line moving.

Turning onto final approach, I could see the glider in front of me tracking to touch down near the painted numbers indicating runway orientation on the hard surface. With the glider's landing imminent, I was focused on landing short, to be in good position to connect for the next glider in line for the tow, somewhat oblivious to the fact that my closing speed had increased. Airplanes naturally fly patterns a little faster than gliders, which is important to know for judging safe spacing. The problem can be exacerbated by traffic that is tightly packed, the SOP for today.

Recognizing that the separation distance was going to be tight, I slowed the tow plane to around 55 knots, above stall but still low in energy, and uncomfortable. Yes, it was all going to work out, but I also remember making a mental note to add in a little more distance the next time around.

The view, from behind and above, provided an excellent indication of the glider's position and progress. Once on the ground, it would roll out beyond the line-up and then clear left onto the grass. My challenge was to land on the numbers (painted on the runway threshold to indicate compass orientation), then decelerate quickly to be in a good position for the next tow.

Although it's impossible to see the main wheel of the glider as it contacts the runway, there are other cues. Modern gliders are constructed out of fiberglass and other composite materials, which makes them strong, light, and flexible. The trick, then, is to look for the downward deflection of the wing tips. It's usually very pronounced, and a sure sign the glider has stopped flying and is on the ground. This time, though, the deflection was huge, right down to the surface. What happened next was even more dramatic.

With the glider appearing to be on its way to leaving the runway, I began the flare. All good, and with a little less energy than typical, I could be sure of an easy deceleration. Except that the glider wasn't exiting. Instead, it was slowing, then stopping, on the runway, emitting blue smoke from underneath—a wheel brake jam. And—holy shit—I was moving! My speed, 45 knots, may be slow in the air, but on the ground that's fast, we're talking really fast. No way to stop before reaching the glider!

To visualize the setup, imagine the tow plane touching down on the runway, and the glider, stopped on the runway, about 150 feet ahead. To the left of the runway, there is a line of gliders, with no spaces in between. Right of the runway, it is clear of aircraft, and for a good reason. In that direction, there is a gradually descending hill and ravine, populated with small trees, brush, and boulders from the original clearing of land for the airport.

What about flying away? This would have been a good option before touchdown, but on the ground, powered down, still traveling at 45 knots but slowing, and with only a little over one hundred feet of clear runway available, well, that would be pretty exciting. The consequences of a failed go-around are not appealing.

I steered the plane to the right, into the prickly bushes and down the hill. Ceiling and visibility out the windscreen suddenly went from unlimited to a green zero-zero with leaves and branches whacking the aircraft. The sound of trees breaking was deafening. And the airplane wasn't slowing, either, the downhill run adding speed. Estimating course and direction mostly by feel, I turned the airplane back to align with the runway, hoping I had passed the glider, and headed for the north end of the ravine.

*A young Adam serving as a tow pilot for the Region 1 competitors.*

Once there, I calculated the airplane would emerge onto the shorter unoccupied east side emergency grass runway.

The change in course turned out to be fortuitous. The trees thinned out, the sound of branches crashing diminished. And the airplane was slowing. The only downside was the formidable rise on the north side, much steeper than the west side, my entry point.

Emerging from the ravine, as I'd expected, the airplane's trajectory tracked the hill's upward slope into air. It was much like launching off a giant ramp. Despite being far below flying speed, there was still plenty of kinetic energy available to become airborne, albeit briefly. With several feet of altitude beneath me, and no flying speed, there was little to do but wait for the unceremonious, jarring drop to the ground. Should be a crowd pleaser, I thought.

*Bang!* And so began the first day of the 1985 New England Regionals, the Soaring Society of America's Region 1 competition. More than 40 pilots vying for the top slot within their designated classes. Charged with the task of flying a predetermined route, the pilot finishing in the shortest time wins, for the day. After four to six days of competitive flying, the pilot with the best combination of scores wins the event.

Key to making the event fun and fair for the contestants was ensuring adequate tug capacity. The rules call for each glider to be towed to a maximum altitude of 2,000 feet AGL, where they release, enter the start gate, and begin the race. Weather conditions can change rapidly, so the idea is to get as many gliders airborne as possible, in the shortest timespan. Competition rules limit start window times, so it is important that all gliders be airborne in time to comply.

To do this, Sugarbush Soaring, sponsor of the event, and Myndy Woodruff, the commercial tow plane operator, arranged to have three L-19 Bird Dog tow planes available. All three would be operated simultaneously, a choreography of staging on the ground, traffic avoidance in the air, and rapid fire sequencing of the multiple take-offs and landings necessary to launch the fleet quickly.

No one expected to start the day with a near death experience. The prospect of a glider landing hard enough to damage its

*Myndy Woodruff.*

landing gear and lock up the brakes was just not on the radar. Happily, the damage to the L-19 was mostly cosmetic—some scuffed paint along with a few grass stains on the leading edges from the encounter with the ravine's flora. The outcome could have been a lot worse.

Despite the near miss on this day, flying at Sugarbush Airport had evolved to be a lot safer than it was in the Macone days. The former proprietor's departure ushered in a new era of commitment to professionalism. The member-run club, Sugarbush Soaring, employed greater emphasis on training and proficiency, while the new tow plane company, Laundramatics, the name derived from the successful coin-operated laundromats owned and run by Myndy, provided well-maintained tow aircraft piloted by talented, mostly seasoned pilots. Myndy's policy was simple: "Make no junk," meaning the management would view any damage to the aircraft very negatively.

Towing gliders in a production environment is a very good teacher. It is challenging enough just flying the Korean War vintage conventional gear (tailwheel) L-19, renowned for its squirrely handling on the ground and tendency to ground loop. The name, Bird Dog, refers to the plane's original purpose, identifying enemy positions on the battlefield. Couple that with dragging a 1,300-pound glider aloft under variable weather conditions; the pilot's hands are full. Ironically, the best soaring days often are the worst, in terms of conditions, for the tow pilot. Sugarbush Airport is situated in a valley running north to south, well known for its proximity to Mount Ellen and Lincoln Peak to the west—the Green Mountains that, on many days, supply an amazing wave. Glider pilots love the setup. The lift is close to the airport and often starts at a low altitude, making tow duration shorter. But with wave above there is often rotor beneath, and rotor can cause severe turbulence while on tow, sometimes leading to upset. I recall one encounter with rotor in which the tow plane suddenly rolled upside down, uncommanded, while the glider, only 200 feet behind, remained upright. Fortunately, the glider pilot, seeing a dim future for the connection, wisely decided to release. Yet wave days are what glider pilots long for, consistent lift, all the way up into the flight levels.

Turbulence can be scary and even dangerous, but what takes out most tow planes is adverse wind—strong crosswinds and tail winds on landing and takeoff. At Sugarbush in particular, wave days, are bad because the prevailing wind is almost always out of the west, perpendicular to the runway. The same is true of lift originating from the ridge to the east of the airport. All this makes for a test of tow pilot judgement and skills, and much dancing on the controls to be sure everything turns out right.

*L-19 tow pilot operations.*

The gliders themselves can pose a danger to the tow pilot. It is the glider pilot's job to steer in a way to minimize the control forces imparted to the tow pilot. Following at a similar elevation and slightly left of the tow plane (to help correct for P-factor) is the correct technique. Students have a hard time with this, and often are out of alignment, requiring the tow pilot to apply maximum rudder and even stick to address. On one tow that I recall, shortly after takeoff the glider student pilot hauled back on the stick, catching the instructor off guard. The glider zoomed upward, pulling up the tow plane's tail, pointing its nose at the ground. Fortunately, there is a release handle in the tow plane—bye-bye, glider. Still, with the ground rushing up, the time it took to find and pull the handle seemed unsettlingly long. It was a combination of surprise and centripetal acceleration—the tendency of everything, including the left hand trying to reach the handle below, to fly upward toward the ceiling, the sudden transition from level flight to a nose dive making the airplane and its contents, notably me, momentarily weightless.

There are many threats. One that ought to be inexcusable is fuel exhaustion. I make this statement acknowledging a "Never again!" entry in my logbook, recalling a fuel management error that nearly cost me the aircraft. Here is where the focus on production can lead to bad outcomes.

It was SOP at the time to start the day with full tanks. The L-19 carries approximately 22 gallons of AVGAS on each side, the switch, selection made by the pilot using an overhead valve handle. Keeping track of the remaining fuel is fairly easy in the L-19, with the left and right tank gauges indicating quantity mounted inside the cockpit where wings join the fuselage.

The goal is to execute as many tows as possible before stopping to refuel. The question is, how close to empty is too close. The target is one-quarter full on one tank, empty on the other. We thought we had worked out a procedure that, when done properly, would exhaust the fuel in the to-be-emptied tank while high in the air, with plenty of time (and altitude) to switch to the fuller tank. If the engine sputtered, the sputter would be momentary. Seemed like a good idea at the time.

The procedure was always to take off and land on the fuller tank. Then in the climb, after most of the fuel needed to do the tow was consumed, the pilot would switch to the emptier tank.

In hindsight, it is clear the idea had two major weaknesses. First, it required a lot of tank switching, especially when close to that quarter-full tank level. Adding this task to the to-do list for a pilot already handling many other challenges (e.g., winds, bad glider pilots, turbulence.) likely didn't serve to lower risk. Second, a quirk in the L-19's fuel system makes the engine more likely to quit during a dive (say, after the glider releases) than a climb, due to fuel exhaustion. This may seem benign, and it would be, provided the pilot followed SOP and switched the selector back to the tank with more fuel prior to landing. But what if the pilot were to forget?

Although we ran the engine at a relatively high 2,000 rpm in the descent to prevent shock cooling, the power needed and corresponding fuel required remained low; an advantage of going downhill. Only when the airplane was configured dirty, flaps out, in the pattern, would larger amounts of power once again be required. It is precisely at this point, with the wrong tank selected, airplane low to the ground, nose low, power requirements increasing, that the engine would quit. How could the pilot fail to switch the selector properly to the fuller tank? The question is far from academic because forgetting to switch is exactly what I did, one beautiful summer day, while striving for the most tows ever.

There is nothing quite like that sinking feeling when an engine quits near the ground. Here, for your consideration, I present another excellent example of the panic response. My action, certainly unrehearsed, was to switch to the fuller tank (good) and then to flip every panel-mounted switch to "on" (fair) in the hope that one of them would be the electric full boost pump. At altitude, the engine almost always comes back once the tank with gas is selected. But sometimes, due to vapor lock or something similar, it takes some boost to finish the job. Up high, there is time, worst case several minutes, to solve the problem. Down low, engaged in a rapidly descending, deteriorating, final approach, the time available is mere seconds, so I wasn't going to wait to see if I needed the boost pump.

Those watching from the glider staging area said the tow plane momentarily disappeared from view when it descended into the rough cut that led up to runway 22's hard surface. And from the pilot's perspective, the surface of the runway was definitely ahead and above. Mercifully, the engine did come roaring back, but not before the L-19 snagged some tall grass with its tail. Climbing out of the cut was a sight to be seen with the L-19 barely flying, by now mostly hanging on the thrust from the propeller. Fortunately, the airplane was very light—one of the few advantages of having so little fuel, so it all worked out. While not particularly graceful, I recall making it to the hard surface, barely.

This makes it sound as if we were all terribly well-intentioned, prudent, only occasionally a little off in our procedures. While mostly true, I did go through a period of high confidence—cockiness—in my flying. There was nothing overly reckless going on, though I did once chase a motorcycle down the airfield after a long day of towing, nearly snaring it with the tow rope. What could be more fun? I thought I was keeping a safe distance from the target during the chase, but I had forgotten about the heavy metal ring whipping

*Steve Maynard, Sugarbush tow pilot.*

around at the end of the 200-foot rope. The rope-ring assembly came within inches of wrapping round the motorcyclist. Had it made contact it would have caused serious injury, for sure. Not good! I got in a lot of trouble despite my best efforts at covering it up. Myndy meted out a 30-day suspension.

It wouldn't be the last time a tow rope led to trouble. This tale begins with two tow planes and two gliders flying in formation on the short cross-country from Sugarbush Airport in Vermont to Lake Placid Airport in New York. I was flying the smaller fabric-covered PA18 Super Cub while Stevie Maynard, a fellow tow pilot, commanded the larger more powerful L-19 Bird Dog. The Club had been recruited to fly for an "I Love New York" promotional ad to be shot in and around the Olympic Village, and we were bringing all the necessary inventory—planes, pilots, line-crew—to get the job done. I had been tapped for the camera plane flying for the commercial, while Stevie would tow the subject glider into the right position for me, plus cameras and cameraman, to follow. Bill Stinson, our senior instructor, would pilot the glider during filming. In hindsight, it's unclear whether our Part 91 operation exactly met the standards for supplying these services. I recall thinking that there was nothing in the Regulations preventing us from being filmed while towing or flying gliders. Later, though, while actually flying the PA18 Super Cub, burdened by a bunch of cameras taped to its exterior, and a cameraman on his belly in the back, operating everything, it did occur to me that a Part 135 flight-for-hire certificate would have been handy. In fairness, the late 1970s was a time when the FAA was just beginning to make the distinction clear.

Perhaps a preview of the excitement ahead, our landings at Lake Placid did not go unnoticed. We arrived to see a distraught man had just arrived at the FBO, and he was yelling something about someone destroying his prize pine tree. The poor clerk at the desk, entirely innocent, had no idea what he was talking about. And we, the pilots et al., out on the ramp, tying the aircraft down for the night, retrieving bags, were only peripherally aware of the doings inside.

The loud complaint was not without cause. Later that evening at dinner we learned from an I Love New York production staffer that our tow ropes had played a part in the man's distress. The scene unfolds at the injured party's residence, just outside airport limits and directly in line with the runway. There, the injured party was hosting a late lunch with friends, in his solarium, on the southeast side of his house. The first sign of trouble was not the tow plane flying overhead. Being in the approach path meant airplanes were flying over the house all the time. No, it was the sound of the extra-long (for cross-country towing) 400-foot yellow polypropylene rope slicing across the roof shingles, the attachment ring dinging loudly in concert, trailing behind, that got everyone's attention. Still, everything probably would have been okay had the rope-ring not decided to wrap around the man's chimney. Bad for sure, but still not the end of the world. What should have happened next was a rope break. Sometimes, when towing gliders into rough air that is threatening to overstress one or both aircraft, or when the release mechanism fails, pilots intentionally break the rope at altitude, to achieve a safe separation. Unfortunately, in this situation, the extra-long rope convenient for cross-country towing, also provides for greater resiliency. Pulling forces, e.g., resistance to the brick chimney, are maintained for a longer period of time.

So the rope didn't fail, but the chimney sure did, and that would have been sort of okay had it not crashed down on the solarium's glass roof causing it to shatter, sending glass everywhere, soon to be followed by a direct hit on the perfectly set dining table underneath. In keeping with what must have seemed like a take-no-prisoners policy, the tow plane with rope and, now, chimney in tow finished the job by demolishing the solarium structure, along with a nicely manicured pine tree just outside. The good news was that, after encountering the roof shingles, chimney, solarium roof, dining table, solarium structure, and prized pine tree, the rope eventually broke as it was supposed to, and the tow plane landed safely at the airport.

Fortunately, there were no injuries. And as for the damage, production companies always have a fix-it person, someone with a big checkbook. The problem was solved at the airport, long before we, the Sugarbush team, ever became fully aware. As for the guilty party: Stevie was initially blamed because his airplane had the 213 hp engine for the job. The evidence, however, pointed to me.

Lieutenant Columbo: "Just one more thing, sir. First, you were missing half of the tow rope after landing."

Me: "Well, I thought I caught it on the airport's perimeter fence, but never investigated to be sure."

Lieutenant Columbo: "And the need to add full power on approach, just at the end, prior to landing, to keep flying, what about that?

Me: "Yes, well, that's true."

Lieutenant Columbo: "Officer, arrest this man!"

Who would have believed that a 150 hp Super Cub could pull down a chimney? Of course, if you watch the show, you know the Lieutenant's hunches are usually right.

*Preparing for one of many different L-19 flown photo missions.*

Although some I Love New York production team members were a bit bleary-eyed due to the previous night's imbibement (a vocational hazard), everyone managed to arrive at the airport on time, 7:30 am, for the day's filming. The weather was perfect, sunny with light winds, so the director decided to compress what originally had been planned as a three-day shoot into one, a lot to pack in as it turns out.

Working with a large production company has advantages beyond just having the means to compensate for the occasional mishap. There is literally an army of people to grease the skids, directly and indirectly assuring the best possible result from the shoot. Completing three days' worth of work in one was just another day at the office for them. There were "fetch it" folks who, among other things, organized a magnificent lunch later in the day. The menu had an incredible hot pastrami sandwich, authentic for sure, and certainly one of the major highlights of the project for me.

The Sugarbush team's focus, of course, was on the flying, especially after learning what the director had in mind for the aerial work. The script was straightforward, at least in principle. The glider would be towed toward the Olympic ski jump, where it would release, align in the direction of the jump, and then follow it down, skimming just above the jump. The camera airplane would be tucked in close, slightly behind and above the glider, perfectly framing the shot, focused on the glider, the ski jump in the background. Any worries?

First, the ski jump is about a half mile from the threshold to runway 32; the airport's nearest runway. Far! Second, the elevation at the bottom of the jump is only about 100 feet higher than the elevation of the runway. The glider would need sufficient energy both to complete the aerial work and make it back to the airport. There was the additional challenge of piloting the camera plane to precisely synch up with the glider at just the right place, slightly prior to reaching the top of the jump. Assuming that worked out, all that remained was the small matter of following the glider down the jump in tight formation.

The flying members of the Sugarbush team decided on a divide and conquer approach. Bill, with Stevie as tow pilot, would work on learning how to navigate safely to the jump, while I got comfortable flying a heavily burdened (with cameras) Super Cub. At some point during the day we would put the whole thing together, a beautifully choreographed masterpiece of cinematographic excellence.

Bill is a talented glider pilot, later becoming the FAA's glider examiner for the region. After a few attempts, he was comfortable lining up with the jump and following it down. Going fast was the key to success: providing enough airspeed to make back to the airport. But high speed increased the challenge for the camera airplane I was flying. We discovered this on the first attempt. Bill whizzed by, going about 110 mph, reaching the bottom of the jump as I reached the top. For this to work, he would have to slow down, and not just because I was having trouble catching him. The director wanted a longer scene. While the target footage would add just a couple of seconds, that's a lot in percentage terms if the entire shot is supposed to be only eight seconds long.

We compromised on 80 mph. While barely enough to make the airport, the slower glider speed made it more likely I could catch and keep up. On a good day the Super Cub might reach 115 mph in cruise. With the drag caused by the open door, the camera operator hanging out, and all the cameras on the ornate wing strut system, max speed was more like 95 mph at best.

The parameters for synchronizing the aircraft established, we took up the next challenge: tucking up tight to get the perfect shot. Close formation flying is hard, and potentially very dangerous, unless both pilots are skilled and on their game. Formation flying is even harder with dissimilar aircraft.

And these were two entirely different categories of aircraft (glider and air-plane), following a ski jump. Well, here's to the Olympics, the name of the game that day.

Neither Bill nor I had a lot of formation flying experience prior to the I Love New York job, so we decided to work slowly up to what the director had requested. On each attempt, the camera plane would get just a little closer to the glider. It took ten tries before we were anywhere near the zone, and even then syncing our speeds in such close proximity proved to be dif-ficult. The goal was to maintain a constant distance, close, but not too close, risking a collision. Tough! A situation where persistence pays off? Although it took all day, we finally got the shot the production company was after. Actually, we got it twice, the second time just in case the camera operator had forgotten to put film in the camera.

Excluding the chimney affair, I look back fondly on the I Love New York campaign project. There was some improvisation, normally not a good thing in flying, but the steps we took to accomplish the task were deliberate and pretty well thought out. To the extent there was exposure, the sources were clear. Low-level flying means fewer options in case of a problem, like an engine failure or, in the case of the glider, insufficient energy to get back to the airport. Securing a bunch of unapproved equipment to the airframe turned me into a test pilot to some extent. Yes, it is assumed there will be more drag, but what about potential control issues caused by an out of cen-ter of gravity (CG) problem, especially lateral CG, the lateral envelope not mentioned in the airplane's approved flight manual. For this reason, we did conduct several Super Cub test flights, adding more equipment each time. Only with the flight envelope confirmed, did the camera operator join me in the back.

The motorcycle incident aside, the word "cocky" really fails to capture what was going on in the tow department at Sugarbush. I personally did thousands of successful, safe tows, many under tough flying conditions. Most of the other pilots can make the same claim. There were problems, but not because of poor judgment or lack of skill. To the extent there was dan-ger lurking, familiarity and complacency presented the greatest threat. In some ways, despite all the risk factors in play, the Lake Placid adventure was safer because it was novel. Everything had to be invented, carefully consid-ered, and practiced; new skills developed along the way, along with a sharp-ness of focus. This is not to say that the I Love New York adventure didn't up the challenge, or that towing gliders is boring—far from it. It's just that the irony of the routine—everything working out well, the same way every time—is that very occasionally it doesn't, as some of us have discovered. Whether it's risking accidental fuel exhaustion, or having a glider stop suddenly on the runway, landing with a tailwind to expedite production, flying irregular patterns, touching down just a little too close to parked aircraft, success doesn't necessarily mean it was safe. Yet all the tow pilots working at Sugarbush, including me, did some of these things, and more. Happily, no tow pilots were killed (or seriously injured), during my towing tenure, which lasted about eight years, but there were accidents. Most, but not all, tow plane wrecks were due to ground loops, a natural hazard. One pilot flipped an airplane over onto its back noseward, due to an ill-timed rapid reversal of wind direction. The wind got under the horizontal stabilizer and pushed the airplane over, aided by the L-19's rather forward CG. Actually, knowing that CG was an issue, some of us would add weight behind the passenger seat in the back. In fact, a case of oil had been placed as ballast in the overturned airplane's rear baggage compartment. Unfortunately, most of the oil had been consumed feeding the airplane's hungry O-470 engine over the course of a number of months of flying.

The scariest accident involved Fuzz Taylor, an ex-United 747 captain. Shortly after finishing a tow, he experienced a complete loss of elevator control. He did all he could, making a relatively controlled crash into the trees. Luckily, Fuzz, while scraped and bruised, walked out of the woods okay.

*Tow pilot memories—a rebuilt L-19 was added to our personal fleet in 2011.*

The plane, however, was pretty much destroyed. Fuzz was not at fault. The root cause was a failed, difficult-to-inspect pulley that had chafed at, and ultimately broken, the cable, demonstrating how easily and innocently routine can go rogue.

Flying tow planes taught the difference between remembering things and learning them. Anyone with a good memory can remember facts and events. People who can learn have the potential to become wise. The two are not mutually exclusive, but in flying it is what is learned that has the greatest value. I flew many tows over the years but remember only a few of them—the really scary ones. Yet, each flight, remembered or forgotten, taught me a little bit more about flying. Sure, some of it is muscle memory, a kind of practice-makes-perfect that occurs after doing more than 4,000 tows. The more existential benefit, however, is the development of an innate ability to identify novel worrisome situations long before some "correct" action has to be taken. This is, again, about answering the question: do I want to have be the best pilot I have ever been in my whole life to solve the problem? Better that the problem never has to be addressed in the first place. Pilots with the ability to learn enjoy a big advantage. They leverage their previous empirical and academic experiences in making better decisions, even when the set-up is completely unfamiliar.

I am unlikely to experience another near miss with a glider stranded on the runway. But when I get a land and hold short operation (LAHSO) clearance from the tower at Boston Logan International, landing a jet in heavy crosswinds, the consideration I give it will include a run-through of all the ways to inadvertently fail to obey. This is in the spirit that lower risk operations, in which the consequences of failure are bad, e.g., crashing into another aircraft at the runway's intersection, need special attention. Facts are important. The ability to connect and map unrelated events appropriately, in a useful way, is priceless. Learning is this mapping ability; as it relates to flying, more is more.

### Lessons learned:

**Lesson 1:** Well intentioned, careful and skilled pilots are not completely insulated from danger.

**Lesson 2:** Good judgment is born from a combination of bad judgment, luck, and reflection.

# 10 | Weather or Not, Here We Go (A Sobering Moment)

There are gazillions of weather products out there today, and many are contradictory, or inappropriate to flying or the mission, or just plain wrong. When you're reading forecasts, it's easy to take things out of context or see certainty where there really is none.

I watch our local TV weather every morning, and the day's forecast is usually helpful. When the presenter tells me it's going to rain, I carry an umbrella. The accuracy is about 90 percent in most places, although in Vermont it is likely a little worse because of the vagaries associated with surrounding mountain influences and a large weather-making lake, Lake Champlain, located on the state's western border. But what about four days out or even nine days, which is the typical time frame for television weather forecasts? Beyond broad generalizations—predicting that July in Vermont will be snow-free—long range forecasting is worse than just guessing, because the models often have biases. It's why presenters rarely recap previous forecasts. If they did they would devalue the product. And most people forget the prediction anyway, unless something horrible happens like an unforeseen hurricane. It's all old news!

Most of the time, fortunately, flying demands only a short term estimation. The longest nonstop flight on the planet is about 18 hours so a solid 20 hour forecast of enroute and destination conditions is all that is needed.[1] (The longest TAF is 30 hours.) With today's technology, these forecasts are at least 85 percent correct, especially for well-traveled areas. And for the shorter flights that most of us do, the forecasts are very good, perhaps 95 percent with regard to the parameters being predicted. And for the vast majority of trips, the weather is good, or least not bad. So why is weather sometimes so problematic? Much depends on a combination of the weather (bad versus good), pilot skill and training, and aircraft capability.

---

[1] United Airlines flight from LAX to Singapore using a Boeing 787-9 Dreamliner. Qatar Airlines flight from Auckland, New Zealand to Doha using a Boeing 777-200LR, February 2, 2018.

Approaching the problem from a purely practical point of view, it is the process of deciding to go or not to go that is probably the best indicator of a safe operation. Once aloft, it takes an extremely disciplined pilot to prudently manage the risks presented in real time.

For pilots either lacking an instrument rating or flying a non-instrument certified aircraft, there are inherent limitations. Origin, enroute, and destination weather all have to be good. The word "good" is really about having visibility that is equal to or better than what the FAA regulations prescribe and, as determined by the pilot, sufficient to safely conduct the flight. The weather determination must not only take into consideration conditions at the airport (origin or destination), but also throughout any transitions, climbing to and descending from the enroute segment, for example. At all times, it must be possible to conduct the flight safely using external (outside the cockpit) references as the primary source of attitude control and navigation.

Some days the weather will be good, others not so good. Knowing that the long-range forecasts are notoriously inaccurate, unless the trip is imminent, there is always some chance it won't be possible. The expectation, therefore, should be disappointment; actually going... the pleasant surprise.

VFR pilots experience an additional weather-related distance limitation in their flying. The longer the flight, the higher the probability that unsuitable weather will necessitate a diversion at some point en route. Yes, it is possible for good VFR weather to prevail all the way from Boca Raton, Florida, to Burlington, Vermont, about 1,200 NM, but those occasions are rare, especially in winter. The same is true when traveling east or west—and because bad weather systems figuratively tend to move from west to east in the Northern Hemisphere, an west-bound journey for a fair-weather pilot can be a race with the weather. The wait for a stretch of good weather sufficient for a significant distance can be very long indeed for the VFR-only pilot.

Ironically, for those flying VFR strictly by the rules, weather-related go/no-go decisions are relatively easy. If the weather is good at the origin, destination, and en route, the answer is "go." In all other cases with the possible exception of one, the answer is "no-go" as shown in the matrix on the next page.

| VFR | | | |
|---|---|---|---|
| WEATHER | | | |
| Origin | En route | Destination | Action |
| Good | Good | Good | Go |
| Bad | Good | Good | No-go |
| Bad | Good | Bad | No-go |
| Bad | Bad | Good | No-go |
| Bad | Bad | Bad | No-go |
| Good | Bad | Bad | No-go |
| Good | Good | Bad | No-go |
| Good | Bad | Good | ? |

The one possible exception is weather en route. Good weather at the origin and destination, but bad en route, is interesting because here the go/no-go decision requires considerably greater analysis, compared to the other scenarios.

Bad weather en route as defined by the forecaster does not always spell no-go for those wishing to fly visually. For example, consider an early morning day flight with origin and destination weather forecasted to be clear, but morning fog possibly obscuring valleys and other low-lying areas. Nearby airports may be zero-zero—no visibility at all. Is it prudent to go? In most cases, yes, because the fog likely will burn off as the day warms. In the US it is entirely legal to fly VFR above the clouds, without a clearance, even when the airports below are 100 percent IFR. But what to do about a forecast of good weather at origin and destination, and isolated thunder-storms en route? The answer here is less clear. A go decision would rest on the assumption that the thunderstorms will be, and remain, isolated, the flight conducted in compliance with VFR rules, and at a safe distance from any convective turbulence. Here is a case where an accurate forecast may not be particularly helpful. When the civilian forecast says that there is a 90 percent chance of thunderstorms in an area, and storms actually occur somewhere in the area, only the most miserly among us would not give the forecasters credit for the prediction. But when flying, especially VFR, forecasting the exact location and timing is important, and it is something forecasters still can't do well. Great accuracy, but with no time specificity/precision. This is one of the reasons why even short term television forecasts can be so frustrating. A rain forecast is a composite of precipitation proba-bility, given the expected atmospheric conditions, and coverage area—the percentage of the forecast area likely affected.[2] So, a 50 percent probability of precipitation in a given forecast area, with predicted actual rainfall coverage of 10 percent of the area, processed according to a collection of byzantine formulas, becomes a 30 percent chance of rain. But what if it rains on you? That feels more like 100 percent chance of rain. Yet, because the forecaster didn't specify where exactly the rain would fall, as long as the aggregate/composite number (30 percent) is achieved, the forecaster's record is untarnished.

This is why aviation weather forecasts rarely provide probability estimates specific to a given location or time. Aviation weather specialists acknowledge that, except in very special cases, their models don't have the precision to do it. Only when applicable to a relatively broad area or airport terminal environment do probability statements appear in the forecasts. It is for this reason that flying VFR with thunderstorms in the en route forecast, even if they are widely scattered over a large area, is probably a bad idea. What if a bunch of storms gang up directly ahead? This could necessitate a substantial diversion. And when flying between storms there is always the risk of the gaps narrowing. Weather forms as conditions change. Assuming a juicy atmosphere with lots of energy from the heat of the sun, adding in the orographic effects of wind hitting hills and mountains, the anticipated safe passage, clear of clouds, can turn scary in short order.

Another interesting scenario involves the forecast of undercast (clouds below) en route. This forces the VFR pilot to face the prospect of flying over bad weather on the way to good weather. This, too, is legal, but is it wise? The answer is that it depends. For a private pilot with no instrument rating, flying a non-instrument certified airplane, the set-up should give pause. What if there is a mechanical problem requiring landing prior to the destination? What if the tops are higher than forecasted, higher than the airplane's capacity for climbing? In either case the options are few, because legally and practically, entering clouds is problematic. There really is no alternative but to try to reach a destination that has good weather or do an emergency descent. The prospect of an emergency descent as a non-instrument rated pilot flying a non-instrument certified airplane returns us to the question: "Do you want to have to be the best pilot you have ever been in your whole life?"

---

[2] PoP = C x A, where C = the confidence that precipitation will occur somewhere in the forecast area and A = the percent of the area that will receive measurable precipitation, if it occurs at all.

So, VFR pilots have to consider carefully the implications of bad weather en route. Prospectively, there are some exciting and scary limbs of the risk analysis tree to explore before deciding to go. Feeling lucky? Independent of the answer, if the risk analysis indicates that luck would be required to achieve the desired result—a safe flight—the right decision probably would be no-go. Incidentally, most VFR-rated pilots will admit that, from time to time, luck was an important factor in securing a successful outcome.

In contrast, an instrument rated pilot flying an instrument certified aircraft should feel very safe flying by VFR above the clouds, especially with two-way radio communication with ATC and radar surveillance. Should there be a need to descend through the clouds or complete an instrument approach somewhere, more than likely ATC will accommodate. Worst case, should an emergency descent be necessary, the pilot and airplane are ready and up to the task.

Many who routinely fly IFR elect to fly VFR even when there is an undercast en route. There can be big advantages in routing, and flying in the clear is generally more pleasant than slogging it out in the clouds, which is sometimes necessitated by the constraints of an IFR clearance. Flying VFR also can help when flying out of busy airports like Teterboro, where ATC coordination with nearby airports can take a long time. If it's a nice day at the aerodrome, a clearance to depart VFR is often granted. The only caution is to be sure the weather ahead supports conducting a VFR flight over the undercast. In some busy places, it is difficult to get an IFR clearance after departure. Sometimes declaring an emergency en route is the only way to solve the problem. Independent of the legal questions, the prudent IFR pilot always has a plan to facilitate an IFR flight should the weather turn out to be worse than expected.

Having the skills and equipment needed to fly IFR offers many advantages, including being able to go safely when the weather is bad. But for the instrument pilot planning to fly in instrument conditions, making good go/no-go decisions is actually much harder. Why? The counter-intuitive answer is because for instrument pilots flying in instrument conditions there are fewer legal or practical restrictions than there are for VFR pilots. To put it another way: IFR pilots have more options.

| IFR | | | |
| WEATHER | | | |
| Origin | En route | Destination | Action |
|--------|----------|-------------|--------|
| Good | Good | Good | Go |
| Bad | Good | Good | Go |
| Good | Bad | Good | Go |
| Bad | Bad | Good | Go |
| Bad | Bad | Bad | Go |
| Good | Bad | Bad | Go |
| Good | Good | Bad | Go |

Notice that all actions are go. In reality, not all days are go for the IFR rated pilot. To help determine the right answer, it is necessary to dive deeper into the meanings of *bad* and *good*.

More precisely, assuming a scenario where at least one of the three columns is *bad*, what considerations are important? I submit there are four:

1) The rules governing flying airplanes in bad weather
2) IFR certified aircraft capability
3) The exact nature of the bad weather on that particular day
4) IFR rated pilot physical and psychological state, training, ability, and proficiency

# Number 1

Number 1 is a good place start. There are specific rules that govern what is acceptable weather, visibility and ceilings, for instrument flying and if the trip can't be done in compliance, there is no point in looking at 2 through 4. There are rules about ceiling and visibilities at the origin and destination airports. There are rules about fuel reserves and whether an alternate airport should be included in the flight plan. Everything the IFR pilot needs to know is contained in a thick book published by the Federal Aviation Administration—the Federal Aviation Regulations (FARs). In this book, nothing is left to the imagination. If the goal is to follow the rules, a go/no-go decision is deterministic, therefore theoretically easy.

# Number 2

Assuming Number 1 is a go, it's time to look at Number 2. Is the airplane capable given the likely weather? There are federal regulations about airplane capability and weather. For example, if the origin, enroute, or destination forecast calls for icing, the airplane has to be equipped and certified to fly in known icing conditions to go. Certain types of transponder equipment may also be required to help ATC precisely determine the airplane's altitude and location. And in some countries outside of the US, special collision avoidance technology is mandatory for flying IFR.

But here, rather than rules, the primary concern is a practical one: is the airplane designed and equipped to complete the trip safely (and comfortably)?

I recall an early spring trip years ago, from Vermont to southern Florida in our twin-engine Aztec. The weather along the eastern seaboard was unstable, with isolated storms popping up all the way ahead of a fast-moving cold front.

As light aircraft go, the Aztec was well equipped. It had ice certification, with heated windscreen (on the pilot's side), heated propellers, and rubber inflatable boots protecting the leading edges. It had weather radar on board, one of the keys to traversing convective weather, and a great GPS approach enabled navigator. Unfortunately, the airplane was not pressurized, so all the flying had to be conducted below 10,000 feet. Even with supplemental oxygen for the passengers, the Aztec's normally aspirated engines prevented it from reaching much higher. A pretty rough slog through the weather, despite being able to detect and avoid the worst storms.

Even with weather radar, flying embedded thunderstorms is challenging. At the very least, it can be uncomfortable for those on board. At worst, the radar can lead the pilot down a blind alley, if the storm detection system lacks the power to penetrate the most severe storms. But flying embedded thunderstorms is entirely legal, and even prudent on some days. (On this particular day, not so much.)

In hindsight, there were three problems with the plan.

1) The front was moving fast, with a lot of energy. Although the forecast had us landing at our destination long before it reached our plotted course, the associated instability conducive to creating storms extended far ahead of the front, in this case hundreds of miles ahead.

2) The Aztec is a relatively slow airplane. On a good day it can reach about 160 knots true. In the northern hemisphere, the lower altitude winds that precede cold fronts are usually south westerly, exactly opposite to our direction of travel. The strong head wind got even worse as the front moved nearer, further eroding the safety margin.

   Even very small variations from what is predicted in the movement of a front can have enormous impact on winds. Proof by example, just prior to reaching our fuel stop in Wilmington, North Carolina, our ground speed had slowed to about 115 knots. A nine-hour flight is tolerable, 13 hours perhaps not. More concerning was the prospect of a race with the approaching front, one we could lose due to our slow progress.

3) The maximum practical cruise altitude for the normally-aspirated Aztec is about 14,000 feet, and this assumes oxygen available for everyone on board. So there would be no way to top the bigger storms, capable of towering 45,000 feet or higher. The greater problem: there is no way to see the storms and avoid them visually. As a consequence, the Aztec pilot is relegated to using the range-limited on-board and/or time-delayed NEXRAD (ground based) radar to ascertain the nature and location of storms. Even assuming the Aztec somehow could reach into the flight levels, 18,000 feet and higher, on many days the effort would be for naught. Winds up there can be 100 knots or more, reducing ground speeds to those more typical of driving, further slowing progress, and increasing the risk of collision with the front itself.

By the time we were fueled up and ready to depart North Carolina, storms covered most of northern Florida, leaving the only escape an east bound ocean route. For those who regularly fly little airplanes in Florida, this would be seen as a trap, and one that would be hard to escape without a lot of luck. *Weather forms as conditions change.* With a wet atmosphere the rule, new storms no doubt would be in play over the water. And with no place to land, the only alternative would be a potentially dangerous penetration.

We enjoyed an impromptu stay at a beach hotel in Wilmington. Although definitely not beach weather—driving rain, strong winds, and even a tornado sighting nearby—the hotel had a nice bar and restaurant, a perfect venue to shop for something bigger, faster, and with a climb capability matching the weather.

The Florida story demonstrates that 100 percent compliance with the regulations doesn't mean a trip can be flown as planned, or that it will be a comfortable or convenient flight. Aircraft capability is important. More precisely, accurately matching aircraft capability to the prevailing weather should play a vital role in deciding whether or not to go. The Aztec can be an excellent airplane for traversing the eastern seaboard, just not on that particular day. Had we waited until the next day to leave Vermont, the front would have passed, leaving us with calmer air and a tailwind, perfect conditions for a faster and more comfortable journey in an airplane of this caliber.

Was the trip as described flown safely? The answer is yes, in the sense that there were many ways to mitigate for what turned out to be an increasing risk of being trapped in a fierce storm. Had the trip been over water or a long stretch of land with no suitable airport, the situation would have been different. In deciding to use the Aztec for the Florida mission, we were acknowledging that we might be in for a rough ride, and the trip might not be completed as planned. For those who don't mind a chess game with some interruptions, and are comfortable advancing across the board in increments, the decision to go is probably okay. For those more focused on making it to the end of the game, waiting is probably the right answer. The one caution is that for the player or pilot who decides to go on a tough weather day with equipment not ideally suited to the weather, having the discipline to discontinue the flight before bad things happen is paramount. Continuing in the face of weather that is beyond the capability of the aircraft quickly ratchets up the danger, and a reading of aircraft accident history suggests that some pilots make the wrong choice.

# Number 3

Having decided on number 2, that the aircraft is suitable for the forecast weather, it's time to look at number 3, the nature of the forecast and weather itself. Is the weather inherently safe to fly? The question may seem redundant because presumably we already have concluded that the aircraft is well suited to the task. Not so, because when looking at airplane capability, the problem is posed in terms specific to weather conditions (e.g., thunderstorms, icing, winds, low ceilings and visibilities, etc.) that are likely to be encountered. With number 3, the focus is on the integrity of the forecast and the general weather setup. Is there something about the merit of the forecast or the nature of weather predicted that under some circumstances could lead to failure of available risk mitigating strategies?

## Deep Lows

Starting with the weather itself, the good news is there are only a few truly perilous scenarios to consider. The bad news is that once one of these scenarios starts to unfold, recovery can be difficult if not impossible. High on the list of perils is flying to a destination with a deep low-pressure system nearby. The danger is two-fold:

Deep lows can be accompanied by violent/turbulent weather, especially near the center of lowest pressure. Everything bad, including high winds, heavy precipitation, and low visibilities, can be expected. I personally experienced this exact scenario on a trip to Europe in the CJ3, encountering some of the roughest and most violent weather I have ever seen, which I describe in Chapter 17.

Deep lows often cover a wide area, so if the destination airport proves ultimately unsuitable, it may be a long slog to one that is suitable, assuming the airplane even has the range necessary to make the long slog.

So, stay away from deep lows at the destination airport. Although legal, and potentially within the capability of the aircraft, should landing prove not to be an option, there may be few good alternatives. Deep lows are generally a no-go.

## Icing

Next on the list of perils is freezing rain. Any forecast that includes freezing rain demands extra scrutiny. And while there are mechanisms for escaping a chance encounter (e.g., climbing higher into warm air), the better plan is to wait for the weather to improve before going.

Like most airliners and military aircraft, our CJ3 and CJ4 corporate aircraft are known ice certified. And their anti-ice (and deice) systems are excellent. Even so, as with most known ice certified aircraft, the systems are no match for a freezing rain event, where the entire airplane gets coated. Deice systems only protect the leading edges. Also, this type of ice, often referred to as *clear* doesn't come off easily, even in the protected areas. The only remedy is a rise in the temperature to above 32°F, or a very quick escape, essentially the same thing.

During freezing rain events the added weight of the ice is a relatively minor concern compared to its aerodynamic effects on the control and lifting surfaces. The opportunity for a loss of control event increases dramatically in freezing rain conditions. Everything is degraded, including available thrust, aerodynamic efficiency, and the ability to see out the coated windscreen to establish a good visual reference, which is essential while conducting a safe takeoff and landing. So if there is freezing ran in the forecast at the origin, destination, or en route the flight is a no-go. And while some airplanes are certified in a way that explicitly forbids flying in freezing rain, others aren't, like so much in flying, it's up to the pilot to decide. Here, fortunately, the choice is very easy.

But what about other types of icing? Rime, for example, forms mostly on the leading edges of the airplane in visible moisture—clouds—at below freezing temperatures. Theoretically it is removable by modern anti-ice and deice systems. The answer is that it depends. When pilots report inflight icing, they tend to qualify it as light, moderate, or severe. The determination is subjective, in the sense that making the assessment depends on the pilot's judgment and to some extent the efficiency of the airplane's deicing systems.

The weather service employs the same terminology when forecasting icing, with the following corresponding criteria:

**Light Icing.** The rate of ice accumulation could create a problem if the flight is prolonged in this environment (longer than an hour). Requires occasional cycling of manual deicing systems to minimize ice accretions on the airframe. A representative accretion rate for reference purposes is ¼ inch to 1 inch (0.6 to 2.5 cm) per hour on the outer wing.

**Moderate Icing.** The rate of ice accumulation is such that anything more than a short encounter is potentially hazardous. Requires frequent cycling of manual deicing systems to minimize ice accretions on the airframe. A representative accretion rate for reference purposes is 1 to 3 inches (2.5 to 7.5 cm) per hour on the outer wing.

**Severe Icing.** The rate of ice accumulation is such that ice protection systems fail to remove the ice, and buildup occurs in areas not normally prone to icing, such as aft of protected surfaces and other areas identified by the aircraft manufacturer. A representative accretion rate for reference purposes is more than 3 inches (7.5 cm) per hour on the outer wing.

Ice-certified airplanes are generally able to keep up with light ice, and in some cases with moderate, at least for a while. Severe icing is an emergency, with immediate exit the only remedy.

I have experienced severe icing only once in my flying (so far). It was on a winter's day, arriving in the Burlington, Vermont, area on a return trip from Florida. The setup was classic. A large low-pressure system had formed to the southwest, and was moving in a northeasterly direction. Moisture and cold air in the northeast quadrant lay ahead of the warm front. The weather at the aerodrome itself was actually fairly good, light IFR with a ceiling at 1,200 feet, visibility 3 miles. But, the weather above and around was bad, with light to moderate rime icing reported from 15,000 all the way down to 8,000 feet. Prototypically, this was certainly no place to be in an unprotected airplane.

We entered the clouds with all ice prevention/elimination systems ablazing, expecting the CJ3 to keep up easily. The leading edges of the wings, engine intake, and windscreen all are heated with bleed air produced by the compressor side of the turbofan engines, while the horizontal stabilizer has a robust boot design that inflates periodically, cracking ice formations off, into the air stream. Pitot-static and engine full authority digital engine control (FADEC) sensors are all electrically heated. On most icing days, the systems are overkill, really amazing. But not this day. First, the windscreen iced up. Even at the highest setting, the hot bleed from the engine could clean only a small peekaboo-sized viewing hole on the pilot's side. The left wing remained clean, but surprisingly the right one started to accumulate ice. Tail status was unclear because it is difficult to see the tail and horizontal stabilizer from the cockpit. We had to assume ice was beginning to form there, too.

The asymmetrical icing on the wings was a worrisome novelty. The only thing worse than heavy ice accumulation is heavy ice accumulation on just one side, with the potential to cause a lifting surface imbalance leading to loss of control.

The crew alert lights indicated normal operation, but my initial thought was that one side of the deice system had failed. I even had maintenance check the entire anti-ice system after we landed. They reported "all systems good to go." Apparently, the energy outputs to each side are just different enough that at the very edge of the system's capability, bleed air anti-icing systems display a tendency to favor one side over the other. Had the icing been just a little worse, the clean side would have iced up, too. Not exactly comforting, but good to know.

My most vivid memory of the experience is how rapidly the airplane iced up. The time—from the point of entering the clouds to ice developing on the leading edge surfaces—was 15 seconds, at most. Had the rate of ice accumulation been any worse, we would have had a real problem. Fortunately, the entire episode was over in about 2 minutes. The skies cleared from obscured to something more layered, and the systems easily dispatched what little rime remained.

Our CJ3 story should be sobering for anyone attempting a flight in anything more severe than light icing conditions. Even in light ice, the plan should be to transition in short order to a non-icing environment. The nature of the airplane's deice/anti-ice systems must be considered, too. Not all ice-certified airplanes are created equal. The Aztec is ice-certified, electrically-heated propellers and inflatable boots all around, but I wouldn't tackle anything more than moderate ice, and only for a very short time. Ice adheres as the airplane slows, even in the booted places like the leading edge wing and horizontal stabilizer, presumably due to the lack of wind forces necessary to break the chunks away. The boots are amusing to watch, but not particularly effective. So there had better be a good escape, either warm air below or clear skies above, with tops not very high.

In a big powerful jet the answer may be to go, but only if the plan incorporates a quick exit from the icing environment during the transition. Knowing that it is impossible to protect all wind facing components (e.g., antennas, radar dome, and vertical fins) even light icing exposure should be limited. It may be death by 1,000 pin pricks, but it is still death in the end.

In summary, if freezing rain and severe icing are in the forecast, the answer is easy: no-go. For light or moderate icing, the answer may be go, depending on the aircraft and available escape mechanisms. In all cases, prolonged exposure to icing is a really bad idea.

## Wide areas of low visibility

Similar in spirit to the danger in a deep low, flat high pressure systems covering a wide area deserve a closer look. The descending air that is characteristic of these systems often produces optimal flying weather, but it also can present serious low visibility conditions (i.e., fog, especially in valleys during the late fall and winter). As the days get shorter, fog tends to form earlier and burn off later. And the exact burn-off times can be very hard to predict. The forecasts are often unreliable. Northern Europe experiences this kind of weather in the months of September and October. There can be wide areas of zero-zero conditions and on some days the fog never lifts.

New England has much in common with Europe. On high pressure fall days wide areas of fog are typical, with clearing occurring very late. I recall one fall during the time I lived in Stowe, Vermont, when the fog didn't lift until noon. This went on every day for a month, despite forecasts predicting clear skies at 9:00 a.m. We made a lot of zero-zero takeoffs that month.

Under such conditions, there are hazards in departures and arrivals, but arrivals demand more attention. Because clearing times are unpredictable, the disciplined pilot must have both a plan to divert to a fog-free airport and with enough fuel to get there.

There are other dangerous low visibility weather scenarios, worse in some ways than fog, which eventually lifts. A stationary front can have all the weather, all at once, in one place: thunderstorms, low visibility, ice/freezing rain, etc. It's like being Charlie Brown, having a terrible rainy cloud over your head all the time. The challenge of a stationary front is that it doesn't move in a predictable way. Targeting an arrival with a stationary front overhead requires careful planning and a good escape route. Don't assume a slam dunk landing.

An occlusion (occluded front), which results when a cold front follows a warm front revolving around a low pressure system, is also a problem. Sometimes described as a zipper, as in zipping a trailing cold front with the leading warm front, occluded fronts are worrisome because there is no respite between passage of the warm front and passage of the cold front. This is another example of how the weather near the center of a low can be unpredictable, and, in some cases, very bad.

Low visibility/active weather scenarios demand special caution. To the extent the mission is a go, there always should be an escape plan. Here, the definition of escape is having the means to advance to a good weather aerodrome (ideally VFR, or at worst very light IFR) with robust endurance, the ability to wait out unforeseen bad weather at the back-up (alternate) airport. Otherwise, the mission is a no-go.

## Forecast merit

The last weather consideration is the forecast itself, specifically the reliability of the prediction. In general, new forecasts are better than old ones, and short-term forecasts are better than extended ones. Knowing this, is there a way to do better, to supplement the forecast? One strategy proven successful is to invest in knowing the near term historical and present sequences. Aerodrome hourly reports, known in modern aviation as METARs, are available either side of the route of travel. In particular, review dew point/ temperature conditions described in the METARs and compare them with TAFs, to see if things match up. If the temperatures are converging on dew points either side of—or corresponding with—the route of flight/destination airport, it's time to discount a forecast that says CAVU (ceilings and visibilities unlimited). Typically, when the dew point and temperature are the same, clouds form; fog, near to or on the ground, should be expected. The big danger is if there is a wide area of converging temperature/dew points. Before departing, locate a destination airport or alternate with a better temperature spread. If that is not possible, the right answer is no-go. Very close dew point/temperature METARs, especially toward the end of the day, spell trouble.

# Number 4

So, we arrive at Number 4, the IFR-rated pilot's physical and psychological state, training, ability, and proficiency. The bullet has both deterministic and non-deterministic elements. A pilot not having the training, ability, or proficiency to fly an IFR mission should declare a no-go right away—very straightforward. But what about the pilot's physical and psychological state? Is the pilot physically and psychologically up to the task? Does the pilot possess the ability to make the right decisions? What about when the operational assumptions, leading up to the decision to go, prove wrong? This is a profound question, and one that should be asked by all pilots contemplating a challenging mission. It can be a very tough question to answer.

There is much to consider, including chronic health conditions, sleep deprivation, and recent injury. All of these are important; individually or together they can impact safety. More difficult to determine is mindset. Does the pilot have the will and ability to recognize a bad weather-related decision and then take appropriate action in real time? If yes, there are many practical benefits, including survival.

## Is the expectation too high?

There is an advantage in knowing before going, that a trip is unlikely to be ideal. Once the flight is underway, a kind of momentum can take over. This is especially true of weather-related decision making, where the traps can be difficult to spot. Even the most disciplined among us resist abandoning a plan when things start going wrong. Examples abound in the history of unstabilized approaches to the runway that led to crashes. They were all excellent candidates for a go-around that didn't occur. The NTSB calls it pilot error, and in fact a lot of pilots are susceptible because at the time, and for whatever reason, the risks are not immediately apparent, and follow through prevails. Whether it's *get-there-itis*, or wishful thinking, hoping against hope for improvement or better conditions, opportunities for making bad decisions abound. We have all at some point been subject to the fixation to carry on independent of compelling new data that says the plan isn't working. Flying as a discipline is a posterchild for this, but the same weakness of mindset is a factor in many other challenging vocations (e.g., surgeon). So, unless you are a super-reflective pilot with superb real time risk management skills, or work for a Part 135 charter, or Part 121 airline operation where many of the decisions are made by someone else—chief pilots, dispatchers, weather mitigation people on the ground—the right answer is to make a prudent, reasoned decision before departing. Most of the time, the decision will be to go. On rare occasions, the decision will be no-go. Happily, history and experience prove that in the vast majority of cases, the outcome will be safe.

## Lessons learned:

**Lesson 1:** Weather forecasts extending beyond 24 hours are interesting, but generally inaccurate.

**Lesson 2:** The decision to go demands a very high bar. Once underway, pilots have difficulty standing down even when all the available information says it is the prudent thing to do.

# 11 Ancient Aztec, A Pretty Good Teacher

Childhood memories can leave a lasting impression. While growing up, most of us have been influenced by a character depicted in literature, on TV, or in a song. We idolized the actors more so than the writers, directors, and costume and set designers who deserve most of the credit. We fans blur player and character into a single entity, a guilty pleasure, despite knowing the actors are pretending in order to facilitate good story-telling. William Shatner brought Captain Kirk to life in the original *Trek* series, but he wasn't actually the Captain. Of course, at age eight I was pretty sure Adam West was actually Batman, and Batman was a real crime fighter.

It was while watching the television western *Sky King* that I felt the full blurring effect, but not for Penny, or Clipper, or even the hero, Sky King himself. The character I fell hard for was Songbird, Sky's Cessna 310B. Songbird was *real*. Sky could have been chasing robbers on horseback, or saving Penny from kidnappers, but what electrified me was the sound of those Continental IO-470 engines firing up to do some rescuing. Cessna was smart to volunteer their newly designed and very capable airplane to aid in the story telling. Somehow they knew there would be thousands of wannabe pilots like me watching, all of us thinking *someday I will fly that plane.*

Good things sometimes come to those who wait. Some 40 years later, I was in the market for a twin-engine plane. The C-310R, a later variant of Sky's plane, was at the top of the list. Now, long out of production, this would be a used airplane, and clearly linked to Cessna's Hollywood based approach to marketing and selling. Great commercial campaigns tend to endure.

So why a twin? Beyond satisfying a childhood dream, what does a multiengine aircraft offer over a single engine design? The conventional argument is power plant redundancy: if one engine quits it's a bad day, but not the end of the world; the remaining good engine is still working, available to facilitate a graceful airport landing somewhere.

Our need for a twin was more mission-oriented, however. We wanted flight into known icing (FIKI) capability for winter flying, along with radar to avoid thunderstorms. We also wanted sufficient speed to fly conveniently from Vermont to South Carolina, where my wife Lisa's family lived. While there are a few single-engine designs, like the pressurized Cessna P210, that can do the job, twins tend to be better equipped. Piper, Beech, Cessna and others recognized early on that to offset the higher cost of acquiring and operating a twin there had to be an improvement in utility beyond just engine redundancy. Speed and additional capacity/load carrying were important. But delivering something closer to all-weather capability emerged as one of the most important selling points. The ability to fly safely and routinely on a bad weather day greatly improves dispatch reliability, vital if one's goal is to employ the airplane as a source of dependable transportation.

Lisa and I disagreed about things over the course of our relationship, and even sought therapy at one point, which I found to be quite a bit of fun despite being accused of not taking it seriously. Nothing, however, prepared us for the challenge of working together to find the right twin. Lisa also was a pilot, formerly an airline pilot, and at the time was much more experienced than me. My 100 or so hours in a Seneca 1 were nothing compared to her thousand or so hours flying commuter turboprops and piston twins. She also had an instructor's rating, and was able to teach flying through multi-engine instrument and beyond. Needless to say, Lisa was a very good pilot.

Because Lisa's knowledge and experience vastly exceeded my own, her advocacy for something other than a C-310 carried weight. The issue in her mind was safety, specifically the challenge for a relatively inexperienced twin pilot like me to safely transition from a Piper Seneca to the much faster and considerably more slippery Cessna 310. The NTSB archives are packed with accounts of inexperienced and/or poorly trained fast piston twin pilots auguring in due to wrong decisions made and poor technique applied.

I remained resistant, explaining that there would be mitigations including specialized training in type and a long period of supervised operational experience (SOE)—basically flying with a more experienced pilot riding alongside. Further, I argued who could resist the idea of a C-310? After all, we lived on a horse farm. All that was missing were some Nazi spies or lost prospectors to track down.

*Newly minted Aztec pilot.*

Lisa and I fought long and hard over the C-310. In the end, Lisa prevailed and my childhood dream airplane was nixed. In its place, Piper's Aztec became our ride. Despite its less modern design, slower speed, and bulky appearance compared to the C-310, the Aztec had a reputation for ruggedness and dependability. Piper was also early to implement "known ice" capability in the Aztec compared to Cessna and Beech (the other major competitor), so there were proportionally many more FIKI specimens for sale.

My *Sky King* moment was not to be, but Lisa's victory was serendipitous. The Aztec was a pleasant surprise, despite a few early mechanical problems, including a gear extension failure that occurred on the very first flight. The airplane does a lot of things well. High on the list is its spectacular endurance and relatively long range, the large fuel tank version able to cover about 900 nautical miles. The airplane is also roomy inside, so unless the load is at maximum (5 passengers plus a pilot), there is room to spread out. And it has a fantastic short field landing/takeoff capability, much better than the C-310 or Beech's competitor, known as the Baron. Small grass airports are just no problem. Actually, I came to like the Aztec so much that when our marriage ended, I insisted on the airplane in the settlement.

In addition to delivering on its feature set promises, the Aztec proved to be a very good teacher. Mostly this was about having the tools to go farther and challenge more difficult weather. But the airplane also presented an opportunity to learn more complicated systems, like those used to operate the hydraulically-actuated landing gear and flaps. Our plane, N22ZZ, had a fancy big airplane-style King KFC-200 autopilot that could do coupled approaches. The attitude indicator, despite being mechanical, supported a fantastic flight director function—little wings that popped out on the instrument provided idiot proof guidance when shooting a precision approach. Tucking the little airplane wings displayed on instrument under the flight director wings assured we stayed on course on glideslope, an especially valuable integration tool when hand flying in bad weather. All proved a valuable introduction to the kind of collateral needed to routinely fly fast and far. This is not to say the normally aspirated Aztec was fast. Its maximum speed was 165 knots, more or less, and that was when operating in its sweet spot, at about 8,000 feet.

The principles in play translate well to larger airplanes, even jets. Although in the Aztec days we were spared concerns about sudden loss of pressurization, clear air turbulence (CAT), or the increasingly byzantine standard instrument departures (SIDs) and standard terminal arrival routes (STARs) typical of big terminal areas, we flew in the same airspace when IFR, communicated using the same lexicon, all while executing many of the same procedures from takeoff to landing. In some ways piloting the Aztec was harder, because unlike jet airplanes able to top the weather, we were always *in* it.

## Recurrent Training and Standard Operating Procedures

High on the list of teaching moments, though, flying the Aztec meant embracing recurrent training and adoption of SOPs, more defined preflight planning, routine use of checklists, and much less improvisation. For example, the pre-takeoff brief (even if piloting without a crew) is a prerequisite for responding appropriately in the event of an emergency. In our CJ3 jet, and assuming a copilot, the brief might go something like this: "We are departing from runway 15. Anything (e.g., aberrant crew alert system lights, inability to steer straight, control malfunction) below $V_1$ (a speed set in advance based on weight, temperature and other things) and we will abort as verbally indicated by either one of us. In this event, you will deploy the ground flaps while I apply braking as necessary. In case of emergencies requiring memory items (like a fire or engine failure), I will complete the appropriate checklist items by memory once stopped. Then we will sort out the emergency/abnormal using the checklist. After $V_1$ it is a go. We will continue the takeoff to no less than 2,300 feet. In case of emergencies requiring memory items (like a fire or engine failure), I will complete the appropriate checklist items by memory. We will then locate the appropriate emergency or abnormal checklist and complete the items listed in due course. Depending on the nature of the event, I may ask you to declare an emergency to expedite handling by ATC."

When flying the Aztec as a single pilot, the brief is considerably simpler. There is no $V_1$ (the speed where the crew commits to flying), but there is a balanced field length calculation to be done. Knowing the available runway, balanced field length basically assures there is enough runway to stop or fly away should one engine quit. So, in addition to confirming that the length of the runway is sufficient, it is good to determine a go/no-go speed, usually a bit above $V_{MC}$ (the minimum airspeed needed to insure effective rudder necessary for the airplane to fly straight and accelerate to the best single-engine rate of climb) in case of engine failure. This is all before hitting something. So, the brief might go as follows: "Anything (bad) below 70 knots (the Aztec's published accelerate/go target speed) and we will abort on the runway. Above 70 knots, assuming an engine failure, the landing gear coming up, we are going. Once committed, I will handle identifying, verifying, and feathering the dead engine. Checklist after that."

What if the runway does not meet the balanced field length criteria? "Anything below 50 knots and we will stop on the runway. Above 50 knots and we are going. In case of an engine failure happening above 50 and below 70, the plan will be to throttle back the good engine and make an emergency off airport landing. After 70, the gear is coming up, I will handle identifying, verifying, and feathering the dead engine while accelerating to blue line, the best rate of climb single-engine."

While it may not be prudent to depart from a runway shorter than the balanced field length required, at least there is a plan. In the heat of the moment, when the engine quits at a speed that is too slow to fly away, there won't be the inclination to improvise and risk an almost always fatal stall spin event after takeoff. Even if there is just one person, the pilot, in the airplane, rehearsing appropriate responses to bad events, however improbable, can be very helpful. A word of caution: whatever the plan, be sure to have the commitment to follow through. Resist the temptation to improvise in the heat of the moment.

*New beginnings.*

Incidentally, taking off in a multi-engine airplane from a runway that is shorter than the balanced field length is legal for all Part 91 operations, the rules that normally apply to personal flying. Charter and airlines operations, however, must always satisfy balanced field length requirements.

## Fly light whenever possible

The Aztec teaches another lesson that is directly applicable to larger aircraft, and one that can make up for a multitude of sins. Although almost all twins are certified to fly away at max gross takeoff weight (MGTOW) after an engine failure when operating out of a low altitude airport the outcome in the event of a real emergency is far less certain. Having practiced this at a safe altitude in a number of light twins, including the Aztec, I can testify that a current pilot following the proper procedures can make it work. However, in the heat of the moment, low to the ground, flying away safely on one engine may prove difficult. The NTSB accident database is full of examples where things didn't play out the way the certification test pilots demonstrated. Fortunately, there are ways to mitigate. Very high on the list is flying light. The Aztec is better than most twins on one engine, but it really shines when loaded about 400 lbs below gross. It's a day in the park, plenty of time to identify, verify, and then ultimately feather the dead engine, thereby gaining additional aerodynamic efficiency, leading to better climb performance et al.[1]

This can be true flying jets as well, especially when flying in the mountains. Achieving a safe climb gradient, sufficient to clear obstacles following an engine failure, can be a challenge.[2] Flying out of Aspen in the CJ3 on a bad weather day demands amazing single-engine climb performance, higher than 8 percent for most departures. The airport is 7,820 feet, so both engine power and lift capacity are significantly degraded due to the thinner air. The impact to single-engine performance is so great that with any significant passenger load the normally 1,800 nautical mile range CJ3 is relegated to a fuel load just adequate to reach Denver.

## Longer runways are better

Longer runways are always a good idea. Imagining an engine failure, the outcome likely will be much better if the airplane can either stop safely on the runway or reach Blue Line (best single engine rate of climb) clear of obstacles. So when ATC offers an expedited departure from the airport's short runway, or an intersection takeoff, it's time for a reality check about single-engine performance and options for a graceful recovery should bad engine-related things happen.

## Redundant systems

Much of the focus has been on engine failure and procedures to address. All meritorious in the abstract. But, ironically, modern engines, even piston engines, almost never fail if maintained and operated properly. So in thinking about redundant systems, the dual powerplant, while important in the unlikely event one quits, is probably not the major advantage. Why own a twin? Well, there are other important systems that do fail more often, sometimes at very inconvenient times. In a single-engine airplane, the loss of a vacuum pump or alternator can be a real emergency, especially if there is only one, and if flying IFR, the back-up being some kind of weird manifold pressure powered device. In a twin with redundant vacuum pumps operating off both engines, dual hydraulic pumps, and dual alternators, loss

---

[1] Manipulation of the propeller controls by the pilot to change the pitch of the non-turning propeller. The goal is to reduce the propeller's surface area exposed to the relative wind in an effort to reduce drag.

[2] Climb gradient is the ratio of the increase of altitude to horizontal air distance expressed as a percentage, therefore a still air distance. When relating the climb gradient to ground distance the correct term to be used is flight path angle.

of one is normally a minor inconvenience. Of all the reasons to own a light piston twin, especially if you're intending to operate in an IFR environment, having redundant accessories is it. Over the course of approximately 500 hours of Aztec operation, I experienced only one engine related problem, a cracked cylinder that resulted in partial loss of power from the affected engine during cruise. Accounting for the accessories, there were two alternator failures (occurring on different trips), one vacuum failure, and one hydraulic pump failure. In all cases, the flight concluded in a predictable way, even landing at the intended destination airport.

## Critical engine

The textbooks define the critical engine as "the engine whose failure most adversely affects the performance and handling of the aircraft." On most twins this is the left engine, the assumption being that both left and right propellers are being driven clockwise when looking forward. What's the big deal? Losing the left engine means testing the envelope where the minimum controllable airspeed ($V_{MC}$) is set along with a number of other parameters like aft CG limit and maximum takeoff weight. In cruise and descent phases of flight, losing the critical engine is a non-event, at least when operating below the airplane's single-engine service ceiling. But on takeoff, or at any point in the flight where the airspeed is low and power setting is high, losing the critical engine can be a handful. Why? Well, it's a conspiracy, the critical engine gang, also known in twin-engine flying circles as P-factor, spiraling slip stream, adverse torque, and accelerated slip stream. These are the four factors, each acting in a different way, that make flying a lot harder without the critical engine.

Starting with *P-factor*, also sometimes referred to as descending blade syndrome, the negative influence in play is left yaw, specifically, yaw toward the dead (left) engine. To understand this, it is important to know that even when both engines are operating normally, total thrust from the left and right engine the same, there will always be some engine induced left yawing moment. The reason is that in the scheme of propeller rotation, the downward moving blade always produces more thrust than the upper moving blade. This is because the angle of attack (the bite of air being taken as the blade descends) is bigger. Now imagine the left engine is not operating. There is, of course, the left yaw, expected because the right engine is located outboard on the right wing, only now aggravated, because the thrust originating from right engine's descending blade is to the right of the right engine's centerline, farther out on the wing than the centerline of the engine itself. Hence, an even greater yawing moment. In contrast, notice that the left engine descending blade's thrust while to the right of the engine, is actually closer to the fuselage, more inboard on the wing. So in the event that the right engine fails, while there is still yaw, yaw to the right, the descending blade's effect is lessened.

*Spiraling slipstream* can make directional control even more difficult. Here the concern is the clockwise corkscrew-like flow of air generated by the airplane's propellers, the thrust profile. Similar to P-factor, spiraling slipstream is a problem when the critical left engine quits, allowing the spiral airflow from the non-critical right engine to aggravate a left turning, left banking tendency. But unlike P-factor, should the right engine quit leaving the left critical engine still running, spiral slipstream actually helps the airplane go straight. Why? It's about the tail, or more precisely the way the spiraling air applies greater force to the left side of tailplane. This force counteracts the right turning yaw from P-Factor, decreasing the amount of left rudder needed to go straight.

Third on the list is *adverse torque*—for every action there is an equal and opposite reaction. This one is fairly easy to understand. With the engine and propeller turning clockwise, the airframe, the rest of the airplane, tends to want to rotate counter-clockwise. In normal flight with both engines running, and no other adverse factors in play, torque is a relatively minor issue. But should one engine fail, especially the left critical engine, torque can be an issue. It's not that the torque effect in isolation is worse when the left engine fails. Actually, the total left turning tendency is less when compared to normal operation because one less engine is producing torque. Think about it in terms of a giant conspiracy. While the total torque is less, when the left engine fails all of the other effects, including P-factor and adverse spiraling slipstream, have a new helper, and they're all trying to get the airplane to turn over onto its back.

## Accelerated slipstream, friend and foe

Are there any other advantages/disadvantages twins enjoy? One candidate to consider is accelerated slipstream induced lift. Although both single- and twin-engine airplanes demonstrate accelerated slipstreams, the artificial wind created by the engine/propeller, only twins can lay claim to any real performance benefit as a result. The reason is in the way the engines are mounted and in the aerodynamics. With the exception of the center thrust line designs, sometimes referred to as push/pull airplanes, like the Cessna 337, almost all twins have their engines and propellers mounted on the wings, outboard of the fuselage, with the propellers ahead of the leading edge. During periods when the engine and propeller are producing thrust, this wind produces more lifting force by the section of wing just aft of the propeller. While the affected wing area may seem small, no wider than the diameter of the propeller, improvement in lift capacity can be big, especially when trying to arrest an uncomfortably high rate of descent while flying at a relatively low airspeed. The practical application is the enhancement of short-field performance when making an approach into an airport with obstacles near the end of the runway. Knowing that the angle of approach and the rate of descent likely will be higher than typical, while the airspeed will be lower to avoid consuming more than the available runway, the pilot employs a quick burst of power beginning at the flare to arrest the descent, averting an accelerated stall and hard hit onto the runway. We normally use a little power in the flare when landing the G-44 Widgeon amphibian at our airport in Milton, Vermont. The runway is north/south and only 2,250 feet long, bordered by tall trees about 500 feet from either end. Despite the relatively slow airspeed and fast descent rate, that brief burst of accelerated slipstream delivers a perfect landing every time.

It's important to differentiate the power cushioned flare from landing techniques that employ relatively high power settings to create induced lift at near stall airspeeds all the way to the runway. Dragging the airplane in, to achieve the least possible kinetic energy, risks entering a part of the flight envelope where no matter how much power is applied, the airplane must descend before it can climb again. Known as operating behind the power curve, the practice sets a multitude of traps for the unwary twin pilot, the scariest an almost certain loss of control should one engine fail. Of course, all is made worse by the airplane's close proximity to the ground.

There are other downsides to leveraging accelerated slipstream. Some twin designs have very high clean configuration (flaps up) power-off stall speeds, often much greater than $V_{MC}$. To mitigate, SOPs for airplanes with this characteristic typically require application of some flaps on takeoff to lower the stall speed. The G-44 Widgeon is a good example. Its POH recommends application of 15 percent flaps for takeoff. Why? In most cases there is no issue if both engines are functioning normally, the airplane is flying, well on its way to passing through the $V_S$ airspeed. The engines are serving to lower the stall speed. But what happens if the pilot forgets to deploy the flaps and one engine fails prior to reaching $V_S$, the clean configuration stall speed? The immediate cessation of accelerated slip stream means some loss of lift on the affected side. This, in combination with the other adverse influences—P-factor, spiraling slipstream, and torque—can be a real problem. Will the airplane roll over and crash? Much depends on weight, atmospheric conditions, and pilot proficiency. Even in the best case, a graceful recovery flying away safely, may be a challenge. These are words to the wise for those reluctant to routinely follow POH guidance and/or use checklists.

## Flying away safely

Consider this a self-indulgence, a time to be righteous, like all those critics touting the value of twins in the hands of professionals, while condemning the mostly private, owner pilots, also known as amateurs, who create the bad statistics. Could this be a case where the statistics are accurate, but not particularly precise?

The ability to fly away is the light twin engine airplane's raison d'être, certainly part of aviation folklore and the sales materials offered by the OEMs. Does the evidence support this? Can the Aztec offer additional safety in the aggregate compared to high performance single-engine piston airplanes like the Cessna 210 or Beech A36 Bonanza, similar in speed, but without the engine redundancy? The answer depends on many factors, the primary being pilot proficiency, at least as presented by the mainstream safety pundits. Practiced knowledge of the emergency steps needed to deal with a complete engine failure emergency, especially on takeoff, is a prerequisite for success. No one would argue with that. But what if the emergency never happened? Or more to the point, assuming recovery from such an emergency may require Herculean abilities, best case, should the focus extend beyond obtaining over-the-top, outstanding, perpetual recurrent training.

One of the reasons turbofan airplanes are so safe is that there are almost zero incidences of serious mechanical failure. Although I have experienced literally hundreds of flameouts and fires flying the CJ3 and CJ4 simulators, I have had only one abnormal event in the course of more than 1,000 hours of actual turbofan flying (not even an emergency): a right generator failure. That's it, and it was easily resolved by diverting to the Cessna Service Center, courtesy of the working left generator, able to run everything on the airplane, with the battery offering another 30 minutes, just in case. This is not to dismiss the merit of training. In the case of the CJ aircraft it is key to attaining a better understanding of the systems, FMS, and various ways to engage the airspace environment. All good! It's just to say that we train a lot for engine failures, and they almost never happen in real life. Even when they do, it's a non-event because of the robust thrust reserve available from the working engine, at least when departing from lower altitude airports.

The statistics suggest that light twin-engine airplanes are safer than singles only when flown by a professional pilot. The opposite is true when non-pros, less well-trained/experienced pilots are in command, by a margin of more than two to one. The reason is that flying a light piston twin out of an engine failure is very difficult. The margins are extremely thin, especially when the airplane is heavy, or the airport is high in altitude, or experiencing a high density altitude as has been mentioned earlier. Couple this with what may be a non-deterministic situation (e.g., rising terrain), less than perfect zero-time engines, an aft CG, and the challenge can become insurmountable. Yes, there are balanced field length metrics and other published considerations that are supposed to protect pilots from "no man's land," a place where there is no guarantee the ship will be saved. The problem is that in many cases the operational parameters needed for everything to work out are just too marginal to insure that anything actually will work out. Captain Chesley "Sully" Sullenberger, played by the actor Tom Hanks, explains this nicely in the movie version of the emergency landing he made on the Hudson River after his plane, US Airways Flight 1549, flew into a flock of geese.

He makes the case to the NTSB that human beings tend to be startled by surprise emergency events, and the refraction time is shorter for a crew expecting birds to fly into their engines than it is for a crew with no idea. Refraction time is the period where panic is the emotion in play. While training and experience help shorten the period of panic before rational thought and action take over, there will always be some period of panic. It is for this reason that engine failures in light twins, especially low to the ground, should be considered totally unacceptable, to the extent practical.

## So, how to avoid?

One approach is to adopt a jet airplane-style maintenance program that includes both a formal component-replacement-before-failure program and zero defect aircraft system status as prerequisites to dispatch. Yes, there is a MEL, a minimum inventory of properly functioning systems in the jet that are necessary to legally dispatch. But this is the bare minimum and should not be the norm. No more than one, perhaps two flights max, depending on mission and weather, should be conducted with deferred maintenance items unaddressed. While not governed in quite the same way by the FARs or manufacturer AFM, the same idea applies to light piston twins, at least in spirit, especially older designs where system failures like the loss of the only hydraulic pump can be very challenging. There is no legitimate excuse to have all systems operating at anything less than 100 percent. As for the engines, any anomaly demands immediate attention, especially when vital components like magnetos, accessory pumps, lifters, valves, or cylinders are affected. Maintenance is not the place to be miserly. Trying to milk another couple of hundred hours beyond TBO out of the powerplants, justifying using some kind of good cylinder compression argument, is a false economy. Again, do you want to have to be the best pilot you ever were in your whole life to properly address the emergency?

## Don't do stupid things in twins

The statistics confirm that the menu of stupid things to do in a twin-engine airplane is pretty big. They range from running out of fuel to taking off overloaded. Fuel starvation would seem to be just a flagrant demonstration of incompetence, but it happens surprisingly frequently, even on takeoff! Sometimes the reason is no gas in the tanks, but that's not the only way to do it. Forgetting to activate the low pressure electrically-powered fuel pumps that serve as a backup in case the mechanical engine pump(s) fail can deliver the same result. The point here is that to the extent there are redundant systems in twins, the pilot must systematically employ them. Not all do.

Training and doing stupid things sometimes seem to go hand in hand. There was a twin-engine Beech Baron accident in eastern New York State recently involving a candidate for a multi-engine instructor rating and his instructor.[3] The instructor shut off the left engine at a relatively high altitude to test the candidate's ability to handle an actual engine failure in flight. What transpired subsequently was truly amazing. With the engine shut down and properly feathered, the student requested a single-engine approach and landing. Ironically, the request was not motivated by an enthusiasm to further practice single-engine approach procedures. No, the student wanted to save money by returning to the airport with only one engine operating, consuming less flight time by avoiding an in-flight engine

---

[3] National Transportation Safety Board Aviation Accident Data Summary. Accident Number: GAA17CA061. Plattsburgh, NY: November 14, 2016.

restart. False economy? All of this could have worked out if not for the failure of the student (and instructor) to follow proper Baron single-engine approach/landing procedures. Death by a thousand pricks. Beginning the cascade of events, another airplane threatened to enter the active runway environment. Focus disturbed, the student slowed the airplane near the end of the approach shortly after lowering the landing gear and extending the flaps to "land." (Extending the flaps to beyond "approach" during a single-engine emergency is normally not recommended, even for much more powerful turbofan aircraft.) With airspeed rapidly falling and sink rate increasing, the student applied power to the operating engine, but it was too late to arrest the decay. The Baron's speed had already fallen below $V_{MC}$, a great setup for a fatal stall-spin accident. Fortunately, as the airplane rolled left on its side, the instructor pilot retarded the good (right) engine, saving all from a fiery death. Unfortunately, due to significant altitude loss, the airplane slammed into the runway. All survived, but the airplane was a total loss. Nothing like this should ever have been attempted, except perhaps within the safe confines of a full flight simulator.

My favorite egregious act: an ATP-rated pilot who planned to ferry a light twin-engine aircraft using only one engine. The aircraft had experienced an engine failure the previous day. Fortunately, a colleague persuaded her to stand down on the project before taking off.

## The pilot factor

The reward for improvising, or ignoring formal procedures, is not so great when flying twin-engine airplanes. The integrated nature of the systems, more complicated speed profiles, and less forgiving weight and balance envelopes, all more critical in nature compared to their single-engine brethren, make it difficult to do anything better than the book suggests. While adopting a more formal process may seem time consuming, even inconvenient at times, predictability of outcome is important, especially on challenging days, in bad weather, with heavy loads, on short runways. Yes, better and more frequent training, rehearsing response to abnormals and emergencies to perfection, helps. A bigger factor in success, however, is a hybrid of superior seat-of-the-pants skills and discipline, an ability to adhere to book and other formal guidance while also paying attention to that occasional yellow alert, felt on the back of the neck, suggesting something isn't quite right. Welcome to the world of the systems aircraft, Captain. While the light twin isn't a modern airliner, a fifth generation Air Force fighter aircraft, or

*Adam and Gisela Alpert, newly married, pose in front of their handsome 1979 Piper PA-23-250 Aztec.*

spacecraft capable of carrying astronauts safely into earth's orbit, the class shares a common legacy in that for everything to work out in the end, much depends on the collective knowledge of everyone involved in the design, construction, and testing of the aircraft. All those numbers and procedures we ignore or adopt were developed to increase our chances of success.

Gisela (my new wife) and I flew the Aztec across the country, through the Caribbean Islands, and beyond. It provided excellent transportation while also laying the groundwork for mastering more complex aircraft like the Bell JetRanger helicopter, and CJ3/CJ4 jet aircraft, all designs embracing multiple on-board systems for delivering the advertised functionality and performance. Different aircraft have different systems, but there is commonality in the sense that pilots with system airplane experience know what to look for, what questions to ask. What makes the landing gear go up and down, the flaps deploy; what powers the avionics and other electrical devices, and the thrust needed to become airborne? Are there any interdependencies between these systems, for better or worse? When something goes wrong with one or more of the systems, which procedures come into play? Systems airplane pilots also know the importance of approved checklists and standard operating procedures. Investing in this discipline, with respect to flying, navigating, and communicating in what has become an increasingly complex airspace, affords greater reliability and utility. This is not to mention the added benefit of not getting killed while flying the airplane.

## Lessons learned:

**Lesson 1:** Our therapists said the therapy process was mostly about encouraging a greater sense of self-awareness, reflection, loving communication between partners, and a focus on feeling as opposed to thinking arguments. "We have never saved a marriage!" They said. And so it would be with Lisa and me.

**Lesson 2:** I asked Gisela to offer her opinion. She said she thought the therapists were great!

# 12 | Midlife Aviation Crisis

Men join the gym, dye their hair, have an affair (or two) and then buy a powerful red sports car to complete the stereotype. So begins the chase to recapture youth, fun, better, more carefree times. With life half or more done, a *what the hell* sort of reasoning takes over, leading to all kinds of interesting behavior. Usually, things end badly: divorce, speeding tickets, roots (or unnatural hair color). Looking back longingly, seeking some idealized new lease on life, is like driving a car using the rear view mirror as the sole reference.[1] Keeping watch on the white line behind, while making small corrections with the steering wheel, it is possible to keep the car oriented and in the correct lane without looking ahead. But the technique has its limitations. While good for straights, that first sharp turn can be a real doozie. So be sure not to arrive home from the office with lipstick on that freshly pressed white shirt, or mix up names in the heat of passion. At the very least, resolving a mid-life crisis this way demands significantly greater energy, attention, and financial resources (to help manage the chaos).

Now what to do if the midlife crisis is about flying adventures, imagined but not fulfilled? A midlife aviation crisis. Neither fast cars nor younger pretty girls will quite do the trick. Lovers of aviation embrace the future while also admitting some longing to experience the romance of its past. For those living in modern times who elect to indulge this longing, to recapture aviation's past, get ready to hang on by the tail. It's like driving a vintage automobile after embracing twenty-first-century technology. Those old nylon tires may have been replaced by radials, but the handling experience is, well, very exciting.

Still, who wouldn't want the chance to checkout in a P-38 Lightning or Supermarine Spitfire? Even for non-aviators, these airplanes are beautiful, iconic, and romantic—at least when they're not being used as tools for war.

---

[1] Ask your investment adviser about this, the portfolio management strategy employed. It's likely largely based on rear view mirror thinking, employing tools like Zephyr.

But what are they like to fly? And to what extent is there a benefit to flying them, something to learn, offsetting the danger associated with aircraft age, complexity, and a bias on the part of the designers in some cases, to put performance and mission ahead of comfort and safety?

Much depends on the pilot's experience, the aircraft selected as the object of affection, and training; with the quality of training as the best indicator of success. And some airplanes are harder to handle than others, proffering the prospect of emergencies of the worst case kind, with pilot plus passengers jumping out as the last item in the checklist—outcome dependent on egress technique, altitude, and proper function of the parachute system.

The P-51 Mustang nicely exemplifies the category. It sits beautifully poised on the ramp, displaying a polished aluminum finish. The giant four-blade Hamilton Standard propeller is a work of art, reminiscent of the muscular Art Deco style of the time when the airplane was in service. For those seeking a *Back to the Future* experience, some of the airplane's ground-breaking technology lives on in modern aircraft designs. Mostly, though, the P-51 is a must have airplane for kids drawn to airplanes, whose first P-51 probably came from a kit, a model, personally crafted and lovingly suspended from the ceiling—my bedroom at age 12 a case in point. And in imagining flying the real thing, there is further advantage to being a kid. In addition to infinite energy and relatively few inhibitions, there tends to be a refreshing "how hard can it be?" approach among the young. Perhaps this explains why the only slightly more grownup pilots, who actually flew the P-51 in combat, were so clever in their mastery of the machine, and so successful in conducting their missions.

The P-51 is indeed a big, powerful airplane. Later variants had MGTOWs of nearly 12,000 pounds, fully loaded with armament, fuel and externals. The Mustang is high energy, to say the very least. The entry speed for aileron rolls is normally 210 knots and, for loops, a staggering 260. Cruise speed is 372 knots at 25,000 feet and, with full flaps (at 50 degrees), 110 knots is the short-final target ref speed, about the same as our Citation Jets.

The P-51 also is a systems airplane, with hydraulic gear and flaps, and an advanced cooling design that actually adds thrust (the scoop underneath that funnels air to the water and oil radiators also acts like a small ramjet). If the airplane has an Achilles heel, it is that very close attention must be paid to managing the coolant temperature. It normally runs between 100° and 110°C, automatically controlled by operating an exhaust door at the rear end of the scoop. Anything outside the range is a problem. For this reason, the airplane was not an effective low-level fighter. It was too vulnerable to ground fire; one lucky hit to a cooling line and game over. No surprise, the flying manual emphasizes egress technique, including jettisoning the canopy and diving out the right side (because of slipstream effects). In general, any kind of fire or serious engine power-related problem demands an early exit.

The desire to fly an airplane that has *jumping out* on its checklist does suggest something a bit off about the ambition. But accepting that really bad emergencies can happen is part of the cost of flying airplanes like the P-51. The benefit, independent of the thrill, is that there are good lessons to be learned from high performance, relatively unforgiving designs.

So it was off to P-51 school for me, midlife aviation crisis resolved without risk of divorce, bad hair, or wrapping the red sports car around a tree.

## Getting a fighter started

Just starting the P-51 is a production. It's also telling that for every start, there is someone standing by, in close proximity to the engine, holding a giant fire extinguisher. Hot starts (the engine hot from a previous sortie) are even harder because of the risk of vapor lock as the fuel/air mixture is injected into the cylinders, but all starts demand precision. Given the number of steps, there are a lot of ways to screw it up:

Procedure:
1) Crack the throttle to about a half-inch = 800 rpm/idle after start
2) Boost pump on
3) Slight (half-second) prime
4) Hit the starter button
5) After four blades have turned or combustion occurs, mags to both
6) Mixture auto-lean

I initially found this to be a complex choreography to accomplish. Later, with practice, not so much. All an interesting testament to the idea that the familiar is easy, the unknown daunting. And, incidentally, there is much benefit associated with becoming comfortable with the transition.

It has been said that if you can start an airplane, you're ninety percent of the way there towards flying it. Still, in the case of fighters, some flying instruction is helpful. Consider this a note-to-self for readers who find an unguarded P-51 on the ramp while making a daring escape from an unidentified dictatorship where all involved stand falsely accused of a serious crime and the sentence is death.

# Landing and taking off

Takeoffs and landings have their own challenges. For the novice, the first few can be very interesting indeed. As one might expect, the 1,600-hp Merlin V-12 engine produces a lot of torque. The influence of torque effect while accelerating for takeoff is a real issue. There is also gyroscopic precession, in addition to P-factor and spiraling slipstream. In little airplanes, the gyroscope effect is relatively minor because the propeller systems are light. This is in contrast to the 450-pound propeller on the P-51. Independent of the other factors, just raising the tail during takeoff causes a pronounced left-turning tendency. Analogous to helicopters, the effect of any one control input (power, stick, rudder) must be anticipated. Adding power and raising the tail should always be accompanied by application of significant right rudder. And this is with six degrees of right rudder trim already cranked in.

Landings can be exciting, too. Touchdown speeds are high, so it is important to be tracking straight at touchdown. And given that tools for recovery are limited, a bounce can be a real problem. Unlike lighter tail-wheel airplanes, adding power after the bounce to cushion the landing is unhelpful because of control problems caused by increased torque, spiraling slipstream, and precession. And pilot induced oscillation (PIO), where the bounces get bigger after each hit and risk wrecking the airplane, must be avoided at all costs. Training, now and during the war, teaches a gentle re-leveling and no power changes, with the idea that there is likely still plenty of flying energy to land smoothly. The other solution is to feel for the ground with one wheel after the bounce, an idea presented in Chapter 5. I have applied the technique a number of times myself while flying the P-51 and it has worked every time, though in one case the airplane bounced three times before finally settling down.

# Numbers airplane

The P-51 is indeed a numbers airplane, but not like modern fighters, airliners, or business jets. There is no autopilot and the instruments are primitive by today's standards. Flying the airplane is hands on. Even when the airplane was a tool of war, the pilot had to be careful not to exceed certain limitations, especially when controlling the big powerful Merlin engine. Power had to be carefully set, especially on takeoff. Unlike less powerful singles and twins, the torque available in the P-51 is enough literally to flip the airplane on its back. So takeoff is a sequenced affair. It starts with a static check of systems at 2,300 rpm. Once complete, the brakes are released, and the takeoff begins. The pilot adds power steadily, up to 40 inches of manifold pressure.

*P-51 Mustang two ship training sortie.*

The tail is raised at 50 knots, and power is further increased to 55 inches. The airplane lifts off the runway at about 100 knots. During go-arounds it is also important to feed in the power slowly for the same reason.

Approach speeds are equally important. The initial flap setting of 20 degrees helps slow the aircraft to landing gear extension speed of 150 knots. This puts the aircraft on downwind at approximately 140 knots. The next 10 degrees coincides with turning base and 130 knots. Turning to final, airspeed is reduced to 120 knots with 40 degrees of flaps deployed. On short final, for a normal landing, the last 10 degrees (50 degrees total) are added and the airplane is slowed to 110 knots, the goal to cross the threshold at around 100 knots. Targeting the right speeds for landing is a Goldilocks moment. The pilot doesn't want to be too fast for fear of overshooting, nor does he want to be too slow, risking loss of control. Sloppiness is not rewarded when flying the P-51.

## Stalls and stall behavior

There are generally no stall warning systems in fighters of this era, so knowing how to recognize the onset of a stall is a seat-of-the-pants affair, a skillset emphasized during training. Fortunately, the P-51 is an honest messenger. Both normal and accelerated stalls are preceded by some aerodynamic buffet (vibration). The range of airspeeds where these progressive buffets occur narrows from 76 to 88 knots, clean in level flight, to 72 to 76 knots with gear and flaps down. When clean and in a steep bank (i.e., 60 to 70 degrees) the delta between onset and stall decreases even more, while shifting the speed range upward to 120 to 122 knots. Sensitivity to the buffets, especially when clean and while executing a high-G maneuver is a prerequisite for flying safely. There were a number of P-51s lost during World War II while dive bombing ground targets. These airplanes experienced an accelerated stall during the radical pull-up maneuver necessary to recover at the bottom. Despite the relatively high airspeeds in play, the P-51's wing, feeling the artificially-induced increase in weight, would simply stop flying, the angle of attack too high, max lift capacity exceeded. The right answer was to push the stick forward, unloading the wing. Many combat pilots intellectually knew this, but with the ground rushing up and little altitude to spare, pushing the stick forward, nosing over to facilitate a recovery, was counter-intuitive, and not appealing. The P-51 dive bomb missions were discontinued eventually, thereby solving much of the accelerated stall problem. It also allowed the fighters to focus more on protecting the bombers over continental Europe, the P-51 being one of the first designs capable of providing escort all the way to and from the enemy target.

The P-51 dive bombing experience teaches something else. Understanding the concept of angle of attack, and lift capacity, is important in maintaining both lift and control of the aircraft at all times. Yet many pilots lack a complete understanding of the dynamic nature of the lift required to maintain controlled flight. They tend to assume that flying faster than the published aerodynamic stall speed for the aircraft guarantees safe operation. Airspeed is thus the primary metric that most general aviation pilots lean on to assess their margin and predict how close the airplane is to stalling. While airspeed is a significant factor, on its own it is a relatively poor predictor of lift. To precisely determine how much of the wings' lifting capacity is consumed, wing area, weight, temperature and altitude (for establishing air density), load factor, and center of gravity must all be included in the calculation. It is not always practical to do.

This is one of the reasons why the P-51 can be a great teacher. While the P-51 doesn't have fancy angle of attack systems for gathering the parameters and making the precise calculations as some modern fighter airplanes do, it has its own way of communicating. With the onset of the buffet, the pilot knows the airplane's wing is approaching its maximum lift capacity. The message is don't bank any tighter, or finish that loop with just a little less back pressure on the stick. With the right response, the airplane keeps flying; with the wrong one, bad things may happen. All airplane can bite; it is just that the P-51 is a little less forgiving with regard to the stall regime, and in many other respects.

## The Mustang experience

Assuming money is not a constraint, is owning a personal fighter aircraft a good idea? The answer is that it depends. The P-51 is spectacular in both appearance and performance. Flying it is a power trip for sure, an absolute thrill. No doubt it makes for a better pilot. But the cockpit is hot and noisy. For the pilot no longer 19 years old, it is par for the course to feel tired (and sore) after only a couple of hours of stick time, especially if high-G aerobatics are on the agenda. This is with no one shooting at you and all systems functioning normally. The pilots who flew P-51s during wartime must have been exceedingly brave and robust. I can't imagine doing six-hour sorties, day after day, with dog fights scattered in between. Frightening!

## Other options

There is a whole menu of flying temptations to choose from when deciding how to address a midlife aviation crisis. Flying World War II fighters is at one end of the intensity spectrum, but there are other romantic aviation dalliances to consider. A personal favorite is the two-place Boeing-Stearman, also known as a PT-13, PT-17, PT-18, Stearman 70 and 75, Model 73, and NS-1 through 5—designation depending on engine selection, military branch, and country of service. Yes, this open cockpit biplane was built by

*Boeing-Stearman PT-17.*

the same company that now makes the 737, 777, and a slew of other commercial and military aircraft.

Like the P-51, the Stearman started out life in the military during World War II, though it never saw combat. It was a trainer, likely the second airplane Army Air Corp cadets would fly after mastering a J3 Cub or similar light primary aircraft. The Boeing-Stearman was bigger and heavier, not designed for ease of flying. It served as a platform for young pilots making the transition to combat aircraft, including fighters such as the P-51.

Mastering the Stearman is much about figuring out how to take off, land, and fly without being able to see ahead. Like the Cub it is a two-place airplane with the captain seated in the back. Unlike the Cub, there is almost no forward visibility. A combination of passenger positioning, fabric, wires, and a big radial engine bolted to the front of the airplane makes seeing important features like runways very difficult. Success depends on keen peripheral vision and much craning into the airstream to see what is actually going on.

Why so hard? Before the invention of simulators, the Army used "trainer" airplanes to teach the basics before cadets graduated to bombers, fighters, and transports. The goal was for the training experience to be safe while also realistic, as representative as possible of aircraft like the P-51. The PT-17's visibility was degraded by design, to replicate the fighter-flying experience. The P-51's visibility is not great, but other tailwheel fighter designs are far worse.

The Stearman was built to be rugged, partly in anticipation of abuse from student pilots. Mostly though, the Army wanted the airplane to be fully aerobatic. The Stearman experience in most cases would be the cadet's first exposure to the concepts of aerial combat—loops, aileron rolls, barrel rolls, split-Ss, and Immelmanns.

Cadets also learned energy management in the Stearman. While the original Continental 220-hp engine was powerful for the time, it was bolted to a plane that could weigh as much as 3,000 pounds. Maneuvers had to be thought out and executed with care. Entering a loop at the wrong speed, typically too slow, meant possibly falling out at the top, lacking enough engine to power through. No one actually fell out of the airplane, but suffice it to say, the airplane itself would depart the arc in an uncontrolled way. Students had to up their game, flying the target speeds precisely and applying control inputs in just the right way, an ideal skillset for flying more advanced aircraft.

So how did the Stearman fare with respect to addressing a midlife aviation crisis? I wanted to find out, so I ordered one (actually, a rebuilt 1944 model). At this point, it would pay to do a little accounting. The P-51 experience cost about $17,000—cheap for a midlife crisis, or for anything aviation related, frankly. The cost of a used Stearman varies—on average about $100,000 for a good one. After consultation with experts and my wife, Gisela, who likes new things, it was decided that as close to new as possible was the only option. Total cost: $295,000, including custom paint and interior, plus training at our residence airport in Milton, Vermont. Very convenient.

Despite the Stearman's reputation as a challenging airplane, it is a delight to fly, especially on a calm summer day. But it does demand some adjustment in technique, mostly to address the forward visibility problem. Like many big single-engine tailwheel airplanes, taxiing necessitates a zig-zag course allowing for periodic views of the path ahead from each side. And when landing, it is often advisable to perform a continuous turning pattern to touchdown to ensure an unobstructed view of the runway environment. Because the Stearman has no flaps or other lift-altering surfaces, it is also important to be comfortable with slips, to aid in controlling the rate of descent and to enhance forward visibility. Slip type cross-controlling, right rudder–left aileron, for example, is seldom employed these days. Modern designs incorporate lift-altering devices like spoilers, flaps, and speed brakes that can be controlled from the cockpit, improving on the slipping maneuver that makes some passengers feel uncomfortable. It is a sensation akin to being pushed against the window or drawn toward the aisle sideways. Still there are times when slips can be very useful, even in modern airplanes. Sometimes those fancy lift-altering systems fail.

The engine that powers the Stearman is also worth mentioning. Unlike the P-51's engine, which in many ways resembles conventional water-cooled V-designs typical of some automobiles, the Stearman's engine is air-cooled and round, with the cylinders and pistons mounted at symmetrical angles like numbers on a clock. Known as a radial engine, the design is clever in that there is one master rod that is connected to both the first piston and crank shaft at a single point. The other pistons are connected to the master rod with smaller individual rods and bearings. It is interesting to note that single-bank radial engines like the Jacobs always have an odd number of cylinders and pistons. This is because of the nature, and the firing order, of a four stroke engine (e.g., power stroke, exhaust stroke, intake stroke, compression stoke). By scheduling the power stroke to occur in a skipping fashion—cylinders 1, 3, 5, 7, 2, 4, 6 (assuming a seven-cylinder engine)—each piston can experience all four strokes in the course of two complete revolutions of the crank shaft. The engine runs with less vibration, as well.

Although a thing of beauty, radial engines fell out of fashion after the 1950s, largely because of their weight and poor aerodynamic characteristics. The excellent cooling achieved by having all those cylinders out in the wind also created a lot of drag. This is one of the reasons why, even with the 300-hp Jacobs, the engine we choose for our Stearman, maximum cruise is only about 110 mph. Slow! Demand for greater power/weight ratios also helped to spell the end of radials. Unlike the faster-turning flat opposed and V-style engines, radials could only get more powerful by increasing in size and weight, or by creating banks of radials linked together via a common crankshaft—because of the bulkier mechanisms used to connect the pistons to the crankshaft.

Still, radials had a good run with some of the big multi-bank versions producing 2,000 hp or more. Famous planes like the B-17 bomber and Voight Corsair had them, with aerodynamic performance improved somewhat by cowling elements. There is nothing quite like the beautiful growl of a radial. With the plume of blue smoke belching from the exhaust at start up, it just reeks of romance.

If my midlife aviation crisis had ended with P-51 training and the Stearman biplane acquisition, I could have declared victory, out of pocket only about $312,000 plus gas and maintenance going forward. But the lust for planes didn't stop there. The builder of the Stearman offered a deal on a like-new L-19 Bird Dog, similar to the one I once used to tow gliders. "Buy the Stearman for list," he said, "and I will sell you the L-19 at cost, approximately $130,000." Had the crisis been resolved by the acquisition of just the one additional airplane, that would have been okay.

The final questionable decision had its roots in a chance meeting with Bob "Bobby" Rose, Jr., a former Sugarbush-based pilot and friend from those crazy Macone Sugarbush Air Service days.

We found ourselves on an unpressurized Air North Shorts 330 (the flying boxcar) commuting back to Burlington from Westchester, New York. Bobby had finally realized his ambition to become an airline pilot for one of the regional carriers. He was deadheading home after completing his commercial flying for the month. I was there because before I had finished my business in Westchester the winter weather had turned icy, and the single-engine V35B Bonanza I was flying was no match for the freezing rain in the forecast.

*Citation Jet 3, Boeing-Stearman PT-17, and Grumman G-44 Widgeon.*

Although the cabin noise was deafening, we caught up on things, including Bobby's ambition to sign on with USAir (later American Airlines), a big step up. This was a number of years after the Hayward Tyler flights so I was anxious to learn more. It was good to know that someone was making a go of it in aviation.

I liked the analytical work I was doing. It was interesting, paid well, and offered some flying in between. But piloting single-engine piston airplanes, while fun and certainly practical for some missions, was a far cry from commanding a giant airliner. The fact that I had to leave my Bonanza behind was a reinforcing point. Bobby, sensing my angst, offered an immediate diagnosis. "You are having a midlife aviation crisis," he said. Puzzled, I asked him to explain, my initial concern being that, at age twenty-six, surely I had a ways to go before midlife, at least until I was thirty. Bobby was insistent. He said, "You are having a mid-life aviation crisis and there is only one way to fix it. You need a Widgeon—a flying boat!"

In hindsight, I conclude it was Bobby who likely wanted a Widgeon to address his own aviation crisis, but at the time his words had impact. I had read about LeRoy Grumman, the Long Island–based iron works, and the many amazing amphibian designs that were Grumman's creation. There was the Duck, the Goose, the Mallard, the Albatross, and the Widgeon. The

Widgeon was the smallest in the line: a perfect personal airplane, multi-engine for safety, fast, load carrying, and capable of landing on both water and land. Compelling! Someday, I would own a Widgeon.

Widgeon delayed, but not denied. Only twenty-nine years later, I was ferrying N92L, my very own Grumman Widgeon G-44, home from Houma, Louisiana. It was perhaps not the craziest purchase ever, but it was right up there, as evidenced by the emergency that developed on the very first leg of the ferry home. Arriving at Lexington, Kentucky, one of the planned fuel stops, the right main gear failed to deploy.

Fortunately, my competent and clever aviation consultant, Mickey Dalton, was onboard. And unbeknownst to me he had fortuitously consulted with the airplane's mechanic about certain emergency gear extension scenarios. "The main gear uplocks sometimes stick," had been one of his helpful advisements. Good thing we had tools on-board. Widgeons need a lot of tools, as it turns out.

Happily, after an extended time circling the airport, Mickey was able to remove the right gear shroud and pry the uplock loose with a big screw driver. The right gear shot down. Unfortunately, by this time it was night. Having never landed the bulky flying boat in the dark, and with only six hours total time in type, I admit to feeling some apprehension, even worry. Rightly so! After touchdown, I was barely able to recover from an unfolding ground loop, one that would have rolled us into a ball, had the jerking left turn and right main gear wheelie not been arrested.

Amazingly, airplane and occupants were okay, the sticking gear uplock and near crash landing ultimately traced to a mis-rigged landing gear and aileron system. We celebrated at the hotel bar with three double vodka tonics each—delivered simultaneously. As for the remainder of the ferry, we left the wheels down, with no more night landings after Lexington.

Only about $150,000 in upgrades and remedial maintenances later, the Widgeon was ready to go. My midlife aviation crisis was over. Counting the cost of repairs and the Widgeon itself, about $280,000, plus the other airplanes, the P-51 experience, it added up to $872,000, plus on-going storage, also maintenance that, in the case of the Widgeon, tends to be, well, extensive. Expensive?

Gisela and I are still happily married, in love, a big success when considering how some midlife dalliances conclude. So in my mind the airplanes were a bargain, offering adventure, a great living history lesson, and some new cockpit skills. My only worry: will there be a late-life aviation crisis?

## Lessons learned:

**Lesson 1:** Buying and/or flying old airplanes to satisfy a midlife crisis is expensive, but still cheaper than having an affair.

**Lesson 2:** When possible, find a way to rent (as opposed to buy) that lustful fantasy flying experience.

**Lesson 3:** Widgeons require much fixing.

# 13 | **Wives and Airplanes:** The Great Widgeon Adventure

Many formulas portend a great adventure. Certainly one would involve a beautiful woman, a flying boat, and a dual hydraulic system failure resulting in crippled landing gear and flaps.

Our Grumman Widgeon G-44 is a majestic twin-engine, tail-wheel amphibian, sixty-nine years old with an interesting history. It served in World War II as a light bomber (one bomb) looking for German U-boats off the Gulf Gulf Coast. It was put to work in Africa, ferrying oil workers to offshore rigs, and then it transported US timber company managers to their mills, which were typically located near rivers.

Approximately 300 Widgeons were built, from the early 1940s to the mid-1950s. There are about fifty still flying. When we purchased N92L, with more than 12,000 hours logged, it was marginally flyable; built in 1944, it had been maintained with some sketchy interventions and improvisations. Because the Widgeon is a complex airplane with retractable gear, hydraulics, multiple electrical power sources and intricate structures, including a fuselage that functions as a boat for water operations, inadequate maintenance can be fatal. It took us three years to make it reliable and safe. Even so, it is a continuous work in progress.

It was a beautiful August day in Vermont. Gisela and I had finished lunch at the Sugarbush Airport restaurant and were flying home to Milton, Vermont, 10 nautical miles north of Burlington International Airport. Along the way, we had a brief splashdown on Lake Champlain planned for a photo shoot to be accomplished by my brother, Briar, his residence conveniently located on the east side of the lake in the town of Charlotte. Gisela was not yet a pilot, but she assisted nicely with cockpit duties, including reading the elaborate set of checklists.

We approached my brother's house, and Gisela started the water-landing checklist. Much of what makes water flying safe is knowing the water—wave heights, the presence of debris, wind direction relative to the swells. Anything over a one-foot chop can potentially damage the aircraft.

*Grumman G-44 Widgeon run-up.*

Gisela called out flaps on base leg, and I deployed 20 degrees. Turning to align with the water runway and reconfirming "gear up" for a water landing, I pulled the flap lever for 30 degrees. Nothing happened. I pulled again, watching hydraulic pressure. The gauge read zero! We had a problem.

The Widgeon's hydraulic system is powered by the left engine. A reservoir supplies fluid to the landing gear (two main wheels and tail wheel) and flaps. The reservoir also feeds a hand pump, the standpipe for which is lower than the pipe for the engine-driven pump, preventing it from pumping all the fluid overboard before the hand pump can be operated. In theory, the design preserves enough fluid to operate the gear and flaps manually, at least once.

Realizing hydraulics eventually would be needed for landing, it was time to abort the approach and run through the emergency checklist, deciding first whether the landing would be on water or land. For a water landing, the hand pump would be used to operate the flaps only. Landing without flaps is not permitted because high touchdown speeds can cause the nose of the airplane to submarine underwater. Catastrophic! For landing on land, the pump operates both the landing gear and flaps.

I opted to configure for landing on land. With a stiffening north wind, a water landing was less and less appealing. At seaplane school, I was told the backup hydraulic system never fails. So, with high confidence, I selected gear down and started pumping.

The hand pump is on the pilot's side, with a retractable handle. The manual says a maximum of 24 strokes is needed to extend the gear, though my experience during maintenance was that 10 strokes usually would do it. When the gear position lights still showed red after 30 strokes, I began to worry.

It was 3:27 p.m. in the afternoon. In less than an hour, we had gone from a delicious lunch and scenic tour to a real problem. In addition to failure of the hydraulic system, the landing gear was now partially down, so neither a water nor land landing could be made safely. A water landing with wheels down is a fatal mistake in the Widgeon.

There is a kind of sadness that overwhelms you when it seems as if all options have been exhausted. It is not panic, where rational thought and the ability to make decisions are compromised for some period. It is more the realization that the choices are limited and mostly bad. This is the feeling I remember as we realized together that a crash landing was a real possibility. Gisela asked if it could result in a fire. I didn't really have an answer, except to promise I would do my best to get the airplane down safely.

The worst of times can also be our finest moments. I found myself thinking about all the made-up heroes of film and television. Shows like *Star Trek*, *12 O'Clock High*, and even the movie *Galaxy Quest*, with its slogan "Never give up and never surrender." It pokes fun at the others, but then makes a serious point about working the problem to the end, no matter what. Somehow thinking about valiant fictional characters helped short-circuit the panic.

It was time to take stock. The airplane had been fueled with 160 gallons, prior to the trip to Sugarbush. Endurance initially equal to nearly six hours; about four and a half now remained. We had wrenches, screwdrivers, a hammer, and a special rod that Jim Proft, our mechanic, had fashioned after a conversation about emergency gear extension. I had told Jim it would be great to have some way to get the mains down without hydraulics, so he fashioned a manual extension rod, just in case. The idea was to disassemble the main gear shroud and then use the rod to push each gear down. It was untested.

Cleverly—luckily—we had fully charged cell phones. If we could reach Jim, he could talk us through the landing gear deployment. Gisela managed to reach him; an improbable success given he was lounging on his power-boat in the middle of Lake Champlain.

The Widgeon is noisy, so it took her a few attempts to apprise Jim of the situation. (All those movies and shows that depict perfect cell phone reception in the face of squealing car tires, explosions, general mayhem: totally unrealistic.)

Jim had several ideas, including a radical climb. Because the primary pump's suction pipe was in the aft portion of the reservoir, more fluid would be available. We attempted a couple of high-G pull-ups, hoping to drive the gear down. Nausea was the only result.

A landing at our home airport in Milton was out of the question. Burlington International was the best option. The airport was large, close, and had all the services, including emergency response.

At 3:39 p.m., I declared an emergency with Burlington Approach. This gave us priority and permission to deviate from the FARs if necessary.

Jim had briefed Gisela on landing gear system disassembly and what to do for manual gear extension. Because access to the gear is only available from the main cabin, one of us would have to leave the cockpit to attempt the extension. Although I was the only pilot on board, it was not clear whether my slender Gisela would be able to manipulate the heavy gear mechanism unaided. Furthermore, she was unfamiliar with the gear components and positioning. It was decided. After performing the initial disassembly needed to expose the mechanism, Gisela would have to manage the flying while I worked on the gear.

At 3:59 p.m., I told ATC that I would attempt to lower the gear from inside. Because the process would take time, I requested clearance to enter the airspace between Albany, New York, and Swanton, Vermont, to accommodate our maneuvering. Gisela then took apart the right main gear shroud.

Somewhere in the middle of this, Gisela managed to make a call to my brother, who had been waiting for us in Charlotte. She described the situation as desperate, then proceeded to name a revised set of beneficiaries for her assets, should we not make it. Observing that she had stopped working on the landing gear, I asked what she was doing. Tearfully, she told me she needed to be sure that her affairs were in order.

I wanted to be empathetic, but frankly estate planning didn't seem like a priority at the time. As calmly as I could, I assured her I thought we would be okay, while also emphasizing the need to focus on the immediate problem.

The Widgeon had a new Century I wing-leveler autopilot that could track a navigation signal. We, therefore, decided to climb to a higher altitude and then dial in Albany's VOR ground station so the autopilot could track a straight course. Once established the idea was to trim for a shallow descent, naturally preventing the airplane from stalling while I was in the back.

Gisela monitored the altimeter and called out altitudes. We started at about 5,000 feet, and gradually descended as I worked on the gear. A 100-

foot per minute rate of descent gave us approximately 30 minutes before we would need to start over. With the shroud now removed, I could see the entire gear assembly and the ground below. The gear was clearly unlocked, with its small locking hooks, one on each side, several inches from the catch.

My goal was to pry the assembly outward and down, so the hook could engage, using Jim's special tool and a hammer. The idea was to set the end of the bar on a little shelf in the gear casting about half way down, and then push the gear out. Once the hook was close to the catch, I would use the hammer to force the entire structure to its limits, hopefully making the hook.

The first attempt failed. I couldn't get the gear to lock. I tried several times, applying as much force as I could. I worried about losing the tool through the opening to the ground while hanging on to the bar's handle and hammering on it. That would end any hope of extending the gear manually.

I decided to take a break, to turn around toward Albany, climb and restart the descent. My second attempt was better. I was able to extend the gear fully with the hook partially engaged. There was no green-light gear indication in the cockpit, but I could see the gear and tire were fully extended. Would it hold? I turned my attention to the left side.

The forces needed to pry the left gear out were even higher. Using all my strength, I couldn't reach the limits and I was nowhere near engaging the hook. There was no way I would be able to get the left side locked. My partial success could doom us to an uncontrolled rollout once the left gear collapsed. We had to get the left main down.

I went back to the cockpit to call Jim. The news hardly cheered Gisela, but she dutifully placed the call. By now, Jim was back on shore, getting ready to head to the airport.

Jim speculated there might be some kind of hydraulic lock. Knowing the right side was partially engaged, he suggested the left actuator was sucked in slightly by residual fluid. Since the left and right sides are connected, it made sense that extending one side could cause the other to retract.

We had no access to the actuator, so bleeding the fluid out by disconnecting the tubing was not an option. We were going to have to find another way.

Jim suggested that by applying continuous pressure to the left gear, the residual fluid should bleed out. But how long would it take? Jim didn't know, but he was pretty sure that, with the gear handle down, the remaining hydraulic fluid eventually would dissipate.

I went back to the cabin. Holding Jim's tool firmly on the casting's shelf, I pushed with all my strength. There were two hours of fuel remaining. How long would it take to bleed the actuator?

Jim thought it might take half an hour. I was hoping for sooner. I was exhausted from the previous attempts, and we still had to deal with the partially engaged/locked right side. It had taken an hour and a half to get to this point. In another 90 minutes, we were landing somewhere, gear locked or not.

After twenty minutes, I tried hammering again. Pushing as hard as I could, I started to bang away. Suddenly *Ouch!* I had hit my left index finger knuckle with the hammer. Now I was bleeding all over the airplane.

I stopped hammering and went back to the cockpit. Gisela was incredulous. "Don't we have enough problems already without you thinking up new ones?" she said. I had no comment except to say it "hurt like hell."

The first-aid kit was out for replenishing, so Gisela fashioned a bandage out of industrial-strength cleaning wipes and hair ties, slowing the blood flow to a trickle.

After giving ATC an update, I resumed my hammering. *Bang, bang, bang*—I could see I was getting closer. Finally, with one big bang on the tool, missing my hand by a fraction of an inch, the hook engaged and Gisela shrieked, more or less simultaneously, "It's green, it's green!" We now knew it was possible to fully extend and lock the gear manually. Back to the right side.

It was 4:40 p.m. Bleeding the other actuator had worked. When I went back to work on the right gear, it took only one or two hits before it locked in place. Both the left and right latches were in position, an awesome sight, indeed.

I replaced the shrouds and returned to the cockpit. Although the tail-wheel was still indicating unsafe, I concluded losing the tail skid was an option we could live with.

We reported our success to ATC, and called Jim with the good news. By now, he was on his way to the airport, to be ready to remove the airplane from the runway. With luck, this would involve nothing more than jacking the tail up, lowering the tail wheel, and towing the airplane. But, with no flaps, landing speed was going to be high.

4:50 p.m. A no-flap runway landing generally is not taught at Widgeon school, because most of the work is on the water. So, this would be my first no-flap landing in the Widgeon.

We improvised an approach speed of 110 mph, with touchdown at around 90. The airplane stalls at 98 mph clean, power-off, but with power on it would be somewhat lower. During a normal landing, touchdown speed is closer to 70 mph.

ATC relayed a message from emergency services, who wanted our ETA to coordinate the stationing of equipment. I asked for a continued clearance in the corridor to burn off fuel. I wanted some reserve, but fuel is heavy; less is more when it comes to lowering landing speed. We gave an ETA of 5:50 p.m.

Burlington's runway 15/33 is 8,320-feet long. With flaps, the Widgeon needs no more than 1,800 feet. Without flaps, the landing distance would be longer.

At 5:35 p.m., I said "Burlington Approach, Widgeon 92L, we are requesting clearance to land at Burlington, we would like the long runway today, have Lima."

Burlington Approach: "92L, roger, you can start the turn inbound for runway 33, winds 360 at 6, altimeter is 30.26, and tower has equipment standing by for you, you can call the tower on 118.3"

Widgeon: "118.3, 92L, roger, thank you for the help."

Unbeknownst to us, emergency services and ATC were coordinating for a chase on the runway, once the airplane passed the threshold.

As we turned base, Gisela firmly reminded me there was a checklist to complete. After all the drama, I had forgotten that a checklist was proper and prudent. "I have one job on this airplane and I am going to do it!" she said. She had done so much more, of course, but it was kind of a Sigourney Weaver in *Galaxy Quest* moment.

Fuel pumps on, mixtures rich, props forward. Gear down!

On final, we saw the fire engines waiting: waiting to chase us down and extinguish a possible post-crash fire. I was feeling increasingly confident about the outcome, but I must admit, as we flew by the flashing lights from the emergency vehicles, I still had my doubts.

The airplane touched down smoothly and firmly on the hard surface—the gear held. The tail finally dropped, the scraping of the skid hitting the runway pavement a terrible and yet reassuring sound. The landing had exceeded expectations.

Burlington Tower: "Welcome to Burlington! You can shut down there."

Gisela dutifully went through the shutdown checklist. We were safely on the ground.

The root cause of the failure was a ruptured line on the pressure side of the pump. With the engine-driven pump working, hydraulic fluid ported overboard until most of the fluid in the reservoir was exhausted. The back-up system failed because the height of the reservoir tank's primary system

*A subsequent successful landing on Lake Champlain.*

standpipe was nearly identical to the back-up system pipe. With the for-ward and raised location of the back-up standpipe, whatever fluid was still remaining in the reservoir was unavailable to the suction side of the hand pump.

Damage to the aircraft was limited to the replaceable steel tailskid. The hydraulic system was rebuilt with new flexible high-pressure hose, a new unloader valve, and a new, larger reservoir system employing standpipes raised to the proper height. A separate in-line back-up reservoir also was installed to provide fluid directly to the suction side of the hand pump, in case the primary reservoir experienced a catastrophic failure.

For the Widgeon, there were many more adventures, and lots more maintenance, ahead.

My hand healed nicely.

Gisela enrolled in primary flight school and ultimately received her pri-vate pilot's license. Now, with her new skill set and confidence, she is always there, at my side.

## Lessons learned:

**Lesson 1:** Mechanical systems may fail, but beauty and romance endure.

**Lesson 2:** Access to a star mechanic can be a life saver.

# 14 | High Anxiety: "So You Want to Fly Jets"

I t was a particularly unpleasant winter morning in New York City. The wind howled out of the east, and the blowing, drifting snow only slightly brightened the overhanging gloom. After a pause at the hold point for JFK's runway 4 left, we were cleared to line up and wait.

The weather was reported 400 feet overcast, half-mile visibility, blowing snow, with temperature and dewpoint both at -1°C. Light-to-moderate icing was forecast in the clouds. Though the weather was frightful, the Cessna Citation Jet 525 was fully capable. The airplane uses bleed air to heat the wings, engine inlets, and windscreen, all fed by two powerful Williams FJ 44-1A turbofan engines. A pneumatic boot deices the tail's horizontal stabilizer using service air, also powered by the engine bleed air system.

For this leg it was my turn to fly (pilot flying, or PF). Our chief pilot, Karen "KK" Harvey, assumed the copilot spot (pilot monitoring, or PM). Clearance was Bette 3 departure, right turn 100 degrees after takeoff, maintain 5,000 feet.

"Citation Jet N565JF, cleared for takeoff runway 4 left, maintain runway heading."

With a final check of the annunciator panel ("dark!"), I advanced the throttles to full power and the airplane accelerated. KK called out "airspeed alive," and, "70 knots cross check," "$V_1$," "V-rotate," and then "positive rate," as I lifted the gear handle into the up and locked position. Still accelerating, *poof*, into clouds we flew. Then suddenly and without warning: *BANG!* A tremendous noise from the tail. The annunciator panel flashed red and yellow while the mechanized voice screamed, "Right engine fire! Right engine fire!"

"Holy crap, we're on fire!" I yelled.

The airplane listed to the right as the airspeed decreased. "Fly $V_2$!" KK yelled. I lowered the nose. The deteriorating airspeed moderated but not enough. Meanwhile, the rate of turn was increasing despite application of full opposite left rudder. "Get that nose down!" KK insisted. I lowered the nose further, but it was too late. At 89 knots the stick-shaker activated. The speed wouldn't come back. We were just a few knots short of stalling. I couldn't believe what was happening. We descended in a steep right turn, our options rapidly diminishing. With only 400 feet between us and the ground, pointing the nose down more to gain speed would leave no margin to recover.

"Terrain, pull up! Terrain, pull up!" screeched the voice, piling urgency on top of the cacophony of machine- and human-generated imperatives. I knew we were screwed, but I couldn't—*wouldn't*—give up. Trying to recover from a clearly unrecoverable situation, I wrestled the controls and watched what little altitude was left deteriorate.

Then, suddenly, mercifully, silence.

We didn't actually crash. But we would have if Bill McDowell, our CAE Simuflite Instructor, hadn't intervened and ended the scenario. "Adam," he said, "that didn't go very well. Shall we try it again?"

It was simulator day two, my first in-flight emergency, and one of many humbling simulator adventures to come, as I attempted to achieve a captain type rating in the CE-525 Citation jet.

The journey had begun months earlier with a decision to create a flight department for our family-owned life science tools company. We selected the Cessna's Citation Jet for its comfort, reliable performance and relatively low operating costs. Because the airplane is certified both for single-pilot and crew operation, we planned to staff it with one professional full-time chief pilot, and me. The key to having a great single-pilot flight department is to bring on a great pilot. Furthermore, the key to passing "initial" is having a great copilot. We got all of that and more when we hired KK Harvey.

Simuflite's CE-525 captain's rating initial training requires 50 hours of ground school and 28 hours of in-simulator training. It's a fully-packed fifteen days with just one day off in the middle to catch up on studying (and laundry). There is a mass of material to absorb, particularly in ground school where a typical day might cover power plant, fire protection, fuel systems, flight controls, hydraulics, landing gear, brakes, pressurization, oxygen system, and ice/rain protection. And the next day might cover emergency operations for all these systems.

If the ground school curriculum weren't intimidating enough, one only had to look around the classroom to feel inadequate. During the kick-off, the students (referred to as "the clients" by Simuflite) introduced themselves and shared their flying experience. The first pilot to tell his story said he had retired from Delta Airlines after flying about 25,000 hours in various transport aircraft, including the Boeing 767. This senior captain hoped to keep his hand in flying by working as a freelance charter pilot. Next was a pilot who had earned around 6,000 hours, much of the time acquired flying F-16s. He, too, had retired after a long career and planned to fly for a civilian Part 135 operation. Then there was the AP mechanic who already had an SIC (second-in-command) rating—he could fly and fix the airplane. Having logged 500 hours in my Aztec and another 1,500 in a mix of aircraft including a Schweizer 1-34 glider, L-19 Bird Dog, Piper Lance, and Grumman Tiger, I felt green compared to my type-rated contemporaries.

The classroom presentations were well-organized and comprehensive. Simuflite encourages participation so even the shyest among us eventually had our questions answered. The school maintains a superb set of computer-generated simulation models and employs them liberally throughout the presentations. The models demonstrate the airplane's behavior during normal operation as well as in abnormal and emergency conditions. An animated diagram of the affected system is presented on one screen, and the view from the cockpit on another. I found this learning tool especially effective. I only wish they made a home edition!

Significant classroom time was spent understanding and practicing the airplane's normal, abnormal, and emergency procedures. While the amount of material is tremendous, relatively few memory items are needed to fly the CE-525, and most of these are associated with emergencies. Simuflite publishes a clever short-form handbook containing checklists for the three conditions. On the back cover, the annunciator panel lights are diagrammed in color. Yellows indicate an abnormal condition (bad), while reds indicate an emergency (even worse), such as fire. Each light is labeled with a page number where the proper procedure can be found. If a light illuminates in flight, it is simply a matter of identifying it on the diagram, and turning to the page number indicated. Of course, this works smoothly during rehearsal in the classroom. In the simulator airplane, things get interesting.

Simulflite's CE-525 full motion Level D full motion simulator, a class of full flight simulator (FFS) that serves to satisfy all type rating related flight time requirements, offers a painstakingly realistic experience. The VFR world, with its landscapes, weather, airports, buildings and other aircraft, is only slightly stylized compared to the real thing. (During one approach to Reno Airport, I could easily identify the Hilton hotel with its artificial lake.) The IFR world is completely authentic. Throughout the simulated flight is it practically impossible to differentiate between what is simulated, and what is real.

The simulator training consists of eight sessions, the eighth being the final checkride. Sessions one through seven are all about getting ready for number eight, with no time to spare. Flying as a crew, each pilot has only two hours per session as pilot-in-command (PIC) and two as second-in-command (SIC). Fortunately, due to the simulator's ability to select for the critical phases of flight while layering in applicable emergency scenarios, a vast amount of material can be covered. And though the time may be short, four hours of approaches to minimums with multiple failures and fires certainly feels like forever.

Simulator day three turned out even worse than day two. I performed so poorly that I seriously considered quitting. On the upside, we didn't crash. During an engine failure scenario, however, I became disoriented and botched the execution of an admittedly hard JFK ILS 04L circle to land 31R approach. The ILS has a relatively low minimum descent altitude (MDA) of 700 feet, but on this particular day the ceilings were only 40 feet above that with visibility down to a half-mile. The plan was to break out, establish ground contact, and then turn right to a 90-degree heading in the hope of seeing the 31R's lead-in lights. I never saw the lights, and while bumbling around I managed to cause a traffic collision avoidance system (TCAS) alert with another aircraft prior to executing the miss. I endured a lot of simulated yelling from the tower.

Afterwards, our instructor, Norwood Band, skewered my performance up, down, and sideways. "That was just terrible," he said. Norwood was a Marine carrier pilot, and it showed. He asked if I was a drinking man. "Yes," I affirmed. "Well I suggest you have a few stiff ones tonight and come back tomorrow rested and ready to do better." With order in hand, I headed out to source a couple of straight-up martinis. *Note to file:* flight training is not the time to give up drinking.

All type ratings are tough, but attaining one's first type rating is truly a test of character. It takes more than aptitude, endurance, and the ability to assimilate a mass of information in a short time. Unlike the traditional, slower paced style of flight training, with its many opportunities to hone technique, in type rating school the compressed calendar and volume of material make it nearly impossible to achieve satisfactory performance prior to the final checkride. Gaining proficiency, and passing the checkride, largely depend on the client's ability to comprehend and correct deficiencies communicated during the debriefings. There just isn't enough simulator time to perfect every maneuver prior to the practical test.

Simulator day five was exceedingly difficult. Most of the flying scenarios involved a hot-and-heavy profile, with engine fires and other failures degrading the airplane's performance to the point where any procedural mistake yielded a fatal outcome. The worst of the day's emergencies started with two failed generators while IFR at 41,000 feet, the airplane's service ceiling. (The airplane only has two generators.) An electrical system failure in any jet is real trouble. In the case of the CE-525, multiple systems—landing gear, flaps, automatic pressurization, anti-ice, anti-skid brakes, and so on—depend on electrical power. Lacking a back-up auxiliary power unit (APU) generator, when both of the CJ's engine-driven generators fail, all that's left is the battery to power the ship. With a normal electrical load, unless immediate action is taken, a dual generator failure leaves about ten minutes of power.

If neither generator resets (and they never do in the simulator), you flip the battery switch from "Batt" to "Emer"—emergency power—to turn off all non-critical instruments and decrease the load. The challenge is to get to an airport (preferably VFR) before everything quits—about 30 minutes of endurance on emergency power. In the simulator airplane, of course, the nearest (and only) airport is always low IFR.

It takes an awfully long time to get down from 41,000 feet to pattern altitude. Even more challenging with spoilers not functioning. Diving at 3,500 ft/min to prevent over-speed, it took a good ten minutes to reach Reno's initial approach fix altitude. That left twenty minutes of electrical endurance to set up, shoot the approach, and land. Contributing to the challenge, the steam gauge style Emer instruments in the CJ, a small subset of what is normally available, are scattered across the panel. The pilot's scan must be exceptional. Furthermore, available instrument approaches are limited to the VOR and ILS, all hand flown. There's no working autopilot once the Emer switch is thrown.

To my astonishment, the approach and landing were completed successfully, even though I nearly crashed the airplane. KK was running through the remaining checklist items while monitoring my actions. I looked down for mere seconds to switch to Batt to lower the landing gear and flaps. When I looked up the airplane had rolled onto its left side. Thankfully, being significantly right of course, returning the airplane to level flight effectively centered us on the localizer. A lucky break, and a poetic moment. Coincident with breaking out, runway in sight, the panel flicked to black indicating a complete loss of electrical power. Touchdown and emergency braking ensued.

During the debriefing I asked Norwood if the dual gen failure scenario might come up during the test. He replied, "Everything we do is fair game." I recall muttering something about being doomed as we hurried away.

I had started to suspect that Simuflite instructors viewed owner-pilots less than positively. It wasn't so much about the overconfident, stereotypically Type A pilot who can write out a personal check for the airplane. It was more about the flying experience owners enjoy compared to their professional counterparts. Most pros rise through the ranks flying a variety of piston, turboprop, and then jet aircraft, often operating Part 135 or 121. Theirs is a world in which teamwork is the key to safety, passenger comfort, and operational efficiency. For most pros, cockpit resource management (CRM) is a well-understood and long-practiced concept. Their primary challenge is learning an airplane's systems and the procedures for handling abnormal conditions and emergencies, and to practice test maneuvers. But for the owner-pilot with little, if any, turbine experience, stepping up to a high performance jet aircraft can be daunting. Not only is the airplane, and its systems, unfamiliar, many (most) owner-pilots come from a single-pilot background where there is no crew for CRM. Further, unless the owner-pilot has logged significant instrument time in terminal areas and is current, he or she should expect to hang on by the tail for most of the flight training. Normal, abnormal, and emergency simulator scenarios are typically conducted IFR in terminal environments where the weather is terrible and landing at the destination airport is the exception and not the rule.

As we advanced through the sessions, I got points for attitude but beyond that little praise. Session six seemed to go well. Session seven, the rehearsal for the test, went okay with only one checkride busting mistake—after breaking out for the circle to land at Kennedy, I prematurely disengaged the AP while simultaneously lowering the flaps, which caused the airplane to balloon back into the clouds. Oops.

Each client must receive the chief instructor's blessing to proceed to session eight and take the test. While failure at this point is dreadful for the client, the prestige and credibility of the school and its instructor-contributors also is on the line. Failing the FAA checkride is bad for all parties. To this end, clients needing a bit more polish are offered additional training (such as extra simulator sessions off-calendar), to focus on weak areas.

KK and I went together to seek our blessings. Not surprisingly, KK's performance was ranked in the top-five percent of the class. By contrast, my grade was not discussed, and I knew there was concern. Leaving no room for debate, however, KK stated her conviction that we were good to go. The chief instructor agreed. I appreciated KK's enthusiasm for my abilities, but independent of my chances of qualifying as captain, I fretted I might take her out with some incorrect checklist item or FMS programming error while serving as copilot. No one was more surprised than I was to hear that our checkride was scheduled for 6:00 a.m. the following day.

As with the previous simulator sessions, the checkride begins with an oral test and a preflight briefing. The examiner expects each candidate captain to know all the speeds by heart; many systems questions are asked. The examiner provides the weather and, at a high level, describes the various scenarios that can be expected. They claim there is nothing on the test that wasn't covered at least once during training. And Simuflite's policy forbids the examiner to create more than one emergency or abnormal event at a time during the checkride. (I was told that it is up to the client to create all the others. Ha!) KK and I both passed the oral test, so off to the simulator we went.

I'd been sleeping poorly throughout the training, and the night before was no exception. Thank goodness it was Free Donut Day at Simuflite. Food is banned in and around the simulator, but I considered these to be desperate times, and so I picked up three glazed donuts. I ate one before entering the secure simulator floor and smuggled the other two into the cab. In the event I actually passed, I sincerely hoped any donut crimes would be overlooked.

We decided I would fly first with KK as copilot. Ironically, the examiner had us departing from Kennedy using same runway that had taken us out in session two. Even the weather was similar. Bad omen? Off we went into the slog. The practical test was underway.

Amazingly, the first emergency, an engine failure on takeoff, went well. Per procedure, after $V_1$ we maintained directional control, positive rate-gear up, climbed straight ahead and accelerated to $V_2$, 1,500 feet AGL—flaps up. We leveled off at 2,000 feet, declared an emergency with ATC, and pulled out the checklist. KK dutifully read off the steps and I dutifully executed them. For this particular scenario we were able to restart the engine and continue our journey. Yes!

Next came some steep turns and unusual attitudes while IFR, which we handled smoothly. For the first time in many days, I was actually having a little fun. I didn't even need to sneak a donut.

Following multiple abnormal and emergency approaches at JFK, we headed to Nevada and experienced an explosive decompression at 35,000 feet. Well-rehearsed during previous sim sessions it was glasses off, ox masks on, mask mic on, drop passenger masks, AP off, throttle back, spoilers out, and while executing a left turn, dive for the ground at redline. Knowing the passenger masks work only below 25,000 feet, we hustled down.

The examiner kept the simulator running, which meant we were still in the game. I couldn't believe that after a week of heart-stopping near-death experiences everything had come together so well. I even managed to survive the violent wind shear event at SFO. Two more hours of flying, and we were *done*.

During the debriefing, the examiner reviewed what went well, and what did not. I thought we had handled the test more than adequately, but the examiner thought otherwise. Among other comments, he shared, "During those steep turns, I was pretty sure you would bust. But the computer says you were within the 100-foot maximum deviation, so I have to pass you on that," and, "When you were holding at JFK you flew perilously slow. I was pretty sure you would stall right there, but you didn't stall, so I have to pass you on that, too." In parting he said, "That was one of the worst checkrides ever. Congratulations, you passed."

I left the debriefing deflated, but still, I had passed, thus meeting one of my goals for the training. KK kindly suggested the examiner might be having a bad day, but I suspected not. I did hope it was just that he didn't much like owner-pilots.

A few days later, with our freshly minted ratings in hand, we traveled to Florida to pick up our new-to-us Citation Jet. The real airplane was a pleasure to fly and even better, we experienced no failures or fires. I also knew that, as my terrifying, anxiety-producing flashbacks of wildly-flashing annunciators portending disaster faded, there would be next year's recurrent training to look forward to. That's the whole idea.

**Lessons learned:**

**Lesson 1:** Have a superior first officer by your side during training.

**Lesson 2:** More donuts are better.

# 15 | Welcome to the Modern World

"**M**ister Sulu, course 113, mark 7." We watch as the navigator pushes a few colored buttons on the console and *voila*! The starship precisely alters course. "Standard orbit, Mister Sulu." A few more buttons and the ship is orbiting a yet to be explored planet—even more impressive given the myriad calculations and maneuvers needed to engage a strong gravitational field.

Can it be that operating in outer space is a simpler proposition than navigating the Earth's modern airspace system? Well, at least as imagined in *Star Trek*, Mister Sulu's control inputs suggest great progress in improvements to the human-systems interface needed for intergalactic travel.

Quite the opposite has happened here on earth. While aircraft systems have become more capable, they also have, in some cases, become more difficult and complex to run. This is one of the reasons why frequent retraining is required to stay current and safe. For a pilot flying multiple types of aircraft, maintaining proficiency can be more than a full-time job. Minor differences in procedures among types, while innocent in isolation, can create big problems for pilots switching back and forth.

The news isn't all bad. In addition to becoming more capable, modern systems have also become a lot more reliable. Radios don't fail as often, and the wheels almost always go down when commanded. Management of systems in the cockpit also has gotten better in that there is much less improvisation needed. The appropriate response to a yellow crew alert system (CAS) message on the multi-function display (MFD) in the Cessna CJ4 that says "J-BOX LIMITER OPEN L" is to go to an emergency/abnormal checklist, where both an explanation of the problem and proper actions are recorded. In this case, the alert means there is an open 225-amp fuse in the aft junction box, indicating that if the left generator were to fail there would be no power available to systems drawing from the respective electrical buses on

*Time warp—BioTek's original 1993 Cessna Citation Jet CE-525, the first design in the series, accompanied by our 1981 C-180 Skywagon, the last design in the series.*

the left side. Recommended action: land as soon as practical. Gone is the need to speculate or ponder what to do next.

Many systems in modern aircraft like the CJ4 follow this idea. There is an underlying complexity, but the pilot is largely insulated from the details, needed only to manage a few simple actions in the course of normal (or abnormal/emergency) operations.

Not so for the airplane's flight management system (FMS) that determines weight and balance, runway length requirements, performance characteristics, communications, and more. The FMS is directly involved in navigating the airplane, often from takeoff to landing and everything in-between. Inputs to the FMS control departure and arrival procedures along with non-precision and precision approaches to the destination airport. All of the input parameters need to be set correctly or the airplane won't operate as expected by the pilot (or air traffic control). How hard can it be? Although some systems are better than others, setting them up can be challenging, in part because the inputs required aren't particularly intuitive. Further complicating things are the nomenclature and symbol alphabet— for example, the difference in the color of a script (white versus green) on the primary display—which can change everything. A far cry from Mister Sulu's button-operated Starship Enterprise, safe operation of the FMS in most aircraft demands much pilot interaction and knowledge.

In the beginning, of course, there was no flight management system, just a bunch of instruments, airspeed indicator, altimeter, vertical speed indicator, and outside air temperature, to name a few. The pilot was the system, in the sense that he or she was responsible for integrating all of the independent sources of information into a picture of situational awareness sufficient to safely fly the airplane. Later, when better radios and ground-based navigation systems were introduced, pilots had to add that information to the mix. While challenging, knowing that the pilot had to keep constant watch on a multitude of data sources (the scan), there was less mystery in what the airplane was going to do next. The pilot knew (almost always), because the pilot enjoyed 100 percent direct control.

With the advent of reliable autopilots, automatically maintaining heading and/or altitude, tracking a ground station, the pilot's work load was reduced, even shooting an approach to minimums in the case of the fancier models. Still, the pilot maintained control of the sequence of events necessary to conduct the flight; the autopilot managed only one segment, or leg, of the flight at a time. It was still the pilot's job to determine the legs, using charts and other reference materials, then to control the airplane's component devices, including autopilot. This isn't ancient history. Large transport-category aircraft like the Boeing 707, 727, and the early 747 were operated this way through the 1970s and early 1980s. Even the sleek Concorde, for all its amazing performance capabilities, had little to show for integrated automation in the cockpit. Slide rules, tables, and charts served as computer and memory in that time. I recall the desperate search by one Concorde copilot for the chart needed to calculate how to avoid a sonic boom over Ireland. (British Airways would let passengers visit the cockpit in those days.) The document was in a three-inch stack of charts, graphs, and tables. Fortunately, he found the chart and got the information he needed, likely saving many glass windows across the southwest Irish coast.

The game changer was the invention of fast, relatively inexpensive computers with big memories. It was now possible to store all the trip information, including waypoints and ground stations, needed for navigation. Further, computers could manage the entire trip, feeding the autopilot information not for just one leg, but all of them, in sequence. Later versions of the early flight management systems could control vertical profiles as well as the lateral ones for following the correct course, making it possible to automate departures, arrivals, and approaches with vastly more precision than any human pilot.

The cost of more automation and better efficiency in the cockpit came in the form of increased complexity. The systems required more attention to programming. It was one thing for pilots to make a mistake setting up single legs, or dialing in the correct navigation frequencies. The error would affect only one leg, and it was usually caught early and corrected. But an input error into an FMS incorporating all the legs, including the ones leading up to the approach, sometimes including the approach itself, might not be detected until very late, perhaps while executing a critical procedure, possibly leading to controlled flight into terrain (CFIT) or conflict with another aircraft. Due to the nature of programming, the proper correction could be difficult to determine, and take a long time to execute.

In the case of certain departure and arrival procedures, and approaches, addressing an error can be particularly challenging. Taking over the controls, and flying by hand, may not be a good option because the navigation information formerly provided to the autopilot, now the pilot, could be wrong. In the case of an IFR approach in bad weather, if things are really messed up, there may not be sufficient guidance to do a safe miss—abandoning the approach procedure to try again or go somewhere else. The only recourse then would be to ask the air traffic controller for help.

Pilots do a pretty good job of getting the inputs right and applying proper fixes when they were wrong. Still, there have been accidents related to these systems. One of the most famous involved American Airlines Flight 965 in 1995. Scheduled to arrive at Alfonso Bonilla Aragon International Airport in Cali, Columbia, it crashed into a 9,800-foot mountain nearby. The collision with El Diluvio was due to the copilot's FMS input errors. Four of the 163 people on board survived.

There were several things the crew did to doom the flight. Mismanagement of the FMS, however, led the list. The ILS approach to runway 01 was briefed and loaded, but with the wind calm and skies clear, the tower intending to expedite suggested using the VOR-DME approach to runway 19, a non-precision approach from the opposite direction. The crew accepted the change, even though they were not prepared for it. Unfortunately, things were moving very quickly at this point, and they did not have enough time to program all the waypoints into the FMS before passing over the first one, the VOR that begins the approach. In their haste, they attempted to load a subsequent waypoint on the approach, the Rozo NDB, but it was the wrong NDB—same identifier, just located in a different country. And while all this was going on, they were in a rapid descent, spoilers deployed, in an attempt to reach the altitude necessary to properly make the approach. The incorrectly loaded NDB caused the airplane to steer 90 degrees off course, away from the valley where the airport is located, into an adjacent valley. By the time the error was caught, a 9 mile lateral offset from the intended inbound course had developed—the airplane now lined up with the mountain. The final deathblow occurred when the crew failed to retract the spoilers after the old-style, strictly look-down, terrain awareness warning system (TAWS), sounded the alarm indicating an impending collision. Despite a full power escape maneuver, the airplane failed to clear the mountain. A classic case of CFIT.

What's interesting is that the fatal error was made after the crew realized the FMS had been programmed incorrectly due to insufficient time, and while in the airport terminal environment. In the process of reprogramming, they erred again, setting the airplane on its fatal course. The error was subtle, caused in part by confusion over a chart that didn't quite match what was in the airplane's computer. That's the nature of the beast. Many waypoints in the world have similar or same names. And it is not always easy to confirm that the correct one (for the flight) has been entered. This is one of the reasons most crews require the non-programming pilot to verify what the programming pilot has entered. In isolation, the increased role of FMSs in the cockpit is manageable. Yes, the crew has to take care to know the system well, and to program it correctly for the flight. It is all doable, with a disciplined cockpit and solid training.

There is a new, creeping FMS-related menace, however, especially worrisome when the weather is bad and the cockpit environment busy. With the wide adoption of FMS solutions, and improvements in navigation technology, specifically Wide Area Augmentation System (WAAS) GPS, departure, arrival, and approach procedures that were once regarded as impractical, if not unworkable, have become almost commonplace. GPS-driven departures and arrivals are pretty much everywhere, and GPS approaches, including precision approaches, are increasingly supplementing, if not replacing, conventional ground-based radio systems like ILS and VOR. This could be good news, at least from the perspective of utility and efficiency. But what is sobering is the nature of what's possible. Departure and arrival procedures are more complex now, to accommodate increased traffic and to reduce noise footprint. European airspace—where some procedures are so byzantine they cannot be flown safely without the computer—is a prime example of this. There is also the hybrid nature of some approaches with compound lateral and vertical GPS guidance leading to an ILS (ground-based radio) precision approach and, ultimately, the runway. Burlington,

Vermont, where our jet airplanes are based, has something like this. The pilot flies using RNAV to a waypoint that intersects the course to the runway, runway 33. Upon reaching the waypoint, the pilot or computer must switch the source from GPS-based to ILS for the approach to work properly. "When is it going to flop over?" was a common refrain during those early jet flying days, and during the times the FMS was in control.

The problem isn't just related to flying jets. My single-engine piston Cessna Skywagon has a Garmin 750 FMS that would do justice to many larger airplanes. The Garmin is tremendously capable, and frankly necessary for efficient flying in today's airspace. But as with larger airplanes, in combination with the autopilot, operating the 750 correctly can be a challenge.

By way of example, here's the setup for the same ILS 33 into Burlington International in my Skywagon. Some hints: AP is abbreviation for autopilot; HDG, NAV, GS, APR and ALT are all buttons on the AP. GPSS is an AP mode that increases GPS tracking sensitivity. The reference to needle colors are about knowing the source (GPS, satellite, or ILS, ground based radio), while the needles themselves provide an indication of the airplane's position in space relative to a desired course. All, including a compass rose, make up the horizontal situation indicator (HSI). The HSI, when married with glideslope information, also originating from the ILS ground station, and then shown to the pilot on the primary flight display (PFD) along with airspeed and vertical speed, completes the picture—where the airplane is presently located, relative to where it should be, where it is going next, and how fast. Simple!

1) Select and activate the approach. Confirm the correct Localizer or VOR frequency is in the active box. Confirm AP switch is engaged in FD mode.

2) Use HDG NAV to intercept final approach course (once on vectors go direct to a point on the approach with the INBOUND course activated). NAV source is GPS, **pink needles**. APR should automatically illuminate on the AP display.

3) Use ALT VS to change altitudes.

4) Once cleared for the approach, HDG NAV APR should appear on the AP display. The airplane should be in level flight. Use the full compass format for the PFD. GS will eventually appear to the right of ALT on the autopilot display.

5) Source should automatically switch from **pink** to **green needles** once the lateral and vertical ILS single is received. If it doesn't, manually change the source.

6) On the PFD, look for the **green G + DOT** (right of the HSI) for GS guidance. It should show the airplane below the glideslope. The airplane should be in level flight with the AP showing NAV APR ALT and GS.

7) As the airplane intercepts the glide slope (PFD vertical green DOT centered), ALT on the auto pilot will extinguish leaving NAV APR GS. The airplane will automatically descend using lateral and vertical ILS signals for guidance. In the PFD altitude preselect, input the missed approach holding altitude

8) Should it be necessary to go missed, disconnect the AP, apply full power and reconfiguring the airplane, "un-suspend" the Garmin 750 Navigator, follow the missed approach procedure. The source will automatically change to GPS, **pink needles** if the missed approach waypoint is formed by GPS. If the waypoint is not formed by GPS (e.g., a VOR), the source should be changed manually to benefit from the GPS overlay. On the autopilot then hit NAV(GPSS) ALT VS. If GPSS is not selected be sure to hit NAV twice to get GPSS.

9) Monitor the airplane's progress as the autopilot automatically follows the GPS lateral track while climbing to the altitude input in the altitude preselect.

10) The airplane will automatically enter the hold under autopilot control. It will stay in the hold until additional pilot intervention.

Despite its length, the procedure's steps themselves are relatively easy to execute. Remembering them, in the correct sequence, on the other hand, is difficult and not recommended because of the danger of forgetting or misremembering a step. There are also different procedures for different approaches. If different airplane types are in play, each airplane type likely has its own unique set of FMS/AP procedures, something the pilot must know to make the approaches and other navigations work properly when flying the airplane du jour.

Departures can be problematic as well. There is a famous (infamous) standard instrument departure (SID) procedure out of the Teterboro, New York, airport that involves a compound and precise vertical and horizontal guidance to accomplish correctly. The "Ruudy" departure has airplanes departing off runway 24 climbing to 1,500 feet MSL, leveling off, then climbing again once reaching the next waypoint, then completing a precise GPS orchestrated turning maneuver northbound. The number (e.g., Ruudy 6) is constantly being updated, each increment seemingly representing an increasing degree of difficulty. This is a tough departure to do by hand because of the relatively short distances and rapidly approaching altitude

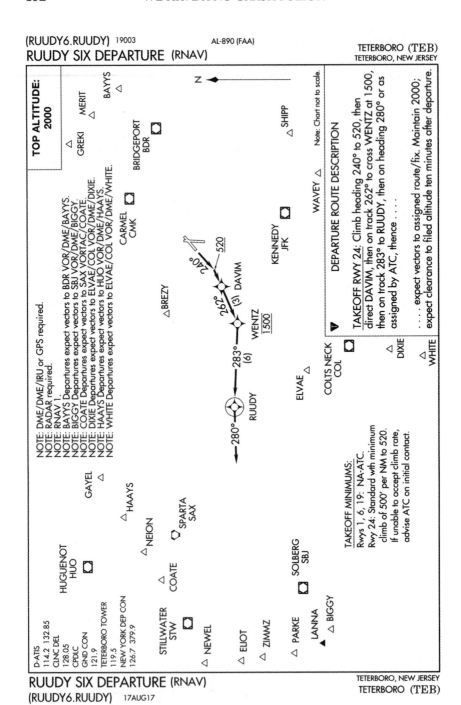

*The Ruudy 6 departure.*

limits, but it is also worrisome to set up in the FMS. The procedure likely has one of the highest bust statistics in the country. Many airplanes fail to adhere to the initial altitude restriction or initiate the turn northbound in a timely fashion. And the errors aren't just academic. Departing from the altitude restriction can put the offending aircraft in direct conflict with southbound-landing Newark traffic.

Ruudy style departures are becoming increasingly common at least partly because the burden of separating airplanes from each other can be shifted from controller to pilot. If the pilot, or more accurately the FMS, follows the complicated departure procedure properly, no conflict will arise. Mess-up the departure, well, at the very least it's warning lights and loud alarms in both the airplane and control tower cab. And likely there will be a government telephone number for the pilot to call once back on the ground.

The funny thing is that much like setting up the C-180's autopilot for an approach to Burlington, the individual FMS programming steps needed to make the Ruudy work are relatively simple. It's just that there are a lot of them, and forgetting a step or doing one out of order is, in a manner of speaking, the kiss of death. For this reason, it is mandatory to confirm the setup is correct before launching into the wild blue yonder. I once had a very close call when I accidentally disabled the autopilot's active and armed modes, essentially the preprogrammed autopilot sequence for the departure, while trying to establish 10 percent flight director pitch up guidance for the time right after takeoff. The only way to know was to observe that these modes were no longer being reported—normally they are shown in very small font in the top right corner of the PFD. Fortunately, being a bit of a worrier, I caught the error just prior to taking the runway, plenty time to make everything right, so no bust this time. The story should serve as a yellow alert to pilots flying these departures. The difference between a perfectly executed Ruudy and one that goes off the rails can be as little as a single errant keystroke.

To the extent there is a perverse consistency between aircraft types, it's the less than intuitive nature of the FMS user interface employed. These things are hard to figure out. Jet schools have special simulators just for learning how to run the airplane's FMS. In smaller airplanes, like the Cessna Skywagon, it's often up to the pilot to devise the necessary procedures. *Pilot train thyself.* While there are good PC-based simulators for individual FMS products like the Garmin 750, totally integrated (with the AP) solutions are rare. Hence the customized procedure. And this idea applies to more than just the Skywagon. Our jet airplanes have a custom FMS/AP setup procedure created by the flight department for every type of departure, arrival, and approach that we do.

The problem isn't just limited to the FMS or other unique complicated onboard systems. The airspace itself, plus demands from ATC, often aggravate the situation. For those who fly into dense terminal areas like NYC, few can say they haven't had a last minute request to set up for a different approach, or a different runway. Which means the programming pilot's head is down, focused on typing on the FMS keyboard, all very last minute, just enough time to complete the input, leaving little or no time to check it. That's not to mention the potential interruption in normal approach and landing checklist procedures, often a casualty of all the attention paid to the FMS. And what about single-pilot ops? The task load can be overwhelming. Although we would like to think the prudent captain would respond with "unable," that is atypical. In most cases the rush is on for fear of the alternative, time in the penalty box for lack of compliance, and back to the end of the line.

There are other weak points in the system. The way ATC clearances are communicated can lead to FMS programming mistakes. Programming a verbally communicated full route clearance, in which all the waypoints have to be written down perfectly and then transcribed into the FMS manually, is especially risky. The risk increases with the length and complexity of the clearances.

The reality is that most pilots work very hard to get the clearance right, and also hope that ATC personnel will catch any significant deviations en route, prior to a conflict or other issue that might affect safety. And to the extent there are errors, most of the time they are caught. The system has proved to be safe, despite the likelihood that errors occasionally will occur in the course of normal operation. Legacy operations often serve as a good safety valve when new technologies are being introduced.

Recent improvements in standardization of systems, especially FMS, have gone a long way toward making the pilot task less onerous and dependent on a convoluted library of proprietary procedures. Even with some convergence, it seems unlikely conventional airplane systems will ever be similar and simple enough to be operated like cars. The differences among car systems don't generally lead to significant deviations from compliance with traffic regulations or, worst case, crashes. Slowing down, or stopping once underway, to figure out how to control the defroster is always an option. The same cannot be said about an airplane's windscreen accumulating ice, obstructing visibility. It is critical that the crew know exactly the right button to push, and the buttons are all different.

Will Mister Sulu's console and procedure suite ever become an earth airspace reality? My guess is yes, but only after artificial intelligence technology is routinely available and accepted. "Siri, please load the approach for Burlington's ILS to 33, vectors to final. Confirm ATC clearance. Execute on my command!" Alternatively, "Siri, I want to land at Burlington!" Another variant, "Siri, get me down, now!" This would be standardization in its truest form, interpreting natural language, with all its variety, to determine intent and then process it into precise and appropriate action. It's the future of aviation and everything else.

But unlike AI in cars—with elimination of the human driver imminent—airplanes with human passengers are unlikely to fly without a human pilot on board for some time. AI will serve as copilot, and the best one ever. How fun is that? There is nothing like having an outstanding copilot, one of the keys to passing simulator school, as previously discussed.

"Didn't you mean to activate the approach, Captain?"

"Why, yes I did."

"Should I activate it for you?"

"Thank you, Siri. Yes."

## Lessons learned:

**Lesson 1:** Cheat sheets are handy to have, each containing all of the actions necessary for conducting the exceedingly complicated procedures flawlessly; all clearly documented, just in case the future is running late.

**Lesson 2:** Inputting needed approach parameters while conducting the approach is like changing a tire at highway speeds. It can be very difficult to stay on the road.

# 16 | Life in the Flight Levels

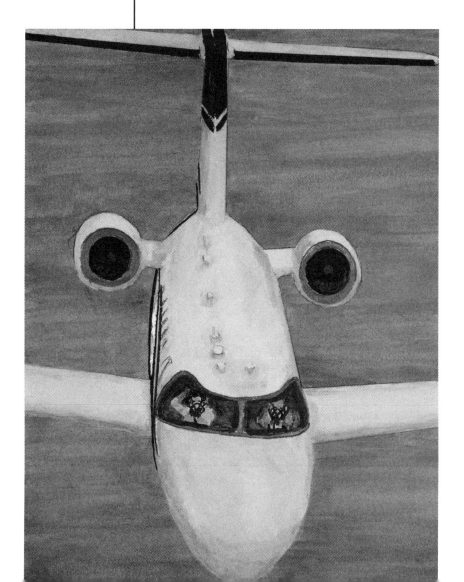

We fly in the upper flight levels, mostly between thirty-five and forty thousand feet, due to a combination of factors that enhance efficiency, comfort, and utility. Up high, airplanes fly faster over the ground while burning less fuel. Up really high, beyond 41,000 feet, there is generally much less traffic, so clearances are easier to get and generally more direct. Often the weather is tranquil, yielding a smoother flight. Icing in the clouds is rare due to the extremely low temperatures and low humidity that are characteristic of the upper troposphere and lower stratosphere. Normally there are no clouds at all, except for those that can be seen thousands of feet below. The upper atmosphere also can be foreboding, potentially dangerous, even life threatening, for some of the very same reasons airplanes operate so well there. Temperatures are cold—so cold that a winter day in New England would seem like a summer heat wave in comparison. Temperatures of -65°F are common, leaving unprotected skin subject to frostbite in less than a minute. The air is so thin that most people will immediately pass out when exposed. Mostly, if anything were to go wrong, it can be a long way down to safety.

The primary concern is maintaining a breathable atmosphere. During normal operation in fan jet airplanes like our CJ3, the task is accomplished by bleeding bypass air from the compressor fan section. The air is then cooled and modulated using a pressurization controller assuring a temperature and cabin altitude that is comfortable. There are other ways to do it. Smaller, pressurized piston airplanes often use bleed air off the compressor side of the engine's turbocharger. Larger modern airplanes like Boeing's 787 use electrically-driven compressors, avoiding the less efficient cooling process associated with bleed air designs. Still, all these systems share a common theme. They convert the outside ambient air, cold and unbreathable in the flight levels, to something approximating the top of an 8,000-foot mountain on a pleasant summer day. And in some fancy airplanes like the Gulfstream G-550 the cabin air mimics a 4,000-foot mountain summit. Interestingly, no airplane delivers a cabin atmosphere that feels like sea level when flying in the upper range of its altitude flight envelope.

So what happens if the system fails? Theoretically, the result can be catastrophic, especially if the failure is related to the pressure vessel itself, the part of the airplane's structure that seals the pressurized air inside. Fortunately, even when the problem originates within the vessel, in the vast majority of cases it unfolds at a pace that allows the crew time to react and get to a lower cruising altitude where breathable air is present. Most airplanes have multiple warning systems to alert the crew should an environmental control problem develop. Occasionally, though, there are failures that trigger a rapid or explosive decompression. The two differ in that explosive decompressions happen so fast and so violently that air cannot escape from the lungs without causing injury.

Most explosive decompressions, but not all, are caused by a targeted missile or bombing of the aircraft. A blown-out window or injury to the fuselage skin by an uncontained engine fan or compressor-blade failure is another possible cause. In both cases, the loss of atmosphere would be almost instantaneous, especially up high, close to or at the airplane's maximum design altitude, leaving cabin oxygen levels so low that without use of supplemental oxygen crew and passengers would pass out in a very short time. The cabin would be very cold, and any remaining moisture would frost the windows. Assuming the blown-out window scenario, there also would be a ferocious wind near the opening. Everything loose in the cabin not sucked out would whip around in the equivalent of a mini tornado. The idea is nicely illustrated in *Goldfinger*, the James Bond movie, when Goldfinger, the character, in an attempt to neutralize Bond, discharges his weapon in the cabin of his Lockheed JetStar aircraft, piloted, notably, by Pussy Galore. The bullet hits a window, causing it to fail, and everything not tied down, including Goldfinger, is sucked out. Bond, saved by hanging onto the interior lighting, and Ms. Galore, restrained by her seatbelt, make a daring escape by parachute. The only thing missing is the fog that would be created when the air is suddenly cooled.

There are almost no sudden or explosive decompression events in modern flying, but sudden loss of pressure is a major feature of pilot training. In the simulator airplane, it is assumed there will be need for an ox mask at some point, partly because the instructor hands out disinfectant wipes to students to decontaminate the masks. (To the school's credit, good hygiene is emphasized throughout recurrent training.) Most scenarios put the airplane very high, 41,000 feet or more, another clue, typically in calm air, nice weather, somewhere above the western plains. Then, suddenly, *without warning*, there is a thunderous bang, followed by the sound of whooshing air. In most airplane types there is also a light that comes on (at cabin altitudes above 10,000 feet) or a series of crew alert system messages (CAS) indicating that atmosphere is venting. The rehearsed response in most flight level capable airplanes is: 1) don ox masks, confirm ox is flowing; 2) throttle back while completing an emergency dive of the airplane including the activation of all possible spoilers/dive brakes to descend as fast as possible, usually meaning redline speed, and usually demanding an off present course turn to avoid possible traffic conflicts; 3) switch mic source to ox mask so crew members can communicate with each other and ATC; 4) confirm passenger oxygen masks have deployed, or deploy them manually; 5) inform ATC by declaring an emergency and providing specifics if prudent and practical.

Even if passengers succeed in donning their masks, in most airplanes, including commercial airliners, passenger oxygen masks don't work well above an altitude of 25,000 feet. Our CJ3 can cruise at FL450 (45,000 feet), so worst case, assuming a rapid decompression event, the passengers may not be sufficiently ventilated for as long as 4 minutes. This assumes the crew takes proper and immediate action, and establishes a descent rate of 5,000 to 6,000 feet per minute, about the maximum for most airplanes. For those harboring a fear of flying, the maneuver requires a dramatic nose-down attitude that feels in the cabin as if the airplane is pointed straight at the ground. There is some dramatic vibration, from the spoilers being subjected to $V_{MO}$ (the maximum Mach speed the design allows). If there is an opening to the outside, there also will be a wind storm in the interior of the cabin. Make it a night flight, with bad weather below, thunderstorms maybe, with their associated lightning lighting the way down. It's the perfect airplane disaster movie.

Rapid or explosive decompression accidents, caused by mechanical or structural problems, are rare but not unheard of. Most are the result of metal fatigue, or in some cases poor maintenance. This was the case with Japan Airlines flight 123, en route from Tokyo's Haneda Airport to Osaka International Airport on August 12, 1985. An incorrectly-repaired rear bulkhead doubler failed shortly after takeoff causing the associated pressure bulkhead to burst open. Although the decompression itself could have been survivable, the violent nature of the event caused the vertical stabilizer (the tail fin) to break off, and damaged all four redundant hydraulic systems operating the airplane's remaining control surfaces. For 32 minutes the pilots desperately improvised strategies to stabilize the aircraft, before crashing into Mount Takamagahara, about 62 miles west of Tokyo. All 15 crew members, and 505 of the 509 passengers on board were lost.

Crews don't typically train for decompression failures like the one experienced by JAL Flight 123, but they do train for loss of cabin pressure events that require an emergency descent. In an unpressurized cabin, or one that has depressurized, most people need supplemental oxygen at altitudes above 15,000 feet. At very high altitudes, where jet airplanes fly, the loss of cabin pressure is for all practical purposes like being in outer space. The time available to don an oxygen mask in the event of depressurization is very short, with useful consciousness equal to seconds. (At 45,000 feet the time of useful consciousness for most people is 9 to 15 seconds.[1])It is for this reason that the FAA has a rule that at least one pilot wears an $O_2$ mask at all times while flying in the upper flight levels. The fear, of course, is that in a decompression event crew members might fail at donning/activating the masks prior to passing out. Back in the cabin there are additional concerns. The passenger oxygen system is not as highly rated as in the cockpit, and the typically lightly-dressed passengers are at risk of frostbite and hypothermia when suddenly exposed to extremely low temperatures.

It is curious that in training for a loss of cabin pressure event in the CJ3 and CJ4 simulator, the scenario has neither pilot wearing an oxygen mask despite the regulations. This seeming lack of compliance may be about giving both crew members more practice perfecting the procedure (e.g., donning the mask properly and with alacrity). But there is also general acknowledgment that as many as 80 percent of Part 91 and Part 135 pilots sometimes disregard the rules about wearing masks high up. And although compliance by Part 121 airline pilots is better, fully half reported not always wearing the masks when required. Perhaps the flight schools are acknowledging that in the real world both crewmembers will be going through the mask-donning drill should the real thing happen.

Without acknowledging our general practice, those who choose not to wear the masks justify their behavior mostly as follows:

1) The masks are uncomfortable to wear for long periods.
2) Some of the reserve $O_2$ will have been depleted by the mask-wearing pilot, leaving less available for passengers and crew in the event of a real emergency.
3) There is the risk of oxygen poisoning, bronchial irritation, and infection caused by prolong mask use.

---

[1] FAA, *Pilot's Handbook of Aeronautical Knowledge* (Newcastle, WA: ASA), 17-4.

From personal experience I can report 1) and 3) are real issues. The masks press against the face uncomfortably and the $O_2$ itself is dry and irritating. One of the risks of simulator training is having to wear a simulator mask that has been worn by hundreds of students of unknown health status. And although a real airplane may have fewer pilots, the same principle applies.

Except for the Payne Stewart Learjet 35 accident, in which either the $O_2$ system failed following a rapid decompression, or the masks weren't donned in time, there are few cases in which not wearing the mask per the regulations has resulted in an accident. Even in Stewart's flight there are indications the decompression may have occurred prior to reaching the upper flight levels, where at least one crew member should have worn a mask.

In terms of relative risk, failure to comply with this regulation doesn't seem to present a big safety issue. It may become moot as newer designs like the CJ4 and Gulfstream G550 adopt automatic descent systems that dive the airplane mostly unaided when the cabin pressure gets too low. In the case of the CJ4 all the pilot has to do is retard the throttles.

But there are other safety concerns with loss of pressure, some of which are not directly related to providing an adequate cabin environment for the crew and passengers.

Traversing long stretches over water or inhospitable land masses (no suitable airports en route) demands consideration of aircraft distance performance at a low altitude in the event of an emergency descent. It is an issue mostly over water, where reaching a suitable airport may require continuing the flight for some time. The need to fly lower to maintain tolerable cabin conditions after a decompression emergency significantly decreases range. This is because airplanes, jet airplanes in particular, tend to fly more slowly and consume more fuel at lower altitudes. To put this idea into prospective, our CJ3 airplane has a range that is more than two times greater at 45,000 feet compared to 15,000 feet. This means should a decompression event occur during a Goose Bay to Reykjavik crossing, dealing with the emergency involves considerably more than just getting everyone ventilated and descending to a suitable non-pressurized altitude. The question now is can the airplane actually make its origin airport, destination airport, or some airport in-between, fuel exhaustion being the primary concern.

Although knowingly flying with a *wet footprint* is permitted under Part 91, most pilots plan their transoceanic flights in a way that, should there be a decompression event at any time, there is always a suitable airport within reach. The same idea applies to an engine failure emergency. The reduction in total thrust produced by what engine power remains almost always means drifting down to a lower altitude. There, in the denser atmosphere, the airplane will fly slower while burning more fuel. In the case of an Iceland mission, a diversion to a Greenland airport is probably the right answer unless the airplane is closer to Canada or Iceland when the failure occurs. The precise determination is made using equal time point (ETP) calculations that take into account the airplane's routing, performance, winds, air temperature, altitudes flown, and fuel load to identify the alternate airport within the shortest flying time should an emergency occur. Key to success, proper ETPs should assure that the airplane can make it to the alternate without running out of fuel.

Different airplane types have different engine failure drift down altitudes that depend on all kinds of factors, including how many running engines are on board at the beginning of the trip. But decompression ETP calculations over water always assume the airplane would dive to 10,000 feet MSL and continue to the alternate airport from there. The reasoning is rooted in physiology—10,000 feet is an altitude at which people can comfortably breathe unaided. It is puzzling, then, that Part 91 regulations require pilots to use supplemental $O_2$ only above 12,500 feet, when flying in an unpressurized aircraft, and only when the time spent there is more than 30 minutes, providing the airplane goes no higher than 14,000 feet. Legally, passengers must be offered oxygen above 15,000 feet.

Although the increased fuel burn at 10,000 feet is still not enough to lead to fuel exhaustion in most cases, in the unlikely event of a depressurization over water, I have always imagined flying the alternate diversion leg much higher, perhaps as high as 25,000 feet. Even with two in the cockpit and five passengers in the back, our CJ3's $O_2$ supply is enough to keep everyone going for at least 44 minutes at 25,000 feet. The greater distance achieved could be as much as 40 nautical miles, more with fewer passengers.

We hope for the best and plan for the worst, but most of the time life at the higher flight levels is better than it is lower down. High on the list of benefits is the benign weather, because most of the storms are below. On days when a line of energetic thunderstorms reaches into the stratosphere, see and avoid circumnavigation strategies work well. Still, even on CAVU days there is lots of weather in play. Specifically, it can be very windy in the upper atmosphere. In general, the winds are zonal, blowing west to east, but they do dive southward and climb northward to some degree. There are also jet streams to consider when flying high. These have the strongest winds and live between 30,000 and 39,000 feet. The northern polar jets

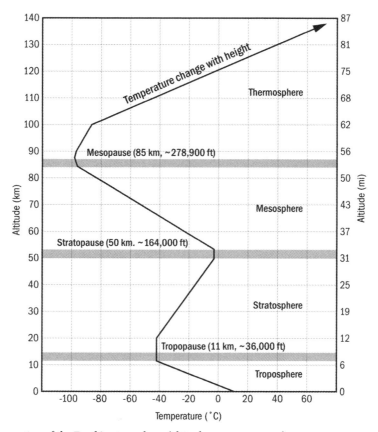

*Cross section of the Earth's atmosphere (altitude vs. temperature).*

tend to meander among the mid latitudes of North America, Europe, Asia, and their oceans, while the southern polar jet circles Antarctica all year round. There are also weaker subtropical jet streams, operating north and south of the equator, and nearer to it, that begin around 33,000 feet and end around 52,000 feet.

The primary consideration given wind in flying is its effect on ground speed for any given route. When traveling west a strong polar jet can slow the flight significantly. On transcontinental routes across America we have had headwinds as high as 150 knots on the bow. In one case the winds were so strong and persisted for so long we had to add another fuel stop to make the destination.

On some days high altitude headwinds can be beaten by flying even higher. There is a general decrease in wind in the transition from the upper troposphere to the stratosphere. At midlatitudes, the stratosphere begins between 33,000 and 43,000 feet, indicated by a temperature inversion (temperatures stay flat or climb rather than fall as a function of higher altitude). In many jets, especially business jets, it's possible to reach the lower parts of the stratosphere within the normal operating envelope. The benefit is a considerably less energetic jet stream, at least theoretically.

Truth is, the go-high strategy doesn't always work. The winds can be the same or even stronger. We have experienced this many times flying our CJ3 and CJ4 westbound over the continental US. Also, there are places on earth where the stratosphere is too high for most airplanes—about 59,000 feet at the equator. And if the winds aren't gentler, the decrease in airspeed due to lower engine power output, typical at higher altitudes, can actually reduce ground speeds.

Of course, a windy day can be your friend, especially when the wind is at your back. Differences in ground speed can be dramatic. For example, our CJ4 cruises at about 430 knots at FL410. Assuming a 120 knot tailwind, the ground speed would be closer to 550 knots. On a trip from San Jose, California, to Burlington, Vermont, that amounts to a savings of more than an hour of flying time, enough improvement to eliminate the need for a fuel stop in Lincoln, Nebraska, or somewhere nearby.

Long haul airlines have exploited the effects of wind and jet streams for many years. In the case of westbound flights to Asia from the US, Great Circle routes are preferred because the northern polar jet tends to be south of the route, lessening headwinds. The return routing, however, is often as close to the northern polar jet as possible. The same idea applies to the Atlantic, where ATC often moves the tracks northward for aircraft flying westbound from Europe to the US during daylight, and southward for their night return, and modifies according to where the jet streams are forecasted to be.

But jet streams present a hazard to airplanes beyond the inconvenience of slowing travel. Clear air turbulence (CAT), a phenomenon associated with the jet streams, can cause injuries, damage, even loss of the aircraft in extreme cases. CAT is invisible and difficult to predict. The jet stream variety is thought to be caused by vertical and horizontal shear around the colder air side of the jet stream, the northern side in the northern hemisphere, near the boundary between the top of the troposphere and bottom of the stratosphere, the tropopause. (The troposphere is where we humans live, at its lowest level, except when flying airplanes.)

The most famous example of the destructive power of CAT was on United Airlines Flight 826. On December 28, 1997, en route from Tokyo to Honolulu, the Boeing 747-100 experienced severe CAT at 31,000 feet, kill-

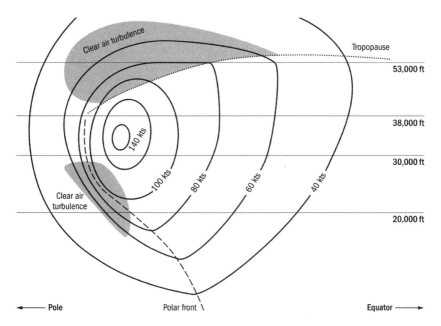

*Clear air turbulence probability depicted in the proximity of the upper and colder edges of the jet stream's core at the boundary between the troposphere and stratosphere known as the tropopause.*

ing one passenger and injuring 15 others. Three crew members also were injured. Fortunately, the crew regained control of the aircraft and returned safely to Tokyo.

I have personally experienced a CAT event once, as a passenger. It was a summer evening in late 1980s, en route from Chicago to San Francisco on a United Airlines DC-10. The airplane had reached its initial cruising altitude, 34,000 feet, in the clear with smooth air. An orange glow from the setting sun bathed the right side of the airplane. The flight attendants were serving cocktails. It started with a burble of light turbulence, immediately followed by several big jolts, as if a huge hand had reached out to shake the airplane. The cabin went silent. There was a moment of smooth air promising the rough ride might be over, but that was not to be.

Imagine an elevator dropping rapidly in free fall. That was the feeling, after the shaking had stopped. Panic and bedlam. The drink cart and flight attendant, both positioned next to me, floated above the floor as nervous flyers in the back screamed. The real insult, though, was the elevator reaching ground floor—*bang!* Whatever wasn't tied down hit the floor abruptly, unceremoniously—a hard landing indeed. Then the plane started flying normally again.

The reality is that the airplane likely was never subject to any significant negative-G load on the way down, although my guess is the sudden stop was at least 2 G, if not more. Although well within the design loading envelop for the DC-10, for anyone not adapted to it, from flying aerobatics or experiencing high-G loads in other ways, as little as 1.5 Gs can feel like a lot.

Fortunately, the seat belt sign was still on, so most of the passengers, including me, were safety belted in. Those who were not picked themselves up off the floor, discovering they were physically okay. The only casualties were in rows 1, 2 and 3 on the right side of the aircraft—those of us in close proximity to the drinks cart: we needed a lot of dry cleaning. Otherwise, all was well, the flight arrived at the destination safely and on time. The passengers had stories to tell. CAT events seldom happen, but when they do life gets exciting.

The rarified air of the flight levels may be foreboding, but there is much advantage to be gained. Even lower down, airplanes that can fly at 20,000 to 25,000 feet, have an advantage managing weather, topping high terrain, and extending range compared to those that operate without pressurization or supplemental $O_2$, generally no higher than 14,000 feet. Even in the flight levels there is a pecking order. The Concorde's initial cruising altitude was 50,000 feet, drifting up to 60,000 over the course of the trip. Very little worry about traffic-related delays up there. The same idea applies a little lower down. The ability to cruise at FL450, well within the capability of many business jets, means flying higher than most conventional airliners can go, therefore with a much better chance of getting a clearance direct to the destination. All good!

While there are risks, the technology that facilitates operating in the upper part of the atmosphere is very good and failures are rare. Still, understanding the potential dangers and appropriate responses in case of trouble should be the pilot's SOP, a prerequisite to staying safe.

There's smooth air up there, at least most of the time, the living fast and easy. But very good to scary bad can happen quick, the cabin cold and breezy.

## Lessons learned:

**Lesson 1:** Keep your seat belt fastened at all times.

**Lesson 2:** Flying really high, into the stratosphere can sometimes, but not always, mitigate for strong headwinds.

# 17 Northern Exposure

Great planning is not always rewarded by a mission that goes according to plan. When our chief pilot showed me the updated weather for Keflavik, Iceland, indicating winds of 75 knots gusting to 86, I knew we were deviating from the safety and comfort of previous transatlantic crossings.

The early-morning flight from Burlington, Vermont, to Goose Bay, Newfoundland, had promised a great week of flying and business in Europe. Our mission was to visit subsidiaries in the UK, Switzerland, and Germany, and distributors in France and Austria. It started out a beautiful, calm spring day. Flying into the sun can be uncomfortable, but after the long, dark Vermont winter, I didn't care.

The trip to Goose in the CJ3 normally takes about two hours, working our way through Montreal, Moncton, and Gander Centers. Goose and Gander are convenient jumping-off points for the transatlantic segment. Since most light to medium jets do not have the legs to fly nonstop to Europe, the trip is typically broken up into three segments, with the middle starting in Newfoundland and ending in Iceland, passing over the southern tip of Greenland.

The landing in Goose was uneventful. It was chilly, but the winds were light with clear skies and unlimited visibility. After refueling, our passengers were back on board, door closed, and prestart checklist complete. Within minutes, we were on our way to Iceland.

Preparing for a crossing is a major activity involving proper determination of weather, routing and altitude. With a range of 1,800 nautical miles, the CJ3 can make the 1,350 nautical mile crossing easily. But the extra 450 miles can be consumed quickly by unfavorable winds, circuitous routings, traffic delays, and deteriorated destination weather. From the weather check prior to leaving Goose, we knew it wasn't going to be a beautiful day at Keflavik, but it was certainly acceptable, with light to moderate winds out of the south and ceilings and visibilities just below VFR minimums. Assuming the forecast winds aloft, we anticipated arriving at the destination with about an hour and fifteen minutes of endurance remaining.

For this leg I would be the pilot flying (PF) in the left seat, while the captain performed the monitoring duties (PM) from the right seat, including navigating and communicating. Typically, we would swap with each leg to maintain proficiency performing the two different jobs.

Since we had already performed our mandatory selective calling (SELCAL) check of the high-frequency (HF) radio prior to arriving in Goose, we were free to follow our flight plan to the coast-out point and beyond. The check confirmed that the controlling authorities, Gander radio and Reykjavik radio in this case, would be able to alert the crew in case of a new clearance or other important information. Using a unique (to the aircraft) SELCAL identifier code, ATC can deliver a special audio tone over the pilot's headset. (HF systems don't have a squelch function, so the volume is normally turned down most of the time to avoid hearing the scratchy noise that is present when no one is transmitting.)

There are many coast-out points scattered along the Newfoundland coast. These points mark where control is conveyed to one of the oceanic control area (OCA) authorities and where the switchover from VHF to HF occurs. For this trip, LOACH, N53 31.0 W057 01.0 was the coast-out point assigned. Convenient to our routing, and about 160 nautical miles northeast of Goose Bay Airport, the only challenge was reaching the assigned cruising altitude prior to crossing. This requirement is not academic. Flying below the assigned cruising altitude before reaching coast-out point can mean potential traffic conflicts with no one on the ground to provide separation. Radar coverage is spotty over the Atlantic, even near the coasts. Fortunately, LOACH provides a nice run from Goose, with plenty of distance to climb to the assigned flight level, 45,000 feet, in time. Still, the controller did mention something about there being 100 airplanes pointed directly at us should there be any delay in the climb.

Coast-out/coast-in points also designate where the tracks begin and end. These are the mostly parallel Atlantic routings along which most commercial flying between the US and Europe is conducted. Very busy roads, and they are moved daily to accommodate weather and traffic. Given the lack of direct radar surveillance over the Atlantic, crews must be very precise with navigation on these routes, staying at assigned speeds and altitudes to assure separation. On this particular day, our routing was north of the track system, so airliners would mostly be south of us, good news because it allowed a straight shot to Iceland, yielding the shortest flying distance possible. This, and great tailwinds, would make our crossing one of the fastest ever, with only one set of equal-time points (ETP) between departure and destination in case of engine failure or decompression. A problem prior to reaching the first ETP means back to Canada. A problem after the second ETP, dictates that it is on to Iceland. Inbetween, we are going somewhere in Greenland. Of course, if the airplane happens to be on fire all bets are off. A ditching in the North Atlantic may be the only alternative.

Upon reaching the OZN NDB in Greenland, the half-way point, our passengers had awakened from a short nap, and were enjoying a late breakfast. The flight so far had been smooth with occasional scattered clouds below. OZN was a mandatory reporting point, so the captain, flying right-seat, reported "Gander radio, N726AG, crossing Oscar, Zulu, November NDB, at 1335, flight level 450, Mach .74, estimating 61N, 40W at 1350, 62N 30W next." She also asked for Keflavik weather and within a few minutes the controller had the sequence: "Keflavik, 1330 weather, winds 200 at 16, visibility five miles, 3,500 scattered, altimeter 29.59."

Mandatory reporting on HF has been a ritual in trans-Atlantic flying since the end of World War II and the formation of the International Civil Aviation Organization (ICAO), the agency that sets rules for international flight operations. The report is always the same: position, time, altitude, speed, and an estimated time for the next mandatory reporting point. Using this information, controllers on the ground track the aircraft indirectly. It's not quite as rudimentary as it was in WWII, when young British women moved miniature wooden airplanes on a giant map for the generals to view, but close. Actually, the people with the equivalent of the wooden airplanes and maps, the controllers, are only once removed from the people talking, OCA radio. The radio people serve only as a liaison, passing messages/information to and from the airplanes and the controllers. As a result, requested changes in routing can take a long time. It's why there are emergency navigation procedures in place should an altitude change, caused by an engine failure, for example, be needed right away.

There are newer emerging technologies for controlling airplanes over the Atlantic. Controller-pilot data link communications (CPLDC) is slowly replacing the voice radio reports, but even this system depends on sending the message through an intermediary.

The reported Iceland weather was more or less as predicted and, feeling confident about the forecast, I told the passengers the weather in Keflavik was better than expected and that we would arrive a couple of minutes ahead of schedule. But weather is fickle, especially in the northern Atlantic.

As we cruised into Reykjavik airspace an hour later, what my right seat colleague was hearing over the radio was nothing like the tranquil forecast I had so smugly shared. Keflavik terminal weather, only an hour since our last cheery weather update, now reported winds of 75 knots gusting to 85. I must have heard it wrong. Then she read the entire sequence. "1440 Keflavik weather, winds 190 at 75 with peak gusts 86, visibility 1 mile in heavy rain, ceiling 800 overcast, altimeter 9752 kPa (28.80 inches of mercury), *airport closed*." In the span of an hour, the barometric pressure had dropped almost three-quarters of an inch. This smacked of a developing intense low. Bad!

We discussed heading back to Greenland, but we had long passed our ETP; there was no way we would make it back with the fuel remaining, even at economy cruise. Further, with the howling tailwinds, now approaching 100 knots, we were being pushed ever closer to Iceland. "We're committed." Decision made.

EMBLA was our coast-in fix for Iceland, where we switched from HF to VHF radio. The Captain made the call: "Keflavik Approach, N726AG, EMBLA, FL450, have Tango, how do you read?"

Keflavik Approach: "N726AG, Keflavik Approach, loud and clear, radar contact 80 miles west of Keflavik, be advised the airport is closed due to weather, state your intentions."

Weather at Reykjavik Airport, about 15 miles east, was even worse, with the same winds, and visibilities down to a half-mile. There was no going back to Greenland, and airports in the UK or Ireland were at least two hours away, well beyond the one-hour reserve we had remaining. The other Iceland airports, on the east side of the island, were pretty far away, too, and had the same, or worse, weather. It was as if the whole country suddenly had succumbed to storm from hell.

It was clear the airport's closed status was going to have to be a formality; one way or another, we would be landing at Keflavik. ATC cleared us to descend to 7,000 and told us to expect the ILS to runway 20. While not exactly into the wind, the runway's orientation offered the best chance of remaining on the pavement after touching down. About 200-feet wide, it could, possibly, accommodate a diagonal landing, if that became necessary.

It was time to share the bad news with our passengers. I didn't want to set off a panic (having just recovered from one in the cockpit), but I wasn't going to be able to pass this off as routine. "Gentlemen," I said, "it's windy in Iceland today, really windy. It's rainy, too. I would expect some bumps, especially during the approach, so you should strap yourselves in tight."

Trying to be positive, I said not to worry, because while the winds were high, they were also for the most part coming straight down the runway. Yes, it would be a bumpy ride, but everything would be okay.

The captain was already setting up the approach in the FMS. To complete the profile, the FMS requires weather information, including winds. It was quite a shock when the computer refused to accept a 75-knot wind speed.

"Try 65 knots," I suggested, but that didn't work either, and 55 knots failed, too. Finally, the system accepted 50 knots. It was becoming increasingly clear that we were going to be test pilots. Evidently, the airplane was not certified for surface winds higher than 50 knots, although there was nothing about this in the limitations. Very exciting, I thought!

The descent from 7,000 to 2,300 feet, glide slope intercept altitude, was rough. The combination of frequent heading changes ordered by ATC and side-gusting moderate turbulence made for a truly wild ride. The rain had picked up, too. The normally quiet cockpit was a roar, the windscreen pelted by cascades of huge drops.

We were getting wind updates from ATC, and the news kept getting worse. The winds were shifting, five, then ten and finally fifteen degrees left of the runway's orientation. Given the CJ3's maximum demonstrated crosswind component of 21 knots, it wouldn't be long before a runway excursion became a real possibility.

Although we had enough fuel for a couple of tries at the runway, we needed another option, should the winds continue to misbehave. Keflavik's layout with two runways at 90 degrees to each other offered nothing better than runway 20.

There was a big apron on the east side of the airport, though, that I happened to notice on the airport diagram chart. Its origin had military roots dating back to World War II and the Cold War. Independent of the legacy, I was thrilled that we might benefit. The outline showed it to be large and sprawling. If it were clear of airplanes and other obstacles, the apron could serve nicely as an improvised omni-directional runway.

We informed ATC that if the winds continued to shift we might have to opt for the apron area. "Is the apron clear?" It turned out the apron was, indeed, clear. We would, of course, try for the runway, once we had broken out from the overcast, but if winds continued to shift I would jog the airplane over to the left and land on the apron. We had a plan!

ATC's final vector, heading 175 degrees, put us on an intercept course. The controller told us to go to Tower, and wished us luck. It was still turbulent, but the autopilot was keeping up. The captain ran the landing check-list, "flaps to approach, gear down (three green, no red), landing flaps are next, and the Tower has cleared us to land."

By now, we were in and out of the clouds and I could see the ocean below. The waves appeared to be 40 to 50 feet high, with swell distances at least 300 feet. White caps disappeared into vapor, ripped away by the ferocious wind.

The autopilot was clearly working hard. Watching the fast action, I wondered how well I would perform, taking over before landing. It would have been a good idea to have tried this in the simulator first.

The captain called out the altitudes, "1,500 feet to go", "1,000 feet to go," and searched for the runway while I monitored the autopilot and other instruments. At 700 feet came the welcome, "runway in sight."

The general location of the first half of the runway was apparent, out-lined by high-intensity runway lights, but the runway itself was gone. In its place was a long rectangular lake, full of white-capped waves. I was pretty sure this would be more of a splashdown than a landing. Still, runway 20 was a welcome sight.

I disengaged the autopilot and lowered the flaps to land position. Simul-taneously, Keflavik Tower reported winds 210 at 78 knots gusting to 85. Great news. If the wind direction stayed between 190 and 210 degrees, run-way 20 would work.

The captain, true to her PM job description, was watching both airspeed and ground speed. I was working pretty hard to stay on course and main-tain $V_{REF}$ airspeed, 102 knots on this particular day. She was to warn me if our speed deteriorated much below $V_{REF}$ before landing.

As predicted, the airplane's ground speed was very slow; at one point only 25 knots. Approaching the runway threshold, it seemed as if we were hardly moving, but the constant jostling turbulence all around was an ever-present reminder that the energies outside were big.

It was now or never to commit to the runway. The last wind report was 205 at 80 knots. Perfect, I thought. With the wind now almost straight down the runway I told the captain I was going for it, and she agreed.

I began the flare, slowing below $V_{REF}$. The airplane gradually descended, responding predictably. The mains touched, kissing the two to three inches of water covering the runway. As the main gear descended deeper into the water, there was a dramatic deceleration, rapidly forcing the airplane's nose down. I tried to compensate with aft pressure on the yoke, but my reaction

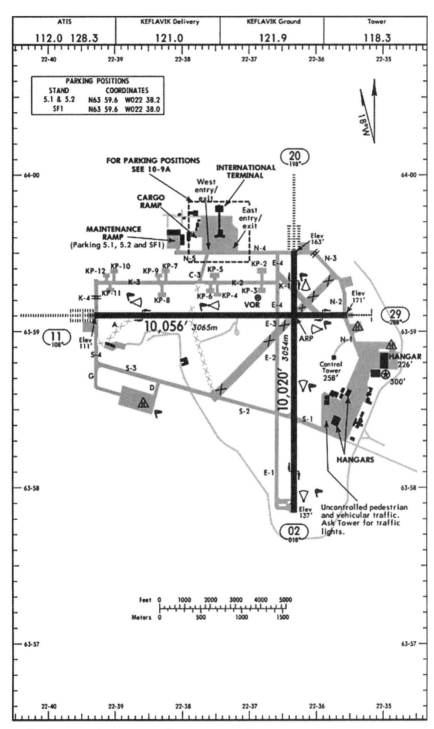

*Keflavik Airport diagram. Note the ramp area to the east.*

was too slow. I thought what a shame it would be, after overcoming all the other adversities, to smash the nose wheel.

When the nose wheel touched, a wall of water showered the front of the airplane. I couldn't see a thing, but it didn't matter. The wind and water drag had brought the airplane to a complete stop, no steering or braking needed. We were more or less on the centerline, down safe, and apparently undamaged.

"Welcome to Iceland," was the refrain from the Tower. "We are very glad to be here!" Was the Captain's reply.

The wind, of course, was still howling. This, in combination with water breaking off the runway's whitecaps and the heavy rain, served to make the visibility out the windscreen terrible. Although we were thrilled to be on the ground, it wasn't clear exactly how we were going to get from the runway to the parking area. And staying on a quasi-active runway didn't seem like a very good idea.

Tower said to continue on the runway and then make a right turn at taxiway Sierra 1 to join Echo 2. We slowly proceeded up the runway, trying to keep the centerline lights sighted off the nose. At the taxiway, I applied power to the left engine while braking, attempting to pivot the airplane around. But, as the tail surface became increasingly exposed to the wind, the airplane refused to turn. Applying more power and more brake, the airplane came around, but now we were facing nearly downwind. With the wind flowing over the control surfaces in the reverse of intended, large loads could be felt through the yoke and rudder pedals. It took the two of us hanging on for dear life to keep the controls neutralized. In 80-knot winds, a full and violent control excursion could do damage. Further, there was a possibility that a control positioned in the wrong way might flip the airplane onto its back. With flying speeds only 20-30 knots more than wind speeds, it wouldn't take much to lose control.

We made it to Echo 2 and were now taxiing with the wind directly behind. We were still struggling, but we had made it about halfway without a problem. If we could make it to the semi-protected terminal and customs area on the north side of the airport, there would be some respite from the wind.

It was not to be. Suddenly, there was an enormous gust that ripped the controls out of our hands. The entire airplane, all 13,000 pounds of it, violently weather-vaned, whipping the nose 180-degrees clockwise. It all happened in a second.

"Goddamn it. What the hell happened?" I said. Of course I knew what had happened, but I was tired, and angry. How much harder does this need to be, I thought?

To the extent there was any good news, the forces on the controls lessened with the reversal of direction. We were right-side up and still in one piece.

The captain called Tower to report status: we weren't going to customs anytime soon. Instead, she requested a clearance to the southeast side of the airport where the military base is located. The plan was to tack, angling the airplane slightly off the wind, southeast bound, and then duck behind one of the large military hangars for protection.

This worked. We traveled south on Echo 2, then crossed runway 20 using Sierra 1. We got to use the military apron after all, as we traversed toward shelter. Once safely shutdown and refueled (to help weigh down the aircraft), we were graciously escorted to a local hotel by FBO staff. We never made it to customs—an unnecessary formality, I guess, post landing in a hurricane.

Our airplane was more fortunate then some. There were six previously-landed airliners, all with a full complement of passengers onboard, ground stopped due to winds. Rock'n'roll, it was not until five hours later before the persons onboard was able to set foot on land.

Amazingly enough, everyone was willing to climb back into the airplane the next day for the trip to Strasbourg. We lined up for departure on our old friend runway 20. With blue skies above and winds down to a mere 40 knots, we blasted off to complete our journey.

## Lessons learned:

**Lesson 1:** Deep lows can form suddenly and be very bad.

**Lesson 2:** North Atlantic weather is difficult to predict.

**Lesson 3:** Maintaining control on the ground, especially in a light airplane on a windy day, is not always a *fait accompli*.

# 18 | **Busted**

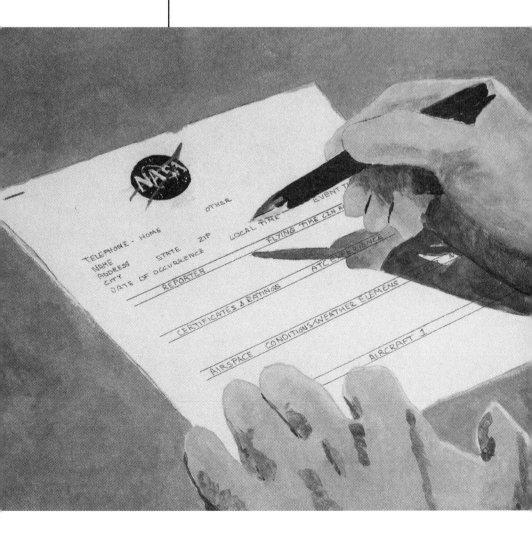

What happens when there is a loss of separation between two aircraft operating in the same airspace? A midair collision is one possibility, although in modern flying this is a rare event. When conducting a flight under IFR, midairs are almost unheard of, especially in North America and Europe where radar coverage is almost universal and the rules that controllers use to determine safe separation are both rigorous and, in many cases, automatically enforced. But loss of separation events, in violation of the rules, do happen, and more frequently than one might expect. Over 500 loss of separation (LOS) events were reported by pilots and controllers to NASA's Air Safety Reporting System (ASRS) in 2016 alone.

When operating in the US, the standards for IFR separation are generally 1,000 feet vertical and either 3 or 5 nautical miles laterally, 5 nautical miles being the criteria when the traffic is more than 40 nautical miles from the radar facility. For airplanes operating above 41,000 feet, the vertical distance increases to 2,000 feet. There are other traffic buffering rules that cover special situations like wake vortex turbulence, and distances that apply to aircraft lined up on the same approach track within 10 nautical miles of the airport. While these minimum separation requirements may seem relatively luxurious, consider that civilian jet aircraft can climb 5,000 feet per minute or more, and cruise at more than 450 knots. That's an altitude increase of 1,000 feet every 12 seconds and a closing rate, assuming the jets are pointed at each other, that would cover the larger 5 nautical mile separation distance (10 nautical miles divided in half) in about 20 seconds, worst case.

Part of the reason there aren't more problems overall is that, except for certain terminal areas, there aren't that many airplanes being controlled. Over parts of the US, the midwest and the western states, the radio can be silent for the entire time needed to traverse a sector. During most of the flight the airplane is cruising at one, or possibly two, assigned altitudes, while following a prescribed route under autopilot control. Because the workload is generally low during these times, errors by pilots and controllers are usually caught before anything bad happens. The departure and arrival phases of the flight, when the cockpit is busy and the prescribed routings and combinations of altitudes are complicated and need to be executed in short order, are when things get exciting. Without careful attention, it's easy to misunderstand a clearance or execute a correctly-understood clearance incorrectly. Even the best pilots and controllers sometimes get it wrong.

Fortunately, there are a lot of safety valves built into the system, so the chances of an actual collision are small. To start, the density of aircraft in the three-dimensional airspace is relatively low. Even in the busy terminal areas, the per-cubic nautical mile saturation point is only about four to six airplanes. And the airplanes normally would be stacked in increments of 1,000 feet, maintaining each airplane's target altitude easily achievable with today's pilot training, instrumentation, and automation. The airplanes are also carefully watched by controllers and their computer-controlled monitor and alert systems, all designed to communicate immediately any potential conflict or violation of the rules. Many of the airplanes have their own collision avoidance technology. Traffic Avoidance Collision Systems (TCAS) I, II, III, and IV have been around for a long time and are mandatory in most larger airplanes as well as airplanes used for commercial purposes. TCAS I provides only traffic advisories, while the other versions also provide a recommended resolution—e.g., dive or climb. All TCAS systems require a compatible and compliant transponder installed in the aircraft to provide the traffic alert or traffic resolution function. Unfortunately, not all aircraft are required to have a TCAS; one of the weaknesses of the system.

We practice TCAS events routinely in the simulator because the real alert, while very infrequent, is quite startling, and the resolution often requires immediate action. Initially the voice says "TRAFFIC, TRAFFIC, TRAFFIC," indicating a potential threat. This report is known as a traffic advisory (TA). Then, in the case of TCAS II and higher, and assuming a true conflict exists, a resolution advisory (RA) is given. The voice says "CLIMB, CLIMB, CLIMB," or "DESCEND, DESCEND, DESCEND," depending on the appropriate corrective action needed to address the impending conflict. There are also more benign, preventive RAs, when the system recognizes a more theoretical conflict scenario. We have experienced this at times when descending to an assigned altitude that is only 1,000 feet above one or more aircraft operating nearby, especially when the descent rate is high. The voice says "ADJUST VERTICAL SPEED," or "MAINTAIN VERTICAL SPEED," when the system senses that, should the airplane continue to descend past the assigned altitude, there could be a collision.

In addition to the initial shock of hearing the TAs and RAs, there is the novelty of having to obey the alert independent of any clearance by a controller. Psychologically, this can be difficult, because pilot training and almost all practical flying experience demands 100 percent adherence to controller instructions. All the more reason to try it first in the simulator. Further complicating the situation, should an actual TA or RA occur, the controller is unlikely to be aware of the event unless the crew reports status. The spontaneous rapid climb or descent on the controller's radar screen will no doubt come as a surprise. For this reason, crews must report TA/RA events immediately after the conflict has been resolved.

Outside of the simulator, I have had only one true TA experience. We were flying our CJ3, about 80 nautical miles east of Lincoln, Nebraska, in the climb, passing through 31,100 feet. The airplane was on autopilot with the target assigned altitude, 33,000 feet, input into the altitude preselect box. Then, "TRAFFIC, TRAFFIC, TRAFFIC," followed almost instantaneously by a raised voice on the radio yelling something like, "I need you at flight level 300." With adrenaline surging, I immediately disconnected the autopilot and dove the airplane toward the controller's altitude target. Meanwhile, the first officer made it clear over the radio that our assigned altitude was actually flight level 330. Although there was no RA, and we did not see conflicting traffic out the window (the skies were clear) or a target on the MFD, apparently there had been a real conflict with another aircraft. This is "a deal" in controller parlance. When you get a direction from Minneapolis Center to call the Minneapolis supervisor, that's bad.

There are essentially three possibilities in a situation like this: 1) the clearance issued by the controller was wrong, but correctly understood, acknowledged, and executed by the crew; 2) the clearance issued by the controller was correct, but was acknowledged, understood, and executed by the crew incorrectly; and 3) the clearance issued by the controller was correct and acknowledged correctly by the crew, and perhaps even understood, but then was executed incorrectly. The FAA assumes number 2, or in some cases 3, at least initially. All spell trouble and are stressful to address. This in addition to the added burden of knowing a near miss with all those passengers onboard may have occurred. Needless to say, staying focused on the mission at hand, finishing the trip to Burlington, Vermont, took extra concentration.

In a case like ours where no accident occurred, the formality that unfolds is mostly about determining whether or not there was a violation. Knowing the root cause, or identifying systemic weaknesses, ironically is secondary, except perhaps as applied to devising defense arguments should the FAA conclude the pilot or controller was at fault. This often pits pilots and controllers against the FAA, essentially adversaries—the nuts and bolts of the FAA's function—focus on enforcement rather than making the system safer and better. Even with new legislation in place, authored by Senator Jim Inhofe, and a big improvement over existing law at the time of the incident, the adversarial nature is preserved.

Fortunately, there is the NASA Aviation Safety Reporting System (ASRS). The FAA, using NASA as a third-party implementer, established this system in 1976 to collect reports on events in which safety may have been compromised. It functions as a repository of incident reports while also categorizing them in a way that is useful for understanding possible operational, procedural, and systemic weaknesses in the National Airspace System. The inspiration for the ASRS was a series of accidents that had occurred under similar circumstances and, at least theoretically, could have been prevented had the circumstances been analyzed properly, appropriate actions taken, and changes in systems and procedures adopted.

ASRS has no enforcement authority, but those who benefit from the system's alerts, reports, and research often take corrective action, especially when threatening hazards, such as a dangerous instrument procedure or malfunctioning navigation aid, are identified. ASRS also takes an interest in human factors (e.g., why some crews fail to understand and execute clearances correctly).

The other novelty is that, to encourage a free flow of reports, ASRS offers both anonymity and in some cases insulation from punishment should a violation be determined. Assuming the report was filed in a timely fashion, and the violation was inadvertent with no accident resulting, enforcement is limited to a recorded violation, with no loss of FAA granted privileges provided there has been no other violation in the previous five years.

So, although the FAA almost always goes after the captain in these cases, the first officer and I both filed a report. I was confident we had gotten the clearance right, but knowing the benefits to safety along with the potential personal benefits, the case for submitting the form seemed compelling. Earlier in my flying, Greg Bean, one of the best flight instructors ever, had advised me to report to NASA whenever I perceived a safety issue. "Report early and often if you see something that isn't safe," was Greg's refrain. True to his advocacy, Greg always had a pad of blank NASA forms in his flight bag—this was before the system went online.

About twenty days later, a certified letter arrived in the mail from Aviation Safety Inspector D'Allura informing me the FAA was investigating the matter—deviation from an ATC clearance. Prior to receipt of the letter, our company mechanic had attempted to download the voice data recorder information for the flight, but the two hour recording loop capacity had been exceeded before landing. So there was no recording of the event by the airplane's system. Still, the FAA would have the ATC center tapes to ascertain the facts.

Airmen have tended to be at a disadvantage in investigations, because in many cases the FAA doesn't have to present evidence in a timely fashion, even when negotiating a possible final action. If the pilot agrees to a lesser charge, like a warning, the evidence may never be disclosed. It's only when the case is brought to court, in front of an FAA, NTSB, or US District Court judge, that the evidence must be shared. Most often the pilot loses.

In our case, after reviewing our polite reply to their certified letter—saying basically that we didn't do it—conducting personal interviews, and likely listening to the tapes, the FAA proposed a warning notice exclusive to the captain. Regarding the tapes, it was hard to know. The inspector said they showed we had violated the clearance, but he was unwilling or unable to share the content directly. Puzzling.

Aviation counsel, having seen a lot of cases like mine, advised against fighting the warning. Since a warning is not technically a violation, there is no punishment. Any record of the warning is expunged after two years—at least that's what they say. Not knowing what was on the tapes made it unclear whether we would prevail should the case go to trial. And once a case goes to court, the FAA is free to look at everything, potentially discovering other inadvertent yet material violations. "Court is unpredictable," was counsel's major theme. I took the deal.

In a way, I regret not taking the next step, facing our accusers and their evidence. Memory can be faulty, but I was pretty sure we had the clearance right. Could it be that we both heard/understood the same thing, repeated it back as heard, and then executed as understood, all the while not getting it right, or as ATC had intended? Possibly. But for this to happen, our incorrect acknowledgment over the radio would have to have been missed by the controller, too. Independent of guilt or innocence, it felt like a lost opportunity to understand what really happened, if only out of an aspiration to improve.

Although we never solved the mystery of the loss of separation event, we did benefit. To start, we changed our SOPs for acknowledging and executing clearances in the cockpit. Prior to the violation the PM almost always was the one to acknowledge clearance over the radio, but the process of executing the clearance and confirming that it was done correctly was more informal. Now, when ATC assigns a new altitude, the PM acknowledges the new assignment over the radio while the PF dials it into the altitude preselect box. Before beginning the descent or climb the PF verbally repeats the altitude set in the box, while looking at the box, and then asks the PM to confirm. In crewed airplanes where there is a captain and first officer, we use PF and PM to refer to different functions being performed in the cockpit. This is different from an anointment of authority. The captain may serve as PM, navigating and running the radio, while the first officer is the one flying, but the captain is the captain, the person ultimately responsible for the safety of the flight.

We also accelerated plans to modify the airplane to support the new satellite-based ADS-B Out protocol, providing much better resolution of the airplane's coordinates and speed to ATC and other aircraft equipped with ADS-B In/Out systems. Although minimal ADS-B Out capability in the aircraft is not legally required until 2020, the considerable improvement in the accuracy and precision of traffic position reporting afforded to ATC made the early investment compelling. Unlike legacy radar with coordinates, direction, and speed information dependent a range-limited ground based system and a relatively primitive aircraft based transponder, ADS-B uses precise GPS information from the satellite network. Therefore, the aircraft position, direction, and speed reported by the ADS-B Out transmitter/enhanced-transponder to ATC or another airplane equipped with an ADS-B In is exceedingly precise. Here, *Out* refers to a unidirectional transmission of location, direction of travel, speed and a number of other parameters unique to the aircraft. *In* facilitates the crew's ability to receive and interpret ADS-B Out information from other aircraft and ATC. In the case of ATC, ADS-B Out transmissions provide the location of traffic, weather, and other pertinent information providing there is a ground station in range. Unfortunately, there are no true ADS-B In/Out based TCAS resolution advisory systems available, yet. Our new 2016 CJ4, for example, is only ADS-B Out equipped, leaning on traditional transponder based TCAS for TAs and RAs. Precise collision-avoidance delayed, but not denied?

Even without a true RA TCAS in the aircraft, ADS-B In/Out promotes awareness of traffic and potential conflicts. Garmin systems, for example, represent threatening aircraft as both a target and a vector from the target, with projected direction and distance estimated over a set period. All traffic relative to the airplane's position is visible, overlaid on a moving map. This real-time tactical information is helpful in projecting the point of a possible collision, and in recognizing threats early—very early. The ADS-B system installed in my Skywagon often warns of worrisome traffic several minutes before ATC issues an advisory.

Would ADS-B In have prevented the conflict over Iowa had it been available and installed? Perhaps. We might have seen the traffic earlier, precisely depicted, viewed it as more of a threat, and therefore made an ATC query, asking to reaffirm the assigned altitude. Speculation? Of course, but like many hypotheticals there is always a chance that, as a result, things would have gone differently.

One consolation was the inspector appeared confident that this was an aberrance, at least in our case. After claiming the tapes were damning, he said, "You will never make that mistake again." Whether the insight was from general experience or from sizing us up as a crew, I don't know. But, so far, he has been right. No altitude busts, or any busts for that matter, since that time.

The loss of separation event was a low point in my flying. I was sure we had operated according to the clearance given, yet the inspector, after listening to the tapes, represented something different. It gave me pause. How was it that a relatively simple clearance—climb to assigned altitude—delivered in a period of relatively low workload, could have been so misunderstood? And by two experienced, practiced, and well-intentioned crew members. Assuming a mistake was made in the cockpit, was the airplane actually in danger? This was the most depressing thought of all, knowing that many lives may have been at risk because of simple pilot error. The highest priority of a captain is the safety of the ship. Was it possible that, due to a simple and avoidable mistake, the opposite played out? Much second guessing.

Independent of the guilt, the altitude assignment mix-up had a menacing feeling about it. This was not like Zurich and the departure procedure in which I accidentally cut the corner slightly on the last RNAV turn, the consequences of the mistake limited to a complaint from the Swiss authorities. The airplane in that case was in the clear, well above any obstructions, with the closest traffic 15 nautical miles away. Yes, somebody on the ground might have been bothered by the noise, but no one would die as a result. True? The problem is that it is hard to know. Not all RNAV departures are so forgiving. In the case of the Ruudy 6 out of Teterboro, New Jersey, failing to stay within the steep climb attitude limits could result in a conflict with traffic landing at Newark. And here the word *conflict* means collision—crash, with everyone dying.

Recognizing that mistakes in flying have unpredictable outcomes which can lead to something very bad happening suggests that in an ideal world there is no room for error; the crew has to get it right every time. Complying with altitude assignments or vectors from ATC demands this kind of perfection. Unless the TCAS says something different, or there is some kind of emergency in play, flying the correct clearance is absolutely paramount to safety. Also, unless ATC indicates otherwise, all RNAV procedures must be flown exactly as published.

It should be pointed out that perfect technique—zero defects—is different from exercising good judgment, although the two are related. For example, it is probably not a good idea to fly when tired or impaired. Mistakes are much more likely under these circumstances. But even the best rested, properly trained, and most current pilots occasionally make a mistake. Pilots are human beings. Human beings make mistakes. Therefore, pilots make mistakes. Not good! But there are ways of detecting errors in advance, or early in their unfolding, or worst case, just in time to avoid disaster.

One thing that helps, in addition to cross-checking between crew members, is to write everything down before acknowledging to ATC. Now there is a written record preserved in the cockpit for reference in case of doubt. But that is not enough. The crew member must read back from the notes. This prevents a situation in which the clearance is repeated back correctly, but not understood. Psychologists say there is something about writing and reading (as opposed to just listening and speaking) that improves understanding, especially when the topic in play, a copied clearance in this case, doesn't quite match what was intended. Here, the read-back to ATC reflects the error, almost always caught by the controller—a good thing given that most pilots will admit that sometimes they need a couple of tries to get it right.

What about learning to anticipate mistakes by gaining insight into potential challenges or, cynically speaking, traps, set by the system, individuals (controllers), or circumstances, many of which can lead to error.

All *Star Trek* episodes start out the same: everything's going well, all systems are at 100 percent; there's even a wedding ceremony underway in the ship's chapel. Then, suddenly, there's a Red Alert. Romulans are attacking

Federation remote outposts with a new super weapon. Their ship is virtually invisible, almost impossible to detect.[1] Who would have guessed?

In the fanciful world of *Star Trek* the protagonist, confronting unexpected, menacing circumstances, inevitably must rise to the occasion. So it is with airplane pilots. And the same questions apply. Were there clues? Should Captain Kirk have been able to anticipate the danger in advance?

Much of the training in the simulator mimics the world of Captain Kirk in the sense that the focus is on emergencies, spontaneous events that require immediate action. An engine failure or fire in the twin turbofan airplane, staged slightly before or slightly after $V_1$, the takeoff speed where the crew is committed to fly no matter what, is a case in point. In the slightly-before scenario, the answer is to throw out all the spoiler/dive brakes then use the wheel brakes to stop on the runway. Slightly-above, well, the right answer is to fly away on one engine. In either case there are a bunch of memorized actions the pilot must perform to assure a safe outcome.

The funny thing about most of the emergency scenarios rehearsed in the simulator is that they almost never happen, especially in modern jet airplanes. This isn't to suggest that pilots shouldn't train for challenging and improbable scenarios. It's just that bad outcomes rarely result from the emergencies pilots train for in school. For example, I know of no real engine fires that weren't handled properly by the crew, resulting in a safe landing. In a way, this is reassuring, a confirmation of the success of the various schools that provide simulator training. The training really works. But as the ASRS data base shows, there have been many close calls in other aspects of flying not covered so comprehensively.

There are lots of ways to lose the ship, but one that is high on the list is complying with challenging, unrealistic controller demands. Complicated late-in-the-game directions from ATC can set the stage for a mistake or, worst case, an accident. In many cases crews are so acclimated to accepting ATC direction they can't muster the courage to say no. I can't tell you how many times we have been on the ILS to 4R at JFK only to be instructed by the controller at the last minute to jog over to the ILS to 4L. It's IMC, night, rough air, and now the FMS needs to be reprogrammed, and quickly. This means head-down for the first officer. Imagine the same scenario, a fast-moving airplane of any type, only this time as a single pilot.

---

[1] *Star Trek*, "Balance or Terror," NBC December 15, 1966, written by Paul Schneider and Gene Rudenberry, directed by Vincent McEveety.

Part of the reason we try to comply is that it is ingrained—the right thing to do. There is also the expectation that saying no means a circuitous, time-consuming rendezvous with another approach, now queued up behind traffic, doomed to the inevitable long delay.

But often it is just lack of proper preparation in the cockpit, the controller largely innocent. I have personally succumbed to this, lulled by the tranquility of the enroute segment only to be confronted by a busy terminal environment that turns everything into a fire drill. Typical of this is a high traffic density airport that may even be experiencing VMC, but suddenly the controller demands some kind of archaic approach. Not expecting a true instrument procedure, and certainly not a back course approach, one that is practiced perhaps once a year in the simulator, chaos ensues in the cockpit.

Setting up for an entirely new approach, or any complicated procedure, in short order is fraught with dangers. The time pressure itself can cause mistakes because everyone is rushing—to find the approach in the FMS, load it, activate it, brief it from the electronic or paper collateral, and then set up the automation to make it happen precisely. A lot of the set up involves typing things into the special FMS keyboard, head-down, in the literal and figurative turbulence of the moment. There is a real risk of succumbing to a creeping paralysis exacerbated by errant inputs to the computer that must be corrected or, in the worst case, are missed, resulting in the airplane not doing what the crew or ATC wants it to do, in time. A herculean effort.

There are some scenarios where the right answer is to abandon automation and conduct a raw data approach, but these come with their own dangers. Is the nav frequency and source input to the PFD correct? Has the omni bearing selector (OBS) knob been set properly for the backcourse, opposite the direction of the approach/alignment for the runway? Here we have a great entry for the "Dark and Stormy Night" literature competition.

Independent of accusations of lack of compliance when, after not doing something they told you to do, they give you a number to call, the most important thing to do is just keep flying the airplane. Going around and regrouping, if necessary, is certainly one good option. Asking for additional ATC support, like a vector/altitude target that is simple to follow, can also help save the day.

Ideally it would be best to avoid the "Dark and Stormy Night" scenario entirely. How? First, I have become hypersensitive to the departure and arrival procedure complexities inherent in flying in the system. If there is time, I study all likely departure and arrival procedures/approaches before the trip, so when any procedure or approach is assigned I have at least some familiarity.

I have also become comfortable delivering a firm "No" to unreasonable requests, such as changing approaches three miles out from the final approach fix (FAF). What are they going to say? "Okay, go around?" That would be fine, given the greater danger of attempted compliance. Sometimes, though, there is cause for a soft no. "N726AG, proceed to such-and-such, fix and hold, expect further clearance time at something hundred hours"—45 minutes into the future. My response: "We can go there, but be advised that approximately five turns into the hold we will need to declare a fuel emergency." Usually, a more expedited solution is the result. The key is to speak your truth.

We have not had a loss of separation incident since the Iowa event and consequent warning letter, but there have been plenty of opportunities for error. In every case, those of us flying the airplane and those controlling it from the ground worked things out without either party being the subject of an investigation—a testament to the largely collegial relationship most pilots and air traffic controller enjoy, and the resiliency of the system.

Still, the adversarial relationship between the FAA and all who use or work within its system promises to be an ongoing story. What's curious is that unlike those who run afoul of the criminal justice system, many *intending* to commit crimes, those caught up in the FAA enforcement tend to be well-intentioned, their mistakes unintentional. Despite the headlines there are almost zero drunk pilots or controllers, for example.

We might wish for a more sympathetic system but the FAA's emphasis on complying with the rules does tend to up one's game. I am definitely more cautious about recording, understanding, and implementing clearances, as a result of the warning I received. The greater worry, however, is that there was some kind of weakness in the system, perhaps one not identified, as is true of almost all unintended non-compliance events. Even with the NASA form program, a great resource, it takes a long time to correlate the data, present it in a meaningful way, derive recommendations for improvement, and then implement the improvements. This is especially true of more strategic problems. Let's face it, pilots have been receiving clearances over the radio in the same way for fifty years. Despite the opportunities for errors intrinsic to this approach, it will be years before something better is universally adopted. In the meantime, pilots, and controllers to a lesser extent, will continue to get it wrong from time to time, with various possible negative consequences.

We fly the system we have, not necessarily the one we want (or need). That's the challenge. It's up to the human pilot and human controller, tips of the spears, to mitigate for its inadequacies.

Still, pilots and controllers, beware. There are evil traps inherent to the airspace system we fly and the FAA regulates. A cautionary tale for sure because when it comes down to good versus evil, evil usually prevails unless good is very, very good, and also very, very careful.

## Lessons learned:

**Lesson 1:** Don't accept clearances that demand a rushed cockpit environment to fulfill.

**Lesson 2:** Airport departures and arrivals/approaches require special attention—"Yellow alert!" to use the *Star Trek* parallel. Complacency is not rewarded!

**Lesson 3:** Write everything down, and in regard to clearances, perform the read-backs from what is written, not from memory.

# 19 Helicopter Odyssey

Approaching the meadow, I pulled back on the cyclic, pitching up slightly, while lowering the collective to bleed off the helicopter's airspeed. The target landing spot was in sight, about 800 feet ahead, a smooth grassy area we had used many times before for practice. Anticipating loss of aerodynamic efficiency as I passed below the effective translational lift (ETL) speed, I raised the collective slightly, providing more power and lift to the rotor disc while simultaneously applying more left foot pedal (the power pedal) to offset the increase in torque. The helicopter continued to slow both in airspeed and vertical descent. But all was not well. The Robinson R44 helicopter, a piston engine-powered helicopter, was becoming increasingly difficult to control, and there was a serious pendulum motion that required increasing magnitudes of cyclic input to address. Now only 20 feet off the ground with near zero airspeed, the oscillations were getting bigger. Anti-torque inputs weren't working properly either, so addressing the increasing back-and-forth yaw was becoming more and more difficult. What was wrong? All systems were operating in the green. Puzzling! I hadn't crashed yet, but the outcome of the flight was now certainly in question. The helicopter was starting to oscillate, and I couldn't control it. "Help!" Then, suddenly, the ship was stable as a rock. I heard my instructor's voice over the intercom. "Now let's try that again." Had Brad not taken over, I would have crashed for sure. And this wasn't lesson one. Loss of control had become a regular event for me.

Figuring out how to fly helicopters has to be one of the most humbling experiences in flying. Attempting it after thirty years of fixed wing experience only makes it worse. Reflecting on those early flights, it is amazing I ever achieved the rotorcraft rating. Much credit goes to Brad Carlson, my primary helicopter instructor. To teach helicopters requires nerves of steel and incredibly fast reflexes. If ever there were a course curriculum in which the student's role is to kill the instructor, learning to fly helicopters is it.

Having all the wrong instincts, a legacy of the years flying fixed wing, lesson one went more or less as expected—badly. Yes, I could fly the helicopter around, kind of like an airplane, but when the task was to slow down or hover for any extended period of time, disaster unfolded. Lesson two was worse, and lesson three a complete failure. After a discouraging lesson four, I was ready to quit. It would have been game over had Gisela not sent me back for more punishment. Through a combination of genuine encouragement and gentle shaming, I ended up back at school trying again to master the craft. More unsatisfying lessons followed, but then suddenly, around lesson seven, I stopped crashing. Yes, keeping the helicopter stable in a hover required 100 percent concentration, but that was a far cry from applying 100 percent concentration and still crashing if not for the intervention of my instructor. Something clicked, and from that point on, progress was measurable. Three months after lesson one, I achieved the private pilot rating, allowing me to operate the aircraft autonomously and with passengers onboard. Later, I upgraded my rating to a commercial certificate, a kind of professional status where charging for flights is permitted under some circumstances. Reflecting on those humble beginnings, it was all quite a miracle.

Why are helicopters so hard to fly? Much of the challenge has to do with the design's inherent instability. In an airplane, letting go of the controls in most cases means little or no change in direction, attitude, or speed. Helicopters naturally develop a rapid excursion that, if not addressed immediately and correctly, most likely leads to a crash. There are technical reasons for this, including the complicated relationship between lift applied by the main blade system or main rotor, proper anti-torque rotor thrust needed to appropriately counteract torque on the fuselage caused by increasing or decreasing lift produced by the main rotor, and a host of other dynamic elements like gyroscopic precession and ETL.

Mostly, though, the pilot has to develop a skill (more of a knack) for anticipating the effect of any one control input on the balance of forces, and using some or all of the other controls available in due course. Developing the right kind of muscle memory is definitely one of the keys, but there is an intellectual component as well. I know of no other flavor of flying where prudent practices seem so difficult to ascertain and then apply, given the special dangers presented by terrain, natural and man-made obstructions, load, temperature, altitude, and wind. Most accidents result when relatively talented pilots operate their aircraft in a high risk way. What's interesting is that up to the point of the accident, many of these pilots believe their actions are entirely reasonable and safe. How can this be?

Many clues were revealed when I transitioned to a jet turbine-powered helicopter, the Bell 206B JetRanger III, one of the most iconic helicopters ever invented. This design is a feature of television dramas from the 1970s, 80s, and even 90s, especially police shows, with the helicopter as prop, or in some cases the star of the show. The 206 has also been a mainstay of real law enforcement as well as the military, with variants in use by all service branches.

In my case, the journey to mastering the JetRanger began with buying a JetRanger. Crazy! While it is not generally a good idea to buy an aircraft before gaining at least a little experience, renting turbine-powered helicopters for training is problematic. Very few schools do it. I was also confident the 206 was the right answer. Its proven design has one of the best safety records of all helicopters, while offering utility and comfort. And frankly, I watched a lot of *McMillan & Wife*, James Bond (in *For Your Eyes Only*, Bond delivers his wheelchair-bound nemesis, the supervillain Ernst Stavro Blofeld, into a tall chimney stack), and *Airwolf*—the JetRanger a feature of all. Very romantic! While not the fastest helicopter, with a cruise speed of around 100 knots, it has a good useful load, and can carry five persons assuming a less than full fuel tank. Perhaps highest on the list, the 206 was reported to be relatively easy to fly, similar in some ways to the Robinson R44 which I had originally trained on.

We purchased our 2003 model in 2013. This 206 was unusual because the previous owner had equipped it with a Garmin 530 GPS navigator and a Garmin 500H EFIS with charts, weather, and synthetic vision. Although the 206 is not certified for IFR flight, the avionics in our aircraft were fully capable.

Next came the search for a trainer to teach me how to fly it. There are a number of companies that do this, including Bell Helicopter, the manufacturer. I chose Lunsford Air Consulting, Inc., out of Palm Coast, Florida, mostly because of their client-oriented philosophy, which included a willingness to customize the curriculum and conduct the training at a location convenient for the trainee. Lunsford has clients all over the US, so coming to our residence was no problem for them.

To start, Lunsford has clients complete an online training course covering the aircraft's systems and operation. There is a quiz after each chapter and a test at the end to judge whether the client is ready to begin flight training. In general, the course is effective, and having the helicopter in the hangar helped with some of the technical references and performing the preflight. Still, mastering the systems out of a book is not the same as mastering them in flight.

The actual flying begins with the arrival of Lunsford's instructor. In my case, it was Mike Tomisich.[1] We started late in the day, so by the time we were ready to fly the sun had set and the transition from twilight to night was well underway. This was no problem for Mike. In addition to his job as Lunsford's flight instructor, Mike is the chief pilot for the Lee County Sheriff's Office in Florida, and an instructor specializing in SWAT training, often flying missions at night with infrared imaging goggles. I did not happen to own night vision goggles (or know how to use them) so adding night to the challenge of learning to fly this unfamiliar aircraft did cause me some pause. Fortunately, SWAT ops were not on the agenda.

Conventional wisdom has it that if you can get the aircraft started, flying will naturally follow. This certainly seems true of the JetRanger in that bringing the 420-hp Allison-C20B turboshaft engine to life requires some finesse. Let's just say there are a lot of ways to cause a hot start, or worse. (Exceeding the engine's temperature tolerances usually means having to do a very expensive tear down.)

The JetRanger is not FADEC-equipped (no computer helping to control the engine), so proper technique requires double checking that the throttle position is set to off before engaging the starter. Introducing fuel into the burner can, where combustion takes place, before establishing adequate airflow from the compressor section is a surefire way to blow up the engine. Mike insisted that care be taken to confirm that both throttle and fuel cutoff switch were in the correct position. He said bad starting technique is a problem for both low and high-time pilots in non-FADEC equipped helicopters. Very expensive, and potentially dangerous!

Once the proper throttle position is established, the pilot engages the starter button located on the end of the collective, causing the starter/generator to accelerate the Ng (Gas producer) turbine and compressor.[2] When Ng reaches between 12 and 15 percent (depending on OAT), the throttle is positioned from off to idle, causing fuel to be introduced and light-off

---

[1] M. Tomisich founded Praetorian Aviation Services, LLC, in 2015. His company provides helicopter recurrent training services for pilots flying the Bell/Textron 206B III and other rotorcraft.

[2] The Ng (gas producer) turbine in the Bell 206 Rolls Royce C-20 engine harnesses the energy from the expanding gases contained in the burner can to run the compressor section. Down flow of the Ng turbine, the expanded gases also drive the Np (power turbine) which in turn powers the transmission and blade system.

to occur. As the Ng percent rises, the pilot monitors the turbine outlet temperature (TOT) to confirm gas temperatures past the Ng turbine are within limits. JetRanger temperatures can go as high as 810°C for 5 minutes, between 810°C and 927°C for 10 seconds, and an astonishing 927°C for 1 second without incurring damage. It is important to hold the start button down throughout the start, leveraging the electric starter's torque as a supplement to the natural acceleration experienced by Ng turbine, caused by the expansion of gases in the burner can. Failure to do this will almost always cause a hot start. Most starts see maximum TOT temperatures in the 700° to 780°C range. In general, lower temperatures are better for increasing the engine's life.

The pilot does not release pressure on the start button until the start is completed (approximately 58 percent Ng). The engine then accelerates to 62 to 64 percent Ng, idle, while the N1, the power turbine, and rotor system accelerate to around 65 percent. After a brief temperature stabilization warm up we increase power to 70 percent Ng at which point the generator is switched on and energized. Finally, once generator power is established, the avionics and radios are turned on and checked for function.

The pre-departure checklist is relatively simple and in some aspects similar to piston helicopters like the R44. A hydraulic check is done at both idle and takeoff power to assure proper cyclic and collective function. A check of proper electrical output is also made along with temperature and pressure for the transmission and engine oil. A final check of fuel pressure, fuel quantity, and turbine outlet temperature (TOT) is also made before departure.

The JetRanger has an illuminated caution panel that communicates abnormal and emergency status. As with many turbofan fixed wing aircraft, a dark panel is good. One or more lights illuminated is bad. "We don't go if there is a light," Mike said. With all indicators in the green and the caution panel dark, we were ready for our first pick-up.

Our personal LED-lit helipad is helpful for finding the helicopter in the dark, but disorienting once inside the ship. The combination of glare and light intensity with a backdrop of darkness makes it hard to gauge height without looking straight down through the chin bubble. There is no way to turn down the LED intensity, so the first few feet taking off or landing can be hard to figure out. *Note to file*, get dimmable incandescent bulbs for the next helipad.

One clear difference between the JetRanger and piston helicopters is the JetRanger's noticeable lack of vibration. When I loaded the disc to pick up the helicopter for the first time, the transition was smooth with no detectable imbalances. But there were initially some pilot-induced excursions and oscillations. The controls of the 206 (especially the cyclic) are sensitive, compared to the piston helicopters I have flown.

That first night of flying was mostly about hovering and figuring out pick-ups and set-downs. We never left our turf airport environment. It was good practice both for mastering the controls and for learning a little more about night flying. Although the aircraft has an excellent landing light system, the night environment is still difficult. This is especially so when ambient light is nil. Loss of reference and disorientation near the ground, even on a good VFR night, is a real risk when flying helicopters. By starting my training after dark and in an unfamiliar helicopter both the nature of the risk and ways to mitigate became clearer. Knowing that personal helicopter flying is statistically vastly more dangerous than flying as a pro, convinced me that learning something about the production world would be valuable. And that's part of what Mike brings. Not only does he fly production missions every day, the missions he flies often are tough, at night or in bad weather.

The next day, we practice more pick-ups and set-downs. Daylight helps. My tendency to over control on the cyclic ceased, in large part due to the better field of view.

The 206 is honest in its responses and smooth in flight. The only source of vibration is aerodynamic buffeting, which occurs at around 100 knots, maximum autorotation speed, also referred to as blue line. This is typical of many helicopters, especially those with a teeter hinge design. We never reached anywhere near red line, 130 knots, but it was clear that operating much beyond the 100-knot blue line speed was not the place to be for a smooth ride.

We did pretty much every maneuver on the FAA Helicopter Practical Test including quick stops, hover auto rotations, jammed anti-torque pedals, failed hydraulics and failed approach to a run-on landing. Unlike the Robinson aircraft, the R22 in particular, hover autorotations are a pleasure in the 206 because of the high mass rotor system. We didn't try it, but Mike claims there is enough energy in the blade system to set the helicopter down, pick it up, and then set it down again without power. Hm!

Unlike the Bell school, Lunsford doesn't have their civilian students practice *full down* autorotations, where the pilot flies the helicopter all the way to the ground without power. Most schools don't. Instead, their focus is on flying the speeds correctly, using collective to adjust glide angle, and hitting the spot. At the end Mike would bring the power in to facilitate recovery into a hover.

According to Mike, Bell's program is somewhat rigged in that they use a special level hard-packed turf and super-smooth runway for full down practices. This mitigates for accidental sideways landings where the skids might catch on a rough runway surface causing a dynamic upset. It also saves wear and tear on the skid shoes if the touchdown turns into a run-on landing with some forward speed.

Acknowledging the risk-lowering benefits of power recovery, there are still ways to get into trouble. During the third day of training, while practicing straight-in autorotations I found myself in a situation where the forward speed needed to flare had deteriorated. I compensated by pitching the helicopter up further to arrest the descent, but before stopping forward movement and leveling the ship a significant descent developed. In response, I pulled up on the collective, but it was too late. The descent continued. The instinct is to keep pulling, but Mike stopped me before the ship exceeded torque limitations—100 percent for 5 minutes and 110 percent, unintended, for 5 seconds. The next thing that happened was a big bounce triggered by the two rear-skid DART Aerospace Bearpaws abruptly contacting the turf surface. Normally used to help stabilize the helicopter when landing in deep snow, they left quite a large divot behind.

The subsequent inspection revealed no damage (except to the lawn), but my hard landing was a good lesson beyond just wanting enough kinetic energy to complete the flare properly. The JetRanger is easy to over-torque, with the end result likely damage to the transmission. And this is not just when practicing autorotations. Care must be taken when arresting rapid descents during approach to landing, or when attempting to fly out of down drafts like those typical of mountain ridges, especially true when the ship is heavy. Descent rates should be stabilized to no more than 300 ft/min at no lower than 300 ft AGL.

I asked Mike about the history of successful autorotations following a real engine failure or one of the other system problems like a malfunctioning tail rotor that necessitates depowering the main rotor to maintain control. Most actual emergencies like this end in a crash, or at least with damage to the ship. But often the crew and passengers survive, a tribute to the captain in Mike's view, despite the bent metal. There are, of course, lots of variables including at what point in the flight regime the failure occurs, how high, and over what type of terrain. Mike's point simply is that to the extent the ship is undamaged, all riding aboard will be safe, "and that's what we teach and strive for."

There has been a lot of discussion about loss of tail rotor effectiveness (LTE) in helicopters in general and the 206 in particular. LTE is dangerous because what comes with it is a sudden loss of yaw control followed by a rapid rotation of the helicopter's fuselage around the main rotor mast. Scary! Early variants of the aircraft were equipped with smaller 62-inch tail rotors, sometimes causing the pilot to lose yaw control when subjecting the helicopter to high torque or turbulent flow over the tail rotor. Unfortunately, the larger 65-inch tail rotor used in our ship doesn't completely solve the problem, according to Mike. Good technique remains a must. In general, a landing approach conducted below ETL airspeeds, about 25 knots in the 206—the helicopter operating in the turbulence of its own rotor vortices, with the wind coming from the six to ten o'clock position—is to be avoided. Sudden and dramatic yaw excursions may be experienced, requiring rapid control inputs to recover. And the wind can be unpredictable, so as a general rule Lunsford recommends approaches in which the transition to a hover, operating in ground effect, occurs roughly coincident with falling-below-ETL speeds.

But sometimes the landing area does not allow for this more conservative landing technique. Confined area operations may be required by mission or circumstance. This is what we see on television when the helicopter sets down in a clearing in the woods or on a road surrounded by wires, vehicles, and other obstructions.

We practiced confined area landings and takeoffs in the JetRanger. The turboshaft engine's power and reliability facilitate unlimited climb-outs, especially at lower altitudes. Even with the ship loaded to 3,200 pounds MGTOW, there is plenty of reserve available. But LTE is still an issue, so confined area landings and takeoffs should be conducted into the wind when possible—indicators of wind direction include smoke, flags, waves, moored boats in the summer, and blowing snow in the winter. Of greater concern is engine failure during confined area operations. There may not be enough energy stored in the rotating blade system to make a safe landing even if an autorotation is conducted perfectly. This is because for a gentle landing most helicopter designs depend both on potential energy, derived from altitude, and kinetic energy from forward speed along with the main rotor's own kinetic energy. If flying low, below 500 feet AGL, with no forward speed, the touchdown is likely to be abrupt to say the least, however well-trained the pilot. Most helicopters come with a height-velocity diagram that makes it easy to determine the various combinations of airspeeds and altitude that prevent a safe autorotation. What is apparent is that putting a helicopter to its best use often demands flying in these danger zones. Vertical takeoffs, landings, and hovers in the range of 20 to 500 feet in many cases come with the risk of a crash should there be an engine failure or other malfunction requiring an autorotation.

Mike demonstrated an interesting technique to address the challenge of operating in a confined area on a hot day, heavy, and at a high altitude. The goal was to reach ETL prior to climbing out of a hover, thereby achieving greater lift and hence performance. But how can this be done? The answer is that if the confined area has a diameter equal to 800 feet or more there is normally enough space for the pilot to reach ETL by circling the periphery of the space in ground effect. Upon reaching ETL, achieving improved aerodynamic efficiency, the pilot can then climb the helicopter out following the circular path. The technique doesn't work when the confined area is very small. And the approved flight manual doesn't include this in the performance charts.

I practiced the technique several times. On the first attempt I had the ship properly circling left, but became fixated by the proximity of trees to the right, so I was too slow to reach ETL. The next try was better. Still, the required bank angle and speed made me uncomfortable. I recall feeling grateful to have escaped the confines of that small space, and determined that for future missions I would avoid hot and heavy departures without a long run straight ahead.

Then there is settling with power, also known as vortex ring state (VRS). This peril has the helicopter rapidly descending in the turbulence of its own rotor wake, usually with low or no forward airspeed. A following wind can make matters worse. Curiously, adding more power only increases the downward acceleration of the air below, with the helicopter soon following. The only way out is to fly out of the turbulence somehow.

The conventional approach to VRS counsels pitching the helicopter forward, the idea being to fly into clear air straight ahead. More recently, the schools have begun to teach Vuichard recovery, named after the inventor-pilot Claud Vuichard. In the JetRanger, because the tail rotor is mounted on the left side, with the main rotor rotating right to left, the maneuver involves banking the ship to the right while also applying power pedal (the left pedal) in rapid fashion. The result is an immediate exit to the right, out of the turbulence. In helicopters manufactured by Eurocopter and Airbus, with the main rotor turning from left to right, the technique is to bank left, instead. Either way, the helicopter exits the downward-moving air.

Settling with power is not just academic. It has led to a lot of crashes. One of the more notable involved the loss of the lead helicopter used in the attack on Osama Bin Laden, then hiding in Pakistan. Caught in a hovering descent, the helicopter hit one of the perimeter walls of the compound where the Al Qaeda leader had been in hiding, and broke apart.

Mike's teaching method is very much about applying principles in a practical way. We didn't operate with the doors off, for example, as helicopters often do on television, for photographic and certain extraction missions, but we did discuss both speed and CG limitations of these operations. The JetRanger is unusual in that, doors-off, the maximum speed is dramatically reduced, to 69 knots with the front doors off and 87 knots with only the rear doors removed. Mike emphasized the importance of obeying the speed limits. Failure to do so can cause the 206 to experience cyclic reversal, in which airflow over the horizontal stabilizer is disturbed, making the ship more difficult to control. Note: name aside, there is no actual reversal. A negative static stability develops requiring increasing amounts of aft cyclic to remain stable at higher airspeeds.

There is also the issue of mast bumping, inherent in many Bell designs. Unloading the rotor system (pushing overly aggressively with the cyclic) can lead to unpredictable main rotor blade excursions, resulting in serious damage to the transmission assembly, and in extreme cases a failure of the mast and main underslung hinge. Unlike rigid blade systems, in which stability is largely independent of loading, the 206 teeter design requires a positive-G at all times. According to Mike, many Bell design aircraft, including some military versions, have been lost as a consequence of these radical push-over maneuvers.

One of the coolest things we practiced was a "landing at own risk" approach to the airport. Sounds dangerous, but the maneuver is mostly about navigating a random course to non-movement areas like FBO aprons, where aircraft are parked and controllers don't have jurisdiction. Helicopters are treated like fixed-wing aircraft in many ways, but there are differences. VFR minimums are lower, clear of clouds being the rule in most cases. More interesting and thrilling, especially at night, is the way helicopters are allowed to traverse the airport environment on the way to the ramp. In the case of Burlington, where we did most of our terminal work, a land at your own risk clearance is usually issued, which, translated, means it is up to the pilot to determine appropriate navigation over the airport environment to the landing spot—no runways or taxiways needed. There are some rules. First, it is considered bad form to fly over other aircraft operating on the field. I once got yelled at for a slow flyby over a squadron of parked F-16s. Fun, but probably not prudent given the risk of foreign object damage (FOD) to the military jet's single turbojet engine, from debris on the ground stirred up by the rotor's downwash. Curiously, making a close approach in front or behind other aircraft is generally considered okay, and it affords a great view. Second on the list, it is typical to inform the controller of any unusual maneuvers expected in due course. A good example would be a sudden course reversal to facilitate an approach into the wind on the way to the landing spot. Although the "own risk" part of the clearance is really about placing the burden of safe navigation on the pilot, controllers don't like being surprised by something truly erratic.

Some instructors (and examiners) dislike clearances away from runways and taxiways because of the potential exposure to the dangerous part of the height-velocity diagram, with no way to perform a safe autorotation. And, independent of an engine failure or similar problem, there are good reasons to use runways, for example when circumstances call for an instrument approach. Usually, though, it's possible to go straight to parking while maintaining proper height and appropriate forward kinetic energy.

Shut down of the 206 is straightforward. The checklist is 1) slowly throttle to idle, 2) wait two minutes, and 3) radios off, throttle to off, generator off. The two-minute cool down period is to prevent coking, which can adversely affect bearings in the turbine section of the engine.

There is a rotor brake mounted on the ceiling that can be engaged at between 38 percent and 30 percent rotor rpm. It is very effective, providing the pilot pulls steadily on the handle. Pumping is not recommended. Once the rotor has stopped, the master switch is turned off.

The entire training typically runs four full days, but we finished in three plus the first night. There is no allocated time limit. According to Mike, when the student is proficient, the training is done. I had twelve 206 hours recorded in my log book, and received my official JetRanger 206B graduation certificate from Lunsford Air Consulting. Following an additional eight hours of supervised operation experience with my local helicopter instructor, I was approved by the underwriter to serve as captain.

The celebration was somewhat muted, however, when shortly after checkout I learned what it would cost to insure the aircraft. The premium would approach $45,000 a year. With fewer than 100 hours total time in helicopters, and almost none in type, there was little room for negotiation.

Putting the matter in perspective, $1 million of liability plus $1 million of hull for the JetRanger equals a premium slightly less than twice the amount paid to underwrite all of us flying the CJ3 jet airplane, and with $50 million smooth, in other words 50 times the liability coverage offered on the helicopter. The broker explained: the actuaries expect helicopter pilots with fewer than 200 hours of experience to crash at some point, a tidbit I elected not to share with my passengers. Sobering!

As for the 206, it is an honest aircraft that does a lot of things well. It is versatile, having served in both military and civilian capacities for many years, and performed scouting, police ops, corporate, rescue and a host of other roles.

Bell recently ended production of the venerable aircraft, to be replaced by the new design 505 JetRanger. No doubt the 505 will be more modern and cost effective, but I doubt it will be so well remembered. As for training, Mike will be back next year to help me polish my skills. He promised to bring his night vision goggles. Who knows? Perhaps helicopter night attack and SWAT will be my next endorsement.

### Lessons learned:

**Lesson 1:** Learning how to fly helicopters is hard; harder for older fixed-wing pilots. Giving up, however, is not an option.

**Lesson 2:** Avoid landing with a tailwind, or hovering above 20 feet with the wind coming from the aft right quarter. Also, avoid descent rates greater than 300 feet per minute when near the ground.

**Lesson 3:** Be careful operating at high altitudes, especially in a hover, with loss of tail rotor effectiveness more likely due to low air density.

**Lesson 4:** Fly light whenever possible.

**Lesson 5:** Obtain recurrent training on a regular basis, preferably with an instructor who has experience operating in commercial or professional operations: lifting skiers to mountain summits, logging lumber, setting towers, emergency medical services transport, law enforcement.

**Lesson 6:** Avoid flying over other aircraft when operating in the airport environment.

**Lesson 7:** Practice autorotations only with a qualified flight instructor on board.

**Lesson 8:** Be very, very careful to avoid wires and other ground obstructions. They can be hard to see. Hitting wires is one of the leading causes of helicopter crashes.

# 20 Maintenance Strategies

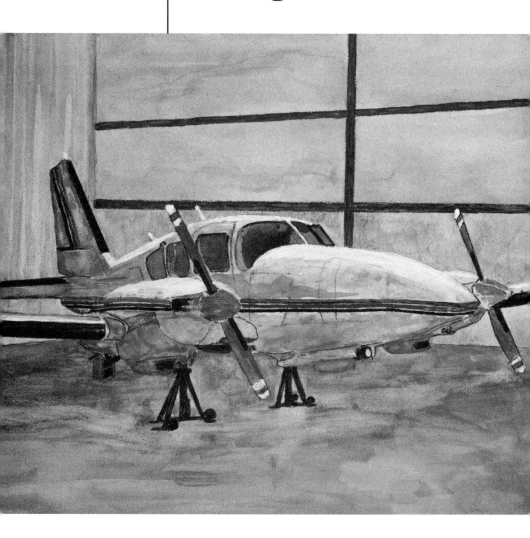

W hen your car breaks down on the side of the road, that's a bad day. To start, you are stranded, at least temporarily. If there is an appointment in your diary, you will probably miss it. Looking on the bright side, you are safe, and the vehicle is, too, though perhaps in need of repair. All in all, a car malfunction is an inconvenience, but in most cases not life threatening.

When an aircraft breaks down—on takeoff, enroute thousands of feet above the ground, or during landing—what then? It's not as if you can pull over and phone AAA. A lot depends on what breaks. Highest on the list of worrisome mechanical problems is anything affecting propulsion, including an engine failure or fire. Fire is worse than failure because along with the potential loss of ability to stay aloft, the aircraft also is on fire, with a combustible—let's say explosive—fuel source perhaps only inches from the flame. There is the potential loss of control due to heat-related shorting of wires and other electrical systems. So in addition to the risk of explosion from the fuel, there is risk of explosion from loss of control—key structural components being overstressed and failing. It's debatable whether it would be better to blow up in the air or on the ground following an uncontrolled impact. Even if the aircraft were to remain controllable, there likely would be smoke in the passenger cabin, making it difficult to breathe, or see. In the cockpit, the pilots would be confronting the same challenges as the passengers, while trying to keep the aircraft flying, working through a myriad of emergency procedures in the hope the aircraft and all aboard can be brought home safely. Daunting! For this reason, airplane engines of all types and designs receive extraordinary attention. There are rigorous maintenance schedules even for the smallest airplane engine. The result: there are almost no engine failures or fires in the modern aircraft fleet.

But not all fires start in an engine. On September 2, 1998, near Halifax International Airport, a Swissair McDonnell Douglas MD-11 en route from New York City to Geneva experienced an electrical fire in its passenger entertainment system—the system that operates the screens on the seat-backs, personal TVs that play sitcom reruns and second-tier movies.[1] The crew depowered the aft passenger cabin electrics, including the entertainment system, but too late. The ceiling insulation around the system, and other combustibles, were ablaze. Further, disabling the electrical power to the cabin turned off the ceiling circulating fans, creating a vacuum that directed the fire to the cockpit, damaging critical systems including the autopilot. The fire spread to the right engine, which had to be shut down by the copilot. The crew fought the flames, while also attempting to reach safe harbor; the captain even left his seat in an attempt to extinguish the flames lapping at the cockpit door. Only 16 minutes from the moment smoke was detected, the aircraft plunged into the sea at 345 mph, killing all 229 passengers and crew.

There were many lessons learned from this accident, starting with emphasizing the urgent priority of getting on the ground as quickly as possible, should there be a fire in flight. The Swissair procedures had the crew dumping fuel to reach an acceptable maximum landing weight, a time-consuming procedure. Crews are now taught to land immediately, in some cases even when a suitable airport not available. There are also new rules governing the materials that can be used in aircraft construction, based on their fire-promoting, or fire-retardant, qualities. Still, how could a short in some wiring take out a giant MD-11?

One consideration is that while all systems may not be created equal in purpose or efficacy, all theoretically present a danger, even the seemingly superficial ones like entertainment. They must be designed, maintained, and operated recognizing that, like turbofan engines that go off the rails, the consequences of any system failure can be very bad.

Say your television blows up. Worst case it calls for a simple evacuation out the door and a call to the fire department. Not so in an aircraft, where it can be a relatively long time to a safe landing. In aircraft, *zero defect* is the target. All systems, no matter their purpose or redundancy, must be working and maintained to the highest level.

But is zero defect practical, or even possible? The answer is it depends. When it comes to larger aircraft like the MD-11, there are almost no flights conducted with absolutely everything installed functioning perfectly. Fortunately, the problems are usually minor—a failed passenger reading light or a part of the air conditioning system not working. Sometimes bigger

---

[1] Swissair Flight 111

things break, like an auxiliary power unit (APU) used to start the turbofan engines and provide back-up electrical power to the aircraft. In this case, the engines may have to be started with a special kind of ground power unit (GPU) and both engine-driven generators must be operational. Use of an approved minimum equipment list (MEL) allows crews to defer maintenance on the APU and certain other systems, providing sufficient redundancy is preserved. The idea is that even when there are known defects in systems and subsystems, because the aircraft is designed to operate that way, the aircraft is also, by definition, defect free.

In the case of non-turbine powered smaller airplanes, weighing less than 12,500 pounds and operating under Part 91, there really isn't a true FAA-governed MEL beyond minimum instrumentation/equipment needed to fly in good and bad weather and certain air spaces. Yes, both engines must be working to fly a twin-engine aircraft, and by law all FAA Airworthiness Directives and mandatory service bulletins issued by the manufacturer must be addressed, but beyond that there is much variability among aircraft in both the reliability of the equipment and the aircraft's true flight readiness status. Here, in conference with maintenance, it is up to the operator and/or pilot to make the call. And here is where it is determined, depending on the call, whether the flight will be routine or over-the-top scary.

The scariest flights tend to be in airplanes with little or no maintenance history. Ferry fights like the one described in Chapter 6 often fall into this category, because while the pilot may be well versed in the type, he or she doesn't necessarily know the individual aircraft. Studying the maintenance logbook helps, but sometimes the true story is hidden, often to grease the skids on the sale. So it was when I bought our Cessna Skywagon C-180. The logs looked great, but then about three-quarters of the way home the transponder quit—and while flying IFR in IMC over Baltimore. The failed transponder by itself wouldn't have been so bad, but shortly afterwards the single VOR receiver in the airplane failed, too. This meant we would need ATC's vectors to get to better weather, and those vectors would have to be based on a primary target radar signature—no squawking code, no altitude information, in the busy airspace of Washington, Baltimore, and Philadelphia. It took an agonizingly long ten minutes of flying various assigned headings before ATC could make a positive identification. Later I learned that the transponder, a Mode C unit and relatively sophisticated for the time, had a history of problems not revealed during the purchase negotiation. The VOR was a mystery. Because the previous owner flew the airplane only on nice days, it is highly likely he never turned it on.

*Proud new C-180 owner.*

Next on the list of potentially scary aircraft are rentals, including those used by schools. While school fleets and rental aircraft can in general be well maintained, there are lots of opportunities for problems. It is helpful to insist on reviewing the aircrafts's formal squawk sheet. This is different from the maintenance logs, which are hard to obtain on short notice and sometimes difficult to interpret without a trained mechanic. Squawk sheets should be readily accessible, with most entries made by the pilots while flying the aircraft. They're easier to understand and more real time in nature.

Any rental airplane flown by multiple pilots should have a formal squawk sheet. While their primary purpose is to record defects observed during flight for later maintenance, each individual pilot flying the airplane should review the previous squawks. While there may not be anything that would render the aircraft unairworthy, active squawks can provide insight into work-arounds that may make the flight go more smoothly. For example, knowing in advance that the number one NAV/COM radio is only working intermittently, the prudent path may be to conduct all instrument approaches with the number two radio as the primary navigation source. This makes it less likely that somewhere in the middle of the approach there will be a need to switch sources, in the event of a complete malfunction of the number one radio.

Unfortunately, squawk sheets on their own don't guarantee a defect-free airplane. Yet that is what we wish for, especially when tackling a tough mission or when flying older designs, that may lack the robustness and redundancy we take for granted in more modern equipment. Warbirds, especially those that emerged during and after World War II, can be a notable challenge to make mechanically safe because they tend to have complex, state of the art for the time, systems. It was war, and it was not entirely clear, at least in the beginning, that the good guys would win. The design priority, therefore, was performance and capability, not safety. A combination of thin safety factors and multiple critical systems that, in some cases had to work perfectly for the entirety of the flight for the aircraft to survive, made piloting these aircraft quite heroic. The P-51 Mustang is one example. It was a marvel for the time, but it came with problems. The combination of its single Allison turbocharged water-cooled engine and its cooling system, with plumbing that stretched from the nose to mid-ship, with the radiator mounted just behind a large intake scoop on the belly, made it notoriously vulnerable to leaks caused by enemy fire or even just normal operational stresses. A breach of the coolant containment meant engine overheat, shortly followed by engine failure; the difference between normal operation and a serious problem was only about 10°C. Engine failure almost always led to bailout: a scary and awkward enterprise requiring the pilot to open the canopy manually, release his belts, and jump out the right side of the aircraft hoping to avoid being hit by the tail.

Now imagine maintaining an aircraft like this sixty years after its invention. Assuming there are spare parts to be had, making the airplane at least as safe as it was during the war implies a monumental investment in maintenance. And since the odd crash is socially unacceptable these days, the maintenance has to be much better. Owning and flying a warbird like the P-51 is a commitment.

Airplanes like the P-51 and other advanced fighters from that time are posterchildren, or *posterplanes*, for conservative aircraft maintenance and flight operations. Even given a perfect specimen, design standards for everything from handling characteristics to engine life were less demanding then than they are today—more a reflection of the science and technology of the time than a lack of ambition.

Fortunately, legacy military aircraft almost always come with detailed maintenance and training instructions. In the case of military operations (Mil-Ops), everything was systematized, nothing left to the imagination. Unfortunately, maintenance documentation also was fairly high level, not covering parts typically supplied or repaired. By the time the modern-day curators of these airplanes started looking for spare parts or guidance in making repairs, original manufacturers were out of business, or simply not able to produce or support the parts needed. Worst case, you make your own parts. Hard!

There are ways to get around this. One is to avoid the old-part search and maintenance challenge entirely by substituting a new and better part. Our 1944 Widgeon G-44 flying boat, for example, was outfitted with two new-technology O-470 Continental engines in 1956—the year I was born, incidentally. Those engines replaced the original 200-hp Rangers that came with my airplane. Known as the McDermott conversion, the Continentals solved several problems, the foremost being that the old engines didn't have enough power to fly the airplane should one engine quit. The new engines also were a lot easier to maintain. All in all, the new engines proved to be more powerful, reliable, and efficient. And admitting an upgrade to the 260-hp IO-470 engine design in the 60s (when I was a little kid), even after all these years parts are still available new from the manufacturer.

Much the same has happened with avionics. Most old steam-gauge-looking panels are being replaced with modern electronic flight instrumentation systems (EFIS), graphic engine monitors (GEM), and GPS navigators connected to modern fancy autopilots. The old instrument designs were notoriously hard to keep running and also prone to failure, even in their day.

There is, of course, the inevitable battle between those who want everything authentic, and those who want a reliable flying machine. I chose the hybrid, modern systems installed in the old design aircraft. Retro is the new reliable and fun. When authenticity is the priority, much care is needed to make sure "old" is still serviceable; more often than not, failure of an important part, usually in flight, will be the test.

The caliber of the talent doing the maintenance is a factor, especially for older aircraft; maintenance procedures weren't always spelled out in the service manual. Unlike modern aircraft, beneficiaries of a maintenance steering group and task oriented approach, with directions for troubleshooting and appropriate repairs clearly documented, older aircraft require a mechanic with sleuthing skills. Often the correct diagnosis depends on experience. A good repair requires knowledge of legacy maintenance procedures not necessarily documented or taught in school. Our Aztec had a landing gear retraction problem that escaped diagnosis for years. An unsafe light would come on in flight, about an hour after gear retraction, indicating one or more of the wheels were partially extended. Unfortunately, because

all three wheels shared only one gear unsafe light, it was impossible to identify which was the offending wheel, leaving us to perform a series of retraction tests, with the airplane jacked up, none of which showed any sign of
malfunction. Through the long investigation the gear never failed to extend
prior to landing, though the possibility was always at the back of my mind.
Of more immediate concern was the mounting cost of trying to sort out the
problem—new valve components, new actuator seals, and lots of repeated
testing, with many different mechanics from many different companies.

The Aztec had a very clever landing gear system for its time, in that it
was completely hydraulic with no electronics except for the gear position
sensors indicating gear position. To complete the gear up or down sequence
successfully, a bunch of special valves in an integrated component known
as the powerpack must operate in just the right sequence. The sequence,
remarkably, is triggered by a single panel-mounted gear handle, really just
a pilot operated valve, positioned up or down to retract or extend the gear.
Assuming sufficient hydraulic pressure and hydraulic fluid, no other systems or interventions are involved.

The downside of a system that is mechanical and autonomous, is that
problems are difficult to diagnose. Unlike modern systems, with computers
that produce error codes that point precisely to the root cause, old systems
require a mechanic's insight into the original designer's thinking. So it was
with the Aztec's errant gear system.

Through a fortuitous set of circumstances, the Aztec gear mystery was
eventually solved. Heritage Flight's maintenance manager, Jim Proft, got
personally involved.[2] Old-school in training and experience, he put the airplane up on jacks, with the wheels retracted, and with pressure sensors at
all actuator junctions. The airplane sat for days in the maintenance hangar,
as we all waited for the gear to extend spontaneously. Nothing. Then, on
one exceptionally cold Vermont day, the hangar door was left open for a
period of time, long enough for hangar and contents to cool. Suddenly the
gear extended, pressures falling. The problem was temperature related.

While Jim didn't initially guess temperature as a causal factor, his exper-
imental method set the stage for the clue to make its appearance. Then it
was on to the root cause, perhaps a failed O-ring somewhere in the system
(remember it was a failed O-ring that doomed the space shuttle Challenger).
Ultimately, the problem was traced to an anti-retraction switch, its function
to prevent accidental gear retraction on the ground. Switch is a misnomer:

---

[2] Heritage Flight, FBO based at the Burlington International Airport, circa 2006.

in the Aztec the component is more like a special valve that mechanically remains open as long as there is weight on the wheels to prevent pressure build-up on the retraction side of the actuators. In flight, with falling temperatures, the valve would leak fluid. And because there are no uplocks in the Aztec, the gear would eventually fall. New O-rings installed, problem solved—only eighteen months after the first report of symptoms. Accolades are deserved by Jim, a true renaissance contributor, whom we later hired as our full time mechanic for the company airplanes and my personal vintage fleet.

Aviation maintenance has changed over the last twenty years. The aircraft systems employed now are so proprietary that it is nearly impossible to identify a problem without the real time diagnostic software that is integrated into the aircraft, along with the many diagnostic tools outside to analyze the data that is produced, all with company service headquarters to lead the way. It's a different approach, and one that is becoming more prevalent with most technologies. Rhetorical question: assuming you have the credentials of a competent mechanic, would you be able to maintain your post-2000 model year car in your home garage using conventional tools? Likely not, unless you have access to the dealer's computerized diagnostic system. Same is true with modern aircraft.

Some of it is about defensive engineering and the burden of liability and risk. The manufacturers want to be sure that in case of a crash, their airplane wasn't at fault when it was really the mechanic who installed the engine intake tube without a proper gasket. But it is more about the systemization of aviation and of aircraft. Systemization has many advantages, mostly because it allows greater automation. But its inherent complexity makes it difficult to identify and solve problems without the help of other complex diagnostic systems, internal monitoring, external computers and software, all needed in the mix. This is an ongoing and increasing challenge for both pilots and mechanics, as the question "What the heck does that code mean?" increasingly becomes part of the lexicon.

And then there are helicopters, a special breed of aircraft. If ever there were a case for having active real-time computer-based diagnostics, it would be helicopters. Many modern turbine-powered helicopters, like their turbojet powered fixed-wing brethren, employ this technology. But older models often don't. So much depends on reducing the chances of failure to begin with, especially for parts like blades, hub systems (the connecting assembly for the control system and the main blades), and straps in some designs where there is no redundancy.

Typical of all helicopter designs is the concept of component life limitations. Many helicopter components have an age limit that, once surpassed, renders the component unusable—scrap. Often this is based on total hours of operation; in some cases it is measured in time, expressed in terms of calendar months. Airplanes have life limited parts, too, but far fewer, mostly relegated to the propulsion and landing gear systems.

Even with a very conservative approach to the life-limited part philosophy, failures occur. And in helicopters, a failure can be a real problem. It's interesting to note that about 90 percent of the emergency checklist items in our JetRanger helicopter end with the instruction "Land As Soon As Possible." Translated, the circumstances are dire: land now! So what to do?

Earlier helicopter designs, without fancy FADEC engine systems, vibration sensors, and a host of other diagnostic data collection devices, depend on the pilot for early detection of a problem. The same applies to lower-cost, relatively modern helicopters like the Robinson 22 and 44 models. Abnormal vibrations, in particular, are early signs that something might be amiss. Temperature fluctuations in engine or transmission components, fluid leaks or popped filter bypasses, also demand attention. All this requires close communication between the pilots flying and the maintenance people fixing. And the pilots need to be honest, especially when the cause of the maintenance issue is something they did, such as over torquing the transmission. Optimally, there is a maintenance team that works directly with pilots, and each flight produces a detailed report of any aircraft anomalies observed. Can helicopters be flown safely without a closely-connected proprietary maintenance team? The answer is, theoretically, yes, but with the caveat that third party maintenance must be receptive to routine and formalized communication with the pilots who fly the aircraft. Still, the proprietary maintenance team is more likely to know the particular helicopter and its history intimately, providing service to it and perhaps a few other aircraft in the fleet on a regular basis, while the third party, no matter how good, may be servicing many different aircraft with varying histories flown by lots of pilots.

Assuming proactive and fully engaged maintenance is available, are there any other enhancements to reliability and safety available to the fixed-wing or rotorcraft owner/operator? High on the list is addressing all cosmetic issues, in addition to any that affect reliability, performance, and safety. This may seem counterintuitive, because the quality of the exterior paint or wear and tear in the interior really should have nothing to do with airworthiness, safety, or reliability. But psychology is in play. Achieving zero defect mechanical performance implies that all contributors connected to the operation, including owners, pilots, maintenance staff, and dispatchers, share a common vision. The risk in distinguishing between airworthiness essentials and non-airworthiness issues, like broken cabin paneling or torn seat covers, is that zero defect becomes subjective. Even in helicopters, there are mechanical problems that can be deferred for a period of time. Should they be? No! And not because there is any real danger. It is about instilling the attitude, shared by all involved, that everything must be as close to perfect as possible all the time. This approach is especially effective when new members join the team. They look around, perhaps not immediately seeing everything underlying, but realizing this is a culture that strives for zero defect at every level. With this insight, an almost complete understanding of how to succeed in the organization is achieved. While perfect should not be the enemy of the good, good can always be better—and that's the right attitude when it comes to making flying safe.

If all else fails, and assuming the pilot and client are the same, it may be helpful to remind maintenance that killing the client is bad for business. Remember, don't kill the client! Very effective, in my experience.

### Lessons learned:

**Lesson 1:** Nonessential systems (e.g., entertainment systems) can kill you if not properly designed and maintained.

**Lesson 2:** There is no such thing as a zero defect policy that allows for defects, even cosmetic ones.

**Lesson 3:** Old design and new design aircraft demand a different set of maintenance talent skills. There are few who can bridge the gap.

# Zero Hour:
## Food Poisoning and Other Improbable Crew Incapacitating Emergencies

# 21

**P**ut yourself in this man's place. Aboard a transcontinental plane when suddenly half the passengers including your own son are struck by a paralyzing deadly illness. And then in the midst of the panic and confusion the stewardess tells you to come forward to the pilot's compartment. This is what you find: a pilot-less plane running wild in a stormy sky.

"Can you fly this airplane, and land it?" The physician on board asks.

"No, not a chance," the former fighter pilot replies. The physician fires back, "You're the only chance we've got."

How could he fly a plane again, after the horrible experience that had sapped his courage and ruined his life? But only he, among all the passengers, had any chance at all to save them, even though it was one in a thousand.

So goes the trailer for the 1957 suspense thriller *Zero Hour*, with Dana Andrews, about a group of airline passengers trapped on board an airplane with a crew and half the passengers fallen ill from food poisoning—an innocent halibut dinner—and no one left to fly the airplane.

I saw this movie for the first time when I was about ten years old. It was one of the Saturday afternoon reruns on television. Long out of the theaters, it still had lots of cache. Romance, drama, suspense, derring-do, and a bit of rescuing. What's more fun than that? For me the story also offered something else: the enduring fantasy that, given the same circumstances, I could be that Dana Andrews character, the only person on board capable of bringing the giant radial piston engine-powered Douglas DC-4 in for a safe landing. It didn't matter that I had no flying skills whatsoever, or that I hadn't actually flown in an airplane, yet. These were details. They would not deter me, or get in the way of a good story.

Much later, after obtaining private and commercial pilot licenses, and allowed to fly small single engine airplanes, my fantasy transferred to jets, as I was a frequent passenger on flights from the US to Europe or elsewhere while managing our life science technology business. Here the goal seemed a little more obtainable, given that I already knew how to fly small airplanes. Flying big airplanes, I thought, how much harder can it be? I went so far as to contemplate the frequent flyer bonus miles I would surely be awarded for successfully landing the Boeing 747 unaided. I had witty remarks at the ready for the late night talk show hosts.

Host: Did you get extra miles for landing the plane?

Me: Well, actually, yes. You get the regular miles plus a million more for upgrading to captain.

*Cue the laughs.*

As it turns out, my fantasy is shared by a lot of people, and a lot of pilots. Having interviewed both pilots and non-pilots, the common element seems to be a desire to rise to the occasion and then be recognized for doing so. Of course, we who dream of displaying flying prowess and courage under fire tend not to consider the negative consequences should things not play out as imagined. There is absolutely the possibility that the fantasy in reality ends in total disaster, with the aircraft lost, all on board perished. Every fantasy has a dark side!

So is it realistic to assume a passenger can land the plane? A lot depends on the skill set of the individual, the nature of the aircraft, its condition, the weather, and the capability of the airport facility available. A complex, large, and damaged aircraft, one of the two engines failed, bad weather, short runways, a flying neophyte at the controls: the chances are not good. A private pilot rated to fly single-engine airplanes, a fully functioning light twin, a nice day, a familiar airport with long runways nearby: it seems reasonable to anticipate a successful outcome.

The *Zero Hour* plot has never unfolded on a commercial flight. Crewmembers have been incapacitated, and some have died, en route, but never in groups of two, both captain and first officer. Even when other crewmembers (and on rare occasions, a passenger) have stepped in to help, there was always one flying pilot remaining, fully capable of landing the airplane independently.

In the general aviation world, on smaller airplanes, there have been save-the-day scenarios with passengers taking over. Often the passengers are, or were, pilots, but not always. Most of the time, the outcome is good, everyone safe, although the airplanes themselves may not fare as well. Sadly, the affected crewmember may not fare well either, though usually it is a health-related problem, something other than the passenger's rough landing.

Common factors of good outcomes include good weather, and an airplane that is mechanically sound. There is usually someone, a pilot or instructor, to provide advice and guidance over the radio. This doesn't mean there haven't been passengers asked to fly planes in bad weather, without guidance, while experiencing mechanical problems. It's just that there isn't a lot of evidence, possibly because no one lived to tell the tale.

One thing is certain, the fancy autopilots in many of today's aircraft won't save the day on their own. This is especially true for modern transport category aircraft with automation that is highly integrated into almost every system. Autopilots in older aircraft aren't much better, requiring quirky inputs performed in just the right way for the plane to fly. A passenger-pilot would have to master some aspects of the autopilot to have any chance of survival. Even then, few autopilots can land an airplane, fly it all the way to the ground, by themselves. So, at some point the passenger-pilot would need to take over the controls and manually make the landing. All of this is largely true for business jet aircraft, in which the operational environment is the same or worse, the systems equally complex.

## The setup

As a thought experiment, I have applied the passenger-pilot scenario to our Citation Jet 4 airplane. While unlikely, incapacitation of all flying crew members on the CJ4 is more probable than on a commercial airline because we do on occasion fly the airplane single pilot. (The CJ4 is certified for a crew of one or two.) It's a good test of the idea because the airplane's Collins Proline 21 avionics are almost identical in function and operation to those found in large modern jet airliners. Many regional jets including the Bombardier RJ series use the Collins. Collins is employed on the Boeing 787 for most flight deck functions. Some 757 and 767 aircraft have been retrofitted with Collins as well.

As in the film, our crew incapacitation event would happen up high, during cruise. In the CJ4 this would mean really high, perhaps 43,000 or even 45,000 feet, typical altitudes when traveling long distances. The autopilot would be engaged tracking a prescribed course of geographical fixes or waypoints using an FMS complete with GPS navigator—although the FMS does other things, too. The autopilot's altitude hold mode would be selected, keeping the airplane flying at its assigned altitude.

## How would the passengers know?

It might not be immediately obvious that the crew has succumbed. A kitchen/bar separates the CJ4's cockpit from the passenger cabin. So unless the pilots were unbelted and fell out of their seats, it could take a while before any passengers noticed. On some flights—SOP on commercial airlines—the windowless cockpit door is closed and locked.

## Removing sick crewmembers

When it's finally revealed that the crew is out, not likely to be revived, it becomes clear to the passengers and any unaffected crew members that someone else will have to fly the plane. First, though, they have a weighty problem to solve: how to remove the pilot, or pilots, from their seats. There is no way to fly an airplane without being seated in one of the two cockpit seats. This may seem a straightforward task: 1) stow the seat armrests, 2) unbuckle the pilot or copilot, 3) lift him or her from the seat, 4) carry aft to the passenger cabin. Easy? Not necessarily. To start, it is not easy to lift a person who is unconscious, or dead—a dead weight. It is even harder to dead lift someone seated ahead. Even with all hands helping, it would be a struggle. If the pilot or copilot were heavy, 200 pounds being typical these days due to the hazards of regularly living out of a suitcase, removal may be impossible without causing injury (to those doing the lifting). Of greatest concern is that in the throes of it all, the autopilot is switched off.

There are a number of ways this could happen. It could be as easy as accidentally pushing the red autopilot disconnect button mounted both on the pilot and copilot yokes. There are more autopilot-related buttons just below the glare shield. Included is a button labeled AP that is used to both engage and disengage the autopilot. Push that, and the AP will be disconnected. But accidentally pushing one or more other buttons could do the same, because these govern the source of the autopilot's information. Push the NAV button, for example, and the autopilot will stop tracking the FMS's stored course. Push the ALT button, and the airplane will no longer hold altitude. Just bumping the pilot or copilot yoke in a pronounced way can trigger the autopilot to switch off.

The most likely scenario, though, is that in the process of removing the crewmember, the thrust angle levers—the throttles—get bumped, moved aft, causing engine thrust to be reduced. A lot depends on how much it is reduced by, but anything close to a thrust idle setting means that the airplane would slow and eventually stall, suddenly losing lift. When the plane stalls, the autopilot automatically disconnects.

It's a bit unpredictable what happens next. Safe to say the plane will deviate from its assigned course and altitude. Worse case, the airplane will spin and enter a spiral dive while accelerating toward redline speed. As for the high anxiety felt by the passengers, no doubt it has now been replaced by full-blown raging panic.

While an experienced, well-trained passenger-pilot might be able to save the ship, it's more likely game over, especially if the airplane is operating in IMC. The real lesson is that extreme caution must be taken not to disturb anything while hauling the pilots from their seats, or conducting any other business in or near the cockpit. If the throttles are accidentally moved, be sure to return them to their original position, quickly.

## Who should fly?

Choosing which passenger should do the flying raises interesting questions. On the surface, it would seem the one with flying experience, ideally a licensed pilot. This is probably the right answer in most cases, but it is worth taking a moment to consider that much of the job involves operating a special kind of computer. Someone with general computer skills could be helpful, but more likely to succeed would be someone familiar with automation, controlling complicated systems like those used in energy grids, nuclear power stations, expedition ships, large oil refineries, and, ideally, airplanes. Just knowing how to use a PC isn't enough.

The ideal candidate should also have the ability to listen and understand, to assimilate information. Much of the job of landing an airplane involves taking instructions, and executing them precisely. Without the ability to listen effectively, it is unlikely even a relatively accomplished pilot not schooled in the CJ4 would succeed.

For our thought experiment, let's assume the passenger-pilot looks a little like me when I was making the trips on airliners back and forth across the Atlantic. Although our passenger-pilot has a commercial certificate and is trained to fly small single-engine airplanes in both good and bad weather, he isn't current. Nor has he had any experience flying large transport category aircraft (or business jets), with glass panel EFIS and fancy FMS. Still, he will serve as adjunct captain, the person in charge and the one called upon to manipulate the controls when necessary. For nostalgia's sake, we refer to this passenger pilot as Stryker (Ted Stryker), the Dana Andrews character. We will also assume two other passengers on board, neither of whom have any flying experience. One happens to be a doctor. The other happens to be Stryker's estranged wife, Ellen, played by Linda Darnell in the movie, adding more drama, if there isn't enough already. She helps Stryker run the radios. All this while the doctor attempts to revive the unconscious crew, desperately in need of medical attention. We draft into service the passengers we are given, not the ones we might wish for. As it would be should this entirely improbable emergency transpire. Could they do it?

## Getting help

The first problem would be how to get help. Here, it's assumed the only help would come through the radio, so that's the first thing to figure out. The radio system in the CJ4 is complicated, with multiple frequencies and lots of different source inputs and outputs. Anyone who has struggled with a 1980s vintage hi-fi system would appreciate the challenge.

Assuming the radio/audio panel configuration is unaltered from when the crew was still awake, it might merely be a matter of putting the headsets on and pushing the push-to-talk button mounted on the left side of the captain's yoke or the right side of the copilot's yoke. Be careful, these switches are mounted near the autopilot disconnect switch. Also, they're split switches; both sides must be pressed simultaneously to transmit.

One concern is that by the time the passengers have discovered the state of the crew, the airplane will have sailed by the ATC sector appropriate to the radio frequency selected. The controller, no doubt, has been screaming over the frequency, hoping for a response, but none is forthcoming. Sector distances vary, but for the CJ4 and most jets the time spent talking on one frequency to one controller is no more than about 30 minutes. This is not surprising given that in 30 minutes the CJ4 can cover 220 nautical miles or more.

It's time for Stryker to rise to the occasion. He knows basic radio technique and the nature of the VHF frequency band that is most often used when operating over land. He should know that there is one frequency, 121.5, that is monitored by ATC controllers everywhere, and by many aircraft. It's the emergency frequency. If 121.5 can be successfully entered into the box, the correct transmitter/receiver selected, communication will be established.

Unfortunately, there are a lot of opportunities to fail at this using conventional methods, despite the relatively simple steps needed to accomplish the task. It could be that Ellen dials the right frequency into the FMS or radio control unit (RCU), but inadvertently listens to the wrong radio (there are two, three if the long range HF radio is included). Even assuming best case, having never done it before means it could be a very long process. Some local knowledge could save the day: the CJ4 has a special button on the copilot's side that when pushed automatically tunes Com 1 (the number one radio) to 121.5. But small-airplane pilots unfamiliar with the CJ4 won't know this. A better strategy is to call for help on the satellite AirPhone, a handset normally located back in the cabin next to the CEO seat, as well as in the cockpit. Most business aircraft and airliners have them, and they work like a regular telephone. Further, the coverage is everywhere in the world. (Actually, it might be wise for the passengers at least initially to use the AirPhone located in the back to get help. Prior to unseating the unconscious pilot, someone on the ground could say where the autopilot switch is located, and how to operate it, in case of accidental deactivation.)

If our CJ4 is typical, somewhere in the cockpit there will be documentation with an ATC center or terminal telephone number to call. Another option is to call 1-800-WX-Brief, the Flight Service briefing number most pilots use (and all pilots know) to file flight plans and get weather. Upon reaching them, all available ATC support functions can be mobilized.

The CJ4's flight deck phone has a hand set conveniently mounted overhead on the ceiling, accessible by both pilot and copilot. It's also mostly bullet proof. It might take a few tries, but because Fight Service is a 24/7 enterprise, someone will eventually respond. Also notice that using the AirPhone is something Ellen could do should Stryker be busy, and is especially useful once communication is established and flying duties demand more attention.

## Finding an expert

The next step in the process is a bit tricky. The hope is that the Flight Service specialist can reach a Citation Jet expert, or at least a Collins expert, who can help guide tuning the radios, with more instruction to follow once a plan is established. There may be a general SOP for this at Flight Service, but it won't include an expert standing by to help. This is where the whole scenario can unravel. There are very few Flight Service specialists, or even air traffic controllers, able to talk down a pilot who is unfamiliar with the equipment, let alone one lacking a type rating flying a high-performance jet. More to the point, without a Citation Jet expert available, one experienced flying both the Collins Proline 21 avionics suite and the CJ4 aircraft, the options available to the passengers on board dwindle considerably.

Adding to list of worries, is the constraint of endurance. Fully fueled, the CJ4 carries enough Jet-A to fly at cruising altitude for about five hours. If the emergency unfolds relatively early in the flight and up high, there could be time to prepare Stryker, Ellen, and aircraft for landing. It would be another matter if the airplane happened to be low. Endurance decreases considerably at lower altitudes, because in the denser atmosphere the engines need more fuel to maintain the same air-to-fuel ratio. In either case, when the Flight Service Specialist says "hold please," it would be a good idea to insist that it not be for too long.

Let's assume a CJ4 expert can be located expeditiously, and connected via telephone to the airplane. We'll refer to him as Treleaven (Captain Martin Treleaven), the name of the cantankerous airline captain in *Zero Hour* played by Sterling Hayden, whose job is to talk the passenger-crew down. The first task would be to hash out a strategy. Time is of the essence, so it can't take long. Keep in mind the airplane is moving fast, fuel is being consumed, and potentially good airport options are passing by far below. There are communication logistics to consider. The expert is able to communicate with the people flying the airplane, but has no way of knowing where the airplane is or where it is going.

Some kind of link must be established between ATC, Treleaven, and the airplane. One option would be to get Treleaven to an ATC facility, where he and ATC personnel both would have the means to follow the radar track of the aircraft. That's what happens in the movie. But finding and delivering the expert to ATC may not work, if time is short, and the distance long. ATC could set up a conference call, with both airplane and expert on the line, as well as the terminal airport selected to host the emergency landing. The benefit of a conference call is that all can be orchestrated without the passengers touching anything but the AirPhone.

## The strategy

Next comes choosing the methodology for managing a safe landing. There are three choices: 1) instruct the passengers to hand fly the airplane to a landing, 2) have the passengers operate the computer in a way that would allow the airplane to land itself, or 3) use a hybrid of 1) and 2) relying on the computer for the descent and for lining up with the runway, with the pilot-passenger taking over after that.

The first option would be a mistake, especially if the airplane were up high where proper control inputs are hard to judge. The CJ4 really isn't designed to be hand flown in the flight levels, and between 29,000 feet and 41,000 feet inclusive RVSM regulations require the autopilot be working and engaged. Further, there are complex tasks for Stryker and Ellen to perform that could be compromised if they're too focused on the controls.

The second option is interesting. If the passenger-crew had no flying experience, using the autopilot all the way might be the best choice—even better if one or more of the passengers had applicable computer experience. While the CJ4's autopilot is not designed to fly the airplane safely to the ground, there is an improvisation that could work if there were an airport in range with a precision ILS.

The autopilot in the CJ4 is very good, and although it's not certified for use below 200 feet AGL, we are taught at simulator school to consider ignoring the limitation in the event of a weather emergency with landing visibility and ceiling very, very low or nil—zero/zero conditions. The idea has other advantages over the hand flying scenarios, because with the autopilot in charge on final approach, the passenger-crew would only need to adjust the throttles to target $V_{REF}$ airspeed (the approach air speed to fly), and $V_{REF}$ is easy to see on the PFD speed tape—it is always depicted as a green donut. That reduces the number of things to worry about to one, compared to four (power, roll, pitch, yaw) in the case of hand flying. Theoretically, once the airplane is on the ILS, the autopilot should be able to track it safely to the runway unaided. (We tried this in the simulator airplane during one of our CJ4 recurrent trainings, and it worked out okay. Assuming the simulator is representative, the real-life emergency might work out okay, too. Still, true auto-land autopilots have features the CJ4 doesn't have. Translation: the landing could be safe, smooth, successful. It also could end in a giant fireball.)

Personally, I like the third option, and not just because it aligns nicely with my talk show host narrative. Configured properly, landing gear down, flaps set to land and deployed, the CJ4 flies like a big, fast Cessna-172. It has almost no bad habits. Yes, there aren't a lot of seat-of-the-pants flying clues like wind noise. Nor do the turbofan engines respond to the throttle inputs instantly like propeller airplanes do. Stryker and Ellen would, therefore, have to closely monitor the airspeed on the PFD while also anticipating power demands. Managing power proactively is the key, because $N_1$ (the main power fan) spool up times can be long, with significant power output delivered only at the high end of the range. Still, assuming the weather is good and the airport is VFR, Stryker, a commercial pilot, should be able to hand fly the plane to a landing once it is lined up.

# Navigating to the emergency landing airport

With option three communicated to the passenger-crew, the next step would be to guide the aircraft to a suitable airport. The criteria is simple: good destination weather, long runways, a precision ILS landing system, a radar environment, and a good emergency response team, ideally airport-based. If operating in the US, the chances of an airport meeting this description are good. Even on the East Coast or in the Midwest, where the weather is often bad, an oasis airport is bound to be within range. Some airports will be more ideal than others, partly because of traffic considerations, but all are candidates, given the situation.

Incidentally, at some point in the unfolding saga somebody is bound to ask the passenger-crew about declaring an emergency. The right answer is "Yes, we have an emergency"—the goal being to establish priority and expedited handling. Once it is generally known that the crew has become incapacitated, someone on the ground likely would declare an emergency on the airplane's behalf.

With communication established, the hybrid plan agreed on, the next step is getting the airplane to the selected airport's terminal environment. The FMS and autopilot offer many ways to accomplish the task but, under the circumstances, the simplest method should prevail. The FMS in particular is complicated—there are many ways to make a mistake in the programming—and therefore fraught with danger. While in theory the passenger-crew could lay in a GPS course to the airport, even with help, the chances of getting it right are slim. The plan, therefore, would be to use the heading bug to select a compass heading and altitude preselect and vertical speed to set the airplane's descent rate and altitude. Both of these are autopilot functions that can be engaged without touching the FMS.

## Communicating the airplane's configuration, FMS and autopilot settings

Before Treleaven directs Stryker and Ellen to push any buttons, he needs to know how the now-incapacitated crew had set the controls of the airplane. In *Zero Hour*, Treleaven has Stryker describe the control settings, fuel levels, airspeed, and altitude over the radio. He does it flawlessly. Unfortunately, in real life, describing the airplane's status by radio could take a long time, even for one schooled in the systems, and there is a risk of misrepresentation. Still, Treleaven needs the information in order to help. What to do? Fortunately, since *Zero Hour* was made, a secret weapon has been developed to facilitate assessment. It's the internet! Most business jets and airliners now have WiFi and access to the internet. Most people have smartphones. In this case, a picture really is worth a thousand words transmitted over the radio.

## Implementing the first part of the plan—navigating to the emergency airport

Photos in hand, Treleaven now has a good sense of the airplane's status. He can safely instruct Stryker and Ellen to change the heading of the aircraft and begin the descent toward the airport. Under Treleaven's guidance, the passenger-crew will have to perform six actions, in sequence and correctly: 1) throttle the airplane's speed back to 200 knots in level flight, 2) adjust the autopilot's heading knob to the desired heading, 3) push the autopilot's heading button to activate heading mode, 4) dial the autopilot's altitude pre-select knob to the desired descent altitude, 5) push the autopilot's vertical speed button (VS) to activate vertical speed descent mode, 6) use the auto-pilot's thumbwheel knob to select the descent rate—1,000 ft/min being a safe setting. Failing to throttle back properly (to prevent over-speed in the descent), mixing up the sequence or picking the wrong knob or button, and the outcome is unpredictable, probably bad.

All of these knobs and buttons are located on the panel just below the cockpit glare shield. Location and function would have been discussed with Stryker and Ellen prior to activation. The throttles are located on the center console and are somewhat intuitive. Still, the passenger-crew would have to be sure to monitor the speed tape, located on the left side of both the pilot and copilot's PFD, to make sure the plane is flying at a steady 200 knots before beginning the descent. Turbulence can be a factor, making it harder to press or turn the correct button or knob, adjust the throttles properly.

With the airplane descending as commanded, and heading in the right direction, it is time to send another photo, this one of the PFD with air-speed, altitude, and preselected altitude, among other things. But what Treleaven really wants to see is the flight guidance computer (FGC) status information displayed at the top. The presentation is cryptic, even for jet pilots. But there is a big reward for deciphering the strange symbols, abbre-viations—an accurate account of what the autopilot is doing, and what it is going to do next. Important!

Stryker and Ellen will have to perform multiple similar turns and descents under the guidance of Treleaven and ATC, prior to reaching the terminal area. Assuming this has been done, the airplane will arrive in a clean configuration (no flaps or gear deployed), level going about 200 knots under autopilot control.

## A real life mission

As an example, let's assume a routine trip, from Boca Rotan, Florida, to Burlington, Vermont. Somewhere off the coast of southern North Carolina, the emergency occurs. Given the time needed to get organized, contact Flight Service, obtain the expert, the nearest suitable airport could be Kingston, North Carolina (KISO). While off the straight line to Burlington, Kingston, has many advantages. The airport is big, with a wide runway more than two miles long. Kingston has an ILS available for runway 05. And there is very little airline traffic at Kingston, mostly freight.

Gisela and I actually made an emergency landing at Kingston in the Aztec when the left engine began to show signs of failure. With the engine shut down as a precaution, emergency declared, we made an uneventful fair-weather landing on runway 23. I have to say, I have never seen so many emergency vehicles in one place. All safe; the only consequence was some anxiety-related indigestion, having consumed in flight a delicious meal prepared by friends at the Franklin County, Virginia, airport, from where we'd just departed.

For Stryker and Ellen, with Kingston determined to be the emergency airport, the next step would be to get configured for landing. Once level and within 20 miles of the airport, Treleaven would have the passenger-crew confirm the airplane is at or below 200 knots. He would then instruct them to lower the flaps to the approach setting, by operating the handle to the right on the center console. Ellen, surrogate copilot, performs the task, because the handle is on the copilot side of the cockpit. Care must be taken not to lower the flaps at more than 200 knots airspeed, because of the risk of damage to the flap system and surfaces, worst case rendering the flaps inoperable. The airplane is still on autopilot, on an assigned heading that ideally should be the intercept course for alignment with the runway. Under autopilot control, the airplane will have descended to 2,100 feet, the altitude appropriate for becoming established on the ILS to runway 05 at Kingston Airport.

As for what happens next... In the movie, Treleaven and Stryker are at odds because of history, a failed fighter mission in which Styrker, as squadron leader, took tremendous losses. Treleaven, his then commander, has doubts about Stryker, even ten years later. Stryker has his own doubts, as most people would in this situation. He must rise to the occasion. Is the protagonist Stryker, in the movie, up to the challenge? Is the Stryker in our thought experiment? Specifically, how much or how little hand flying would be prudent?

## Use the autopilot to fly the approach?

Treleaven, the CJ4 expert, must decide whether to have Stryker disconnect the autopilot and fly the approach to landing by hand, or have the airplane's autopilot do it, requiring the passenger-crew, Stryker and Ellen, to program the computer to intercept the ILS, properly align the airplane with the runway, and start down. If the weather is marginal or worse, it's clear that autopilot is the right answer. CAVU, hand flying the airplane could be a better way to go.

If the decision is to go with the ILS, the passenger-crew would have to 1) input the correct ILS frequency into the FMS or radio control unit (RCU), 2) switch the source from GPS to LOC on the display control panel (DCP) located above the PFD, 3) dial the correct course, 050 degrees, for the ILS using the course (CRS) knob, and 4) push the approach (APPR) button on the autopilot panel—all doable, but not easy to verify via photograph. Unfortunately, WiFi on most aircraft stops working below 10,000 feet, a limit hardwired into the system. So the stream of pictures would have stopped some time ago. But the telephone works, so Treleaven can instruct right to touchdown. More likely, Stryker now would be on the radio, perhaps using 121.5, while Ellen would be on the phone. The beauty of communicating by radio is controllers at the airport can actually see the aircraft, in the air as well as on radar, and can react should any course correction or altitude change be needed.

Of course, there is always the possibility that Stryker and Ellen disobey Treleaven's direction, electing to hand fly the plane in order to expedite, a scenario more in line with the movie plot. After all, the crew needs medical attention. For the moment, though, let's assume Stryker and Ellen continue to fly with the assistance of the autopilot. There are a lot of advantages to this, especially when it comes to making changes in configurations, such as flap or gear positions. Should the airplane require retrimming, almost a certainty, the autopilot would trigger this function automatically. Manual trimming is an option, but it takes practice, not a great idea given all the other challenges Stryker and Ellen are facing.

# The approach and landing

Somewhere before the final approach course, Ellen will be instructed to set the flaps to approach and lower the landing gear, in sequence. These actions are straight forward, with the gear clearly identified by a big wheel located in the middle-left of the panel. Because of the drag of the gear and the flaps, without any change in power settings the airplane will slow from the previously established 200 knots. If all goes well, the airplane's airspeed will stabilize at about 160 knots, near or at the maximum flaps to land operating speed, at which point the flaps can be lowered to that setting.

With the CRS knob set on the approach course, and the heading set at an angle no more than 45 degrees to the left or right of the approach course, it's just a matter of reaching the final approach course intercept, at which point the autopilot will automatically turn the airplane toward the runway. Established on the final approach heading, and passing the final approach fix, the autopilot will automatically begin the final descent.

Once the airplane is on localizer, on glide path, the approach stabilized, and the runway clearly in sight, all Stryker has to do is manage the throttles to slow the airplane to landing speed, $V_{REF}$, 1.3-times the stall speed, disconnect the autopilot by pressing the big red button on the yoke, hitting it twice to disengage the yaw damper as well, and then hand fly the airplane to a landing. Easy! After touchdown, rudder pedals are used for steering, toe brakes for controlling braking, while spoilers, operated by a handle on the left side of the center console, are used to kill the wing's lift. The airplane slows, and eventually comes to a stop.

## Management for success

Unfortunately, even with everyone working together, and leaning heavily on the autopilot, the plan has weaknesses. The biggest risk is setting the autopilot. One mistake and it could be game over, difficult for the passenger-crew to recover in time.

Much depends on weather. If the emergency unfolds in bad weather, the path to success narrows. Tasking the autopilot to fly the approach and landing could work, assuming the instructions from the ground are perfectly composed and presented, and in the air perfectly understood and performed. The sheer number of programming inputs required, the inevitability of mistakes, and the difficulty of identifying and recovering from them in time, foretells less than a happy ending.

In good weather there are more options, but some of the same challenges remain, and there are others, especially on approach, with the airplane configured for landing. Even with the drag caused by flaps and gear, jet airplanes are slippery. Arriving at the correct $V_{REF}$ airspeed requires predicting the airplane's energy as much as two to three minutes in advance. Just chopping the throttles over the numbers won't work, if the airplane is going too fast.

Help from the ground is vital, but there are limits to what anyone can do. One of the most daunting challenges our passenger-crew faces is just figuring out the *switchology*, and doing it in time. When Trelevean says push the APPR button, the crew has to locate the button, push it, and confirm that autopilot mode is engaged. Not doing so could mean disaster. The problem isn't limited to neophytes. Rated pilots transitioning from one type of aircraft to another experience some of the same challenges, especially when upgrading to larger aircraft. While there is some commonality between small airplanes and big ones, jet airplanes and those with propellers, the nature and placement of the controls in the cockpit are often very different. Nowhere is this more apparent than during initial training for a new jet type rating. Even benefiting from previous jet flying experience, and knowing what to look for, much time is invested in learning the layout, where everything is located, and the special ways the switches and buttons and knobs are designed to operate. Unlike the controls in automobiles, which are more or less standardized, airplane cockpits vary considerably, requiring special training and experience for safe operation. For this reason, flight schools often make special non-motion cockpit simulators available to their students, their only function to familiarize pilots with the location of switches and buttons and the basic operation of avionics systems.

One issue we haven't really considered is the effect of stress on the passenger-crew. Passengers seldom get to experience putting on their oxygen masks, let alone flying an unfamiliar airplane without proper training. There is time pressure, the temptation to rush through steps that demand a deliberate approach. And then there is the uncertainty. It's a desperate situation. Even if every instruction from Treleaven and ATC is correct, and perfectly executed in the plane, the most optimistic passenger-crew can't know the outcome until the plane is on the ground. Should the smallest thing go awry, it would be a remarkable passenger who could ward off the inevitable panic and ensuing paralysis. Only in Hollywood!

In the end, the thought experiment becomes a cautionary tale: be careful what you wish for. Some fantasies should remain just that: fantasies. But should this improbable emergency befall you, it would be better to have tried a few simulator landings in type, in case the first one doesn't go according to plan. Also, never order the fish.

## Lessons learned:

**Lesson 1:** Passengers aren't generally called upon to land airliners.

**Lesson 2:** Having some flight training is not a guarantee of success, but it is an advantage.

**Lesson 3:** Rehearsal of the food poisoning scenario in a type equivalent simulator is probably a good predictor of the real life outcome.

**Lesson 4:** Airplanes, especially big jet airplanes, are complicated.

**Lesson 5:** Even acknowledging commonalities among types, the devil is always in the details. Knowing the differences is key to a safe outcome.

**Lesson 6:** To take a plane from flight levels to a safe landing, a passenger-pilot would need to combine extreme self-confidence and improvisational skills in the air with a willingness to listen to and accept guidance from the authorities and experts on the ground. Few can do both. Ego inhibits wisdom and good judgment. Yet wisdom and good judgment are useless without the practical application of ego. I present for your inspection an incapacitated crew aboard a jet speeding at near-supersonic speeds nearly nine miles above the ground, with only the passengers to take the aircraft safely down to the ground. Would you be up to the challenge?

# 22 | The Great Airline Paradox

The lunch menu for the flight from Frankfurt to Washington started with beluga caviar from the Caspian Sea, served with traditional garnishes and melba toast, complemented by a choice of premium vodkas or La Grande Dame Champagne. This, followed by chilled lobster medallions served with Louis sauce and peach-glazed breast of capon with Cumberland sauce. For the main course, a choice of beef tenderloin, squab chatelaine, or trout accompanied by a wide selection of fine vintage wines. To finish, a dessert selection that included Sachertorte and fresh berries topped with French vanilla ice cream, and an assortment of regal ports, cognacs, and other digestifs. Those were the days, the golden age of airline flying. Now, it's a battle just to keep the can, assuming there will be any liquid refreshment at all; a bag of peanuts or potato chips the occasional bonus.

The news isn't all bad, though. Since deregulation ended the golden age, when luxurious accommodation and excellent service were the priorities, airline travel has become cheaper. The number of flights and destinations have increased, at least from larger cities. Flying has also emerged as the safest means of transportation, vastly safer than it was in the 1950s, '60s, and '70s. Much of the improvement is related to standardized training and better technology. The industry is highly regulated now, with most operations systemized, so there is less improvising. The captain is the captain, responsible for the safety of the flight, but any direct contribution to flight planning, aircraft loading, weather analysis, and fueling is largely limited to approving tasks performed by others, or machines. In today's airline environment it's the dispatch specialist who makes the flight work within the rules. Maintenance is mostly predetermined and preventive in nature, done in progressive intervals appropriate to the aircraft and its systems. Internal diagnostics determine an aircraft's wellness before departure and at all times during the flight. Taken together, the system is very safe. Airlines are a bargain, too, at least in terms of absolute cost. But are they good value?

One thing is for sure, the airlines and the system have managed to wring all the fun out of flying. This is especially true in the US. The commercial terminals of many American airports are dirty, crowded, puzzlingly complex, and by definition tortuous, partly because of the multiple functions they perform. They accommodate high volumes of vehicles—ground vehicles, including cars, trains, and shuttle busses, as well as airplanes. They move vast numbers of people. The terminal buildings must be secure, especially on the gate side where boarding and unboarding take place. They must manage an elaborate and awkward passenger screening process, so no bad guys get on the plane. There is commercial activity, beyond buying tickets and paying for excess luggage; to extract maximum dollars from the traveling public airports have become literal shopping malls with stores and restaurants from curbside to jetway door. This is not to mention all that goes on unseen by the passengers—fueling, luggage handling, snow removal, aircraft and aircraft support vehicle maintenance, all while some part of the airport is under construction. Running an airport requires long term planning, investment, an unrelenting commitment to upkeep, all of which the governments—municipal, state, and federal—have difficulty doing consistently on behalf of their clients, the airlines, and the traveling public. It should come as no surprise, that investment in the facility—with its longer cash to cash cycles—is counter to the airline model, which seeks a shorter term return by spending the minimum necessary to extract the maximum possible from the most number of people, without sacrificing safety. (Thanks to the bad economics of crashing, airlines do adhere to a no-passenger-kill policy.)

Nowhere is this model more apparent than in the cabin, where most domestic and some international carriers have been busily reducing the quality of basic service. Coach passengers now pay handsomely for a bit of extra legroom, or to place a small bag in the overhead compartment. Pricing methods are dynamic and opaque, depending on demand, competition, availability, and a bunch of other factors, including passenger demographics, only known to the airlines. It's possible that the same seat on the same flight, other factors such as flight availability being equal, costs you more than it does another passenger, because of your buying history. *Note to file:* miserly consumers may benefit from their miserliness.

Then there is service. Just as it has become impossible to rationalize pricing, it is no clearer whether that bit of extra service is worth the price. The small-print à la carte fees for services like select seating, checked baggage, and carry-on only make it more confusing. No longer can the customer determine true value, because the only tool remaining is price comparison using the advertised unvetted price, the domain where the airlines have the upper hand.

Even if it were possible to do a proper analysis, utility takes precedence over all other considerations. The bottom line is, if you have to get there, and there is only one seat available, and no other options, it doesn't matter whether the menu is Chateaubriand or pretzels, the seat inhumanely small or the size of a Lay-Z-Boy recliner, you're going!

Fundamentally, the airlines have won.

Less apparent is the impact on reliability, getting to the destination on time. Prior to deregulation, airlines routes and pricing were determined by the government, leaving airlines with only two ways to attract customers. One was service—providing the fastest, friendliest check-in, most comfortable seats, best meals, and souvenirs for the kids. The other was on-time performance. There were many delayed flights before the 1980s, but never was there a time when on-time performance was more important to the brand.

It is the opposite in the deregulated airline environment. Here the market has morphed into something truly weird and perverse. Check-ins are crowded, harried, and stressful. Those who fail to pay for a seat assignment and print the boarding pass ahead of time, will be greeted by soulless robot kiosks as the first airline point of contact. Human agents are available, but mostly for extracting additional baggage and change fees, or for involuntary rerouting when the flight is oversold.

Most passengers are on their own for food now. Even in first class, meals are seldom offered unless the flight is long. In the US, first class is mostly about a wider seat, earlier boarding, free alcohol, and perhaps a more generous baggage allowance. Some trans-continental and many international flights offer better menus, but even on the longer routes, the rule for food is less is more.

Delays and cancellations have become more routine, at great inconvenience and irritation to the traveler. The explanation is often weather, but that would be an over simplification. With few exceptions, airline flight scheduling assumes an almost perfect weather scenario—VFR (or very light IFR) conditions almost everywhere in the system. Should a snowstorm develop at or near one of the airports, on-time performance throughout the system usually suffers; airplanes that are needed elsewhere, stuck.

Mechanical problems sometimes delay flights. The incidence is relatively small, however, and remarkable given how the planes are used. Airplane designs are robust, and maintenance services are competent and locally available, at least at major hub airports. Nevertheless, it is not lost on those who monitor the root causes of airline delays that when a delay results from a mechanical issue the airlines must compensate affected passengers—a correlation that could explain the low numbers.

The need for increased security also has made airline travel more complicated and time-consuming. Screening has long been a part of the common carrier experience, but 9/11 brought tougher screening in general, invasive searches, and much longer lines. While not directly at fault, the airlines haven't helped. It's not just the inconvenience of having to arrive at the airport early to ensure time for screening, or the indignity of shoes-off, pockets-empty, jewelry-off, make-up in the plastic bag, carry-on contents in the x-ray machine, body scans. If the process is delayed, because of TSA understaffing or any reason, the passengers who miss their flights are the ones who pay. It may depend on the airline and circumstances, but the fee assessed is where negotiations usually begin.

There are coping mechanisms, including TSA Precheck and Global Entry, that make the security experience more predictable. Still, for the systems to work there have to be gateways established at the respective TSA checkpoints—not always the case. Even when there is a gateway, lines can be as long as those for normal screening. Our government at work.

Then there is on-time performance. An 80 percent on-time performance is average according to the DOT, but that by definition means 20 percent of the time the flight will be late.[1] (Of course, if your flight is late, that equates to zero percent on-time performance.) The measurement is interesting in another way, though, because its focus is largely limited to the flight's departure and arrival times relative to schedule, not how many passengers make it to their destination on time. Ironically, an airline can have relatively good on-time performance and still fail to deliver many passengers to their destinations on time. How is this possible?

The answer can be found in the hub and spoke system the major airlines adopted shortly after deregulation in the 1980s. The change benefited the airlines because it facilitated a consolidation of operations, with major airlines flying the longer routes between the hubs, located in the larger cities, and regional affiliates flying the shorter hops—the spokes. Load factors went up, too, increasing efficiency. Travelers benefited because of the proliferation

---

[1] January to December, 2017, on-time performance for domestic airlines according to the Bureau of Transportation Statistics.

of spokes, connecting smaller airports to the hubs. The downside was the system required most travelers (and their luggage) to fly multiple segments, with connections between. And the connections are the weak links.

It's an acknowledged fact that connections increase travel times. It takes at least 45 minutes to change planes. And the travel distances from spoke to hub to spoke, are inherently longer. At the time of this writing the fastest routing from San Antonio, Texas, to Burlington, Vermont, was 7 hours and 24 minutes, on American Airlines. Incorporated into the itinerary are stops in Dallas and Washington, DC. The great circle route—as the crow flies—from San Antonio to Burlington is 1,497 NM. Dividing distance by time—1,497 NM by 7 hours and 24 minutes—the average speed for the airline journey is therefore 202 NM/hr, or 202 knots. But the Airbus, Boeing, and Embraer airliners that fly this route cruise at about Mach 0.78, or 520 knots. So the increase in distance, because the journey includes stops in two hubs, plus the time taken for each stop—landing and taking off again, changing planes—slows the journey by 318 knots of speed. It could be worse: zonal tailwinds that improve ground speed likely have been figured into the timing. And this, of course, assumes everything goes according to plan. By way of comparison, the company CJ4, which is a bit slower (Mach 0.77 versus 0.78), makes the trip in 3 hours 33 minutes—more than twice as fast than the fastest available airline routing.

And the connections often don't work. The time allowed—45 minutes to even an hour—seems like a lot, but then there's a rerouting or delay, for weather and traffic, and the margin is gone. Our imagined journey from San Antonio to Burlington allows 51 minutes to make the connection in Dallas. Should the plane from San Antonio depart 15 minutes late, still considered on-time by the people who track these things, would leave only 36 minutes. Dallas is a busy airport. Delays in the air, and while taxiing after landing, are not uncommon. But let's assume the overall delay is just 15 minutes. That leaves just 36 minutes to disembark, find the connecting gate, board again. Disembarking on its own can consume another 15 minutes—and keep in mind disembarkation times don't factor in on-time performance. If seated in the front of the plane, and the gate for the next flight is close, you've probably got time. But what if you're seated in the last row and the flight's crowded, and the gate is at the other end of the terminal, or in another terminal? Not enough of a challenge? Irrespective of whether the arriving flight is late, the connecting flight could be leaving on time, or early, or close-early (essentially the same thing), the latter two scenarios are perverse but true, defying explanation except perhaps that the gate needs to be freed up for another late-arriving aircraft.

Running through airports is not a cliché, as anyone who travels regularly knows. And choosing an originating flight with good on-time performance doesn't guarantee a successful connection.

Unfortunately, airlines don't really care if you make your flight as long as most of the passengers do (and on time performance statistics continue to disguise the issue).[2] The economics are inescapable. If you're late arriving at your destination, it costs the airlines nothing. Their only obligation is to provide you a seat on the next available flight. And if there is no available flight that day, unless the delay is the result of a mechanical failure, it's up to you to find accommodation, hotel and food. It can be a long wait during some travel periods, such as Thanksgiving and Christmas, because all the flights are full. Yes, you can swear all you want, never to fly on that airline again, but the airlines know most people come back despite the service. They have to, because where most people embark, the spoke airports, there are few alternatives. People living in hub cities have more options, but their choices also are limited, just in another way. Hubs can be fortresses for the resident airlines. Atlanta is a Delta fortress. Chicago is a fortress for American and United. If you live in one of these cities, more often than not you're going to be flying with one of the dominant companies. If you choose a competitor, it usually means you'll have to make a connection somewhere.

The ultimate co-conspirators guilty of the crime of perpetuating poor customer experience, ironically, are the frequent flyer loyalty programs. Oh no! American Airlines was first, with the modern version in 1981. Now all airlines have them. Frequent flyer programs are attractive because they appear to offer free stuff—flights, hotels, electronics—in exchange for nothing more than loyalty, an unspoken promise to fly the sponsoring airline. And it's tax free. So far, no one has been willing to risk attempting to tax air miles. It's an even better deal for business fliers, who can expect to be compensated by their employers for the tickets, but get to keep the miles.

A confession: I was lured into flying more than a million miles with United Airlines because of their frequent flyer program. The addiction

---

[2] Airlines sometimes pad the schedule and provide certain employee incentives to mitigate for certain high visibility flights likely to be late. Known as gaming the flight, arrival times are adjusted to improve on time performance. Flights often take longer than they should assuming normal routings and airliner speeds, but passengers don't notice because actual arrival times and scheduled times are mostly in alignment. Silke Forbes, Mara Lederman, and Zhe Yuan. "Do Airlines Pad Their Schedules?" Rotman School of Management Working Paper No. 3065986. University of Toronto, Rotman School of Management, November 2017.

started out innocently enough. It felt like a carnival game—win enough points and take home the giant stuffed unicorn. Especially in the beginning, some of the promotions were truly intriguing. One of the offers, shortly after the program was launched, was a year of free domestic coach class travel for anyone who managed to visit every state in the union served by United. (It was a goal that turned out to be unreachable except at great cost, and considerable contortion. A colleague actually succeeded in the quest, but United was the winner.)

It was the prospect of first class travel that attracted me—the luxury seat, gourmet meals, cocktails, the endless attentions of a bevy of beautiful stewardesses, which was their title in those days. A first class ticket is vastly more expensive than coach today, but the disparity was even greater in the early days of deregulation. Coach seats were getting cheaper, as upstart airlines like People's Express, an early low-cost carrier, aggressively competed for the middle-class market. Enter the frequent flyer program. Earned miles, transformed to points, were suddenly a ticket to affordable pampering, the traveler magically "upgraded" and for no extra charge. The program worked for the airlines, too. The overly expensive first class seats were going unsold. Instead of giving up the lure of luxury, the airlines created an auxiliary channel, available only to its most loyal customers. I was hooked. The airlines further secured my loyalty by offering more "free" upgrades along with other amenities like special private lounges, far from the congested main concourses.

Airline companies were among the first to grasp the concept of customer relationship management, and employ it effectively. The agent not only knew your name, he or she could see your travel history, and your personal preferences. And the more you flew with them, the more they made you feel welcome. And the more welcome you felt, the more you flew.

Of course many agents and flight attendants genuinely sought to please, and most of my flights were pleasant. Over many years of travel, some became personal friends and a few were guests at my first wedding.

I met other frequent fliers, some who seemed familiar. I found myself on a Boeing 767 flying from Los Angles to Washington Dulles. Seated to my right was the comic actor Dom DeLuise and his wife, and on my left former football player and actor Ed Marinaro (*Hill Street Blues*, *Laverne & Shirley*, *Blue Mountain State*). By various means, all of us had upgraded to the first class cabin.

Ed kept to himself, focused on keeping a wad of chewing tobacco going. Dom was friendly. We told bad jokes all the way across the country. My only complaint, he had wandering fingers. At lunch, when I was looking the other way, he stole my frosted chocolate cake. His wife scolded him, but it was too late.

The downside of the cozy relationship fostered by frequent flyer programs was that loyalty to a favorite airline at times came at the expense of good travel decision-making. It was possible, for example, to rationalize a costly flight, on the basis that greater rewards come to those who spend more. Even the idea of byzantine routings, increasing the possibility of poor on-time performances, commanded appeal. Longer legs meant more points. For those flying on their own time, paying their own way on a holiday, it could be seen as a reasonable exchange. For those flying on business, the interests of the traveler and the company often diverged—cheaper and quicker not always the loyal flyer's first choice. Some companies went as far as to relegate all business travel logistics to a proprietary travel department. Others adopted strict policies requiring pre-travel approval of proposed itineraries. In most cases, though, the individual traveler called the shots, selecting the airline with the best frequent flier program. I can personally testify to that.

The more serious downside is that frequent flyer programs tend to discourage the kind of competition that could lead to companies improving services—not just proffering more perks. The programs only work when the free stuff costs little to nothing to produce. The free ticket is a case in point. If the seat is going to be empty anyway, it costs the airline nothing to give it away. For the frequent flyer, who gets the seat for points, it's a deal.

One of the reasons that free flights for frequent flyers come at a low cost to airlines is that airlines have restrictions—limited dates, times, and availability—determined by some unknown secret formula. Free seats and seats in general also are cheap to produce because most airlines these days pack their planes with passengers and put their aircraft to almost constant use. To put this in perspective, the typical hub and spoke carrier's average annual aircraft utilization is about 2,500 legs. That's almost seven flights per day for every day of the year. Point-to-point carriers like Southwest fly their planes even more, although their passenger loads are typically less.

Legacy airline frequent flyer programs present a challenge for the upstart competitor intent upon delivering a better experience to the traveler. It's not that the new airline couldn't start a program of its own. The problem is that for the programs to be practical, the costs have to be low. And the only way to do that is to adopt the same practices of the legacy airlines—tight schedules and tightly packed aircraft—which is antithetical to good service and on-time performance. Without some slack in the system, when things go wrong there is rarely an easy, graceful recovery. Even assuming customers are willing to pay more for the ticket in exchange for improved reliability and better service, it seems unlikely the frequent flyer program made necessary by the economics would pass muster. Unless there is a willingness to compromise the brand, good service and on-time performance, free is just too expensive to do.

The result is an airline system that operates using a *management for success* philosophy. Everything has to go perfectly. On sunny days when all is well, the system works. Other days, when there are mechanical problems, bad weather, or inadequate staffing, the system breaks down, at the expense of the traveler's experience. But value is in the eye of the beholder, and the proof is in the success of the airlines and their frequent flyer programs.

The free stuff scenario is far from ideal. Points expire, there are fewer free seats than there used to be, and upgrades are unlikely—except for the most frequent of frequent fliers. Even for the lucky few who manage to go to the front of the plane, disappointment awaits, because like everything else in the airline business, first class isn't what it used to be. Coupled with everything else the passenger endures, bad air, unsanitary conditions, it's amazing anyone still flies with commercial airlines. (I was chronically ill during those frequent flier days.) And, yet, the airlines prosper. The market says low price plus free stuff wins. Must be true! Never has an industry been so handsomely rewarded for delivering inferior product, bad service, and a miserable customer experience—a staggering contradiction on many levels. Perhaps a reflection of our times, the carnival barkers have prevailed and the travelers, most of them anyway, have the airline system they deserve. United Airlines broke that nice man's guitar in 2008, which was sad, but not unexpected. Fortunately, there are travel alternatives for those savvy enough to know the difference between low cost, "free," and a genuinely valuable exchange.

## Lessons learned:

**Lesson 1:** Successful airline travel demands a defensive posture. Allocate at least one day for domestic travel, two or more for travel beyond the borders.

**Lesson 2:** High utilization is incompatible with on-time performance.

**Lesson 3:** Most airline passengers are unwilling to pay for good customer service.

**Lesson 4:** "Free" or cheap trumps all in the airline world!

**Lesson 5:** Management for success produces the most spectacular failures.

# 23 | A Layman's Guide to Flying Private

Imagine the luxury of arriving for your flight five minutes before its scheduled departure. You are ushered through security, onto the tarmac, and right to your plane by two uniformed staff. The luggage pieces, of which there are many, magically transferred by the all-knowing FBO team who expertly identifying those needed for carry-on, while carefully placing the rest in the secure baggage compartment. You and your party board, and in minutes are underway. Premium cocktails and wine await, a delicious lunch or dinner to follow. Best of all, you reach your destination in comfort, on-time, and without any of the hassles normally associated with air travel. Fantasy?

Welcome to the world of private jet travel, where there are no missed flights or lost luggage, and routing and scheduling is discretionary, for the travelers to decide. Need a 12 a.m. departure from Burlington, Vermont, for a 2 p.m. business meeting in Paris? The flight department will accommodate. Should plans change, even while airborne, assuming the new direction can be accommodated safely within operational limits, no problem.

What's more, the routings are direct, allowing for shorter trips and reliable arrival times hours ahead the airlines. Our small flight department has a 97 percent dispatch reliability target, which means 97 percent of the flights must depart and arrive on time. Last year, we exceeded the target and achieved 100 percent, which would be amazing for an airline, but is not atypical for a private operation. The reason: the priorities of most private flight departments are safety, excellent service, on-time performance, and flexibility. Notice that airline companies and private flight departments share only one goal, safety. After that, the divergence is extreme.

Flying privately is less stressful, which is important for anyone anticipating a tough business meeting, needing to arrive rested and alert. And it is just more fun. Passengers accommodated by our flight department almost always board with a big smile. So what's the downside? The biggest inhibitor to flying privately is cost, of course, at least compared to the alternatives. Flight departments flying jet airplanes are expensive by any measure—cost per mile, cost per seat per mile, cost per individual trip, annual cost per passenger flown, and a bunch of other metrics that all compare unfavorably to commercial carriers.

For this reason, starting a flight department can be a hard sell, even for a family owned and operated business, as in our case. Why assume another $600,000 of operating costs when current traveling needs are already nicely addressed by airlines for less than half that amount? Of course, *nicely* is subjective.

Those resistant—my partner-brother was one—tend to offer alternatives, like renting. Not unprecedented for our business; we had organized charter flights for occasional trips to hard-to-get-to places. These were rare, the expense seemed exorbitant. Charter flights are hard to arrange on short notice, because charter companies work, as airlines do, to keep their fleets scheduled to fly as much as possible.

Another solution involves essentially purchasing a share in an airplane and then paying a service fee for overhead—pilots, hangar space, routine maintenance—and a use fee to cover operational costs. This fractional solution solves the scheduling problem; should your airplane not be available, one of similar capability, perhaps owned by other fractional clients, would be dispatched. There are enough aircraft and crews that under normal circumstances a trip can be scheduled within 24 hours.

Fractionals sound ideal, especially for companies with travel demands greater than 50 hours and less than 150 hours. In theory, sharing purchase and overhead is an overall cost-savings. But the savings can be small, because the fractional company must profit from all aspects of the enterprise—from aircraft management, to pilot services, to maintenance, to fuel, even catering. Should the aircraft be purchased or sold, the fractional company makes money then, too, as a broker. And because fractional airplanes fly a lot, they must be sold and new ones purchased as often as every 10 years; late-model year and like-new appearance necessary to preserve the brand. The burden of depreciation is more often than not the end game for the many clients.

There are also *jet cards* available from these companies. Jet cards are targeted at people who need a business aircraft fewer than 50 hours per year. They cost more than charter, but that's offset by greater flexibility in scheduling and the elimination of deadhead leg charges. Of course, the way to eliminate deadhead leg charges is to double the rate charged for the single leg. For example, a one-way flight from Burlington to Boca Rotan using Warren Buffet's fractional company, NetJets, and the 25-hour jet card they offer, costs about $27,000 assuming you're flying on light jet equipment like a Cessna Excel.[1] (There are special promotions, but normally the card itself, branded as the Marquis Card, costs about $220,000 plus the gas used, a little more than $8,600 per hour. The time limit for using the card is eighteen months.)

The clear advantage of fractional and charter companies is easy access to lift. There is no company flight department to manage, no new personnel, no training contracts, no new facilities required, such as hangars. There are no direct maintenance costs, and a much smaller or equal-to-zero capital expenditure to fund. Traveling is as simple as calling a number, and then writing a big check—or the other way around.

Charter and fractional companies have experienced pricing pressures in recent years. Buyers can trawl the travel-on-demand sites online, forcing sellers to bid against one another for business. Getting the best charter deals online may require flexibility with travel dates and times—cheap flights often are the deadhead legs left after someone else's pricier on-demand charter trip.

Finally, there is the DIY option—having your own proprietary flight department, which is what we decided on. There were a number of reasons for the decision, including—honestly—my personal desire to fly jets. Mostly, though, we realized that the demand for business and personal (family) travel would likely exceed the lower volumes necessary to make third party providers cost effective. There is a range, but most experts say that if you fly more than about 200 hours per year, you should consider buying your own jet aircraft.[2] We expected to fly about 250 hours, lower than typical, perhaps, but leaving room to grow. Not to be dismissed was the appeal of knowing both the airplane, its maintenance history, and the pilot(s). While fractional and charter operations are very safe, there is more to being a good pilot than flying an airplane successfully from point A to point B. The pilot is the face of the organization providing lift, so in addition to being competent there is an expectation of affability and accommodation. Also, the pilot(s) need to be comfortable wearing several hats. Some for-profit on-demand operators insist that crewmembers must also clean the airplanes and even organize the catering, especially when away from home.

---

[1] Natalie McDaniel, Netjets NE Sales Representative, New England States, January 2018.
[2] Mickey Dalton, consultant aviation consultant to Constellations Brands, BioTek Instruments, Inc., and several other large public and private companies.

There is not a lot of enthusiasm for this, especially when a pilot union is involved. In a small proprietary flight department, however, everyone must be a renaissance contributor.

Company flight departments vary in size and character, but all who fly jet airplanes have to measure up to a very high standard. This is partially due to regulations, but more often than not the insurance underwriter dictates terms. So, the business person setting up a new proprietary flight department either has to have the skills necessary, or recruit someone who does.

The business person also needs to be able to balance the capital and operating cost of running a safe and effective flight department against the realistic financial targets governed by the size and profitability of the business. When we bought our first airplane, the operating cost was projected to be something like 6 percent of profitability measured by EBITDA (earnings before interest, taxes, depreciation, and amortization). That was a big percentage—less than one percent is more typical—and one of the reasons it was so difficult to get the flight department approved. Another worry is that despite the increase in travel efficiency, the large hit to earnings can decrease value of the enterprise in a significant way. The concern is legitimate, though conventional wisdom in investment banking circles suggests the impact is small, at least for private companies. Ironically, the people who do the valuations tend to assume the flight department would be eliminated if and when the business were sold.

Still, overcoming private flying's startlingly high cost demands a special kind of conceptual sell. Generally, the idea would be to promote the increase in productivity, because travelers would conduct business more predictably and efficiently when not at the mercy of the airlines. It's not an easy hypothesis to prove. Flying commercial airlines is so cheap and flying privately so expensive that there is really no hypothetical to demonstrate lower cost. Even considering the added misery, the need to go a day early, return a day late, squeeze into an increasingly uncomfortable, dirty seat, suffer lost/broken luggage, and poor customer service in general, making a pure financial case for flying privately is difficult to do.

The reality is there is no financial case to be made. Management has to conclude that the high cost of a private air force will be offset by fostering a more motivated, productive, loyal, happy, traveling workforce. There are confluences and synergies to consider; these would be difficult to quantify within a financial pro forma, but the qualitative indicators are compelling. Many times our little flight department has provided transportation for key customers needing a lift to a common conference or trade show, following an airline's failure to deliver. Imagine the return associated with having a captured audience that is all too willing to listen to the perfect marketing and sales pitch delivered over the course of four hours or more.

Proprietary flight departments come in all sizes, and the costs vary accordingly. We started out with a used CE-525 (the original Textron/Cessna Citation Jet) and one professional pilot, plus myself when I happened to be on the trip.

The aircraft was miserly. Flying expense, direct operating cost (DOC), was perhaps $1,000 per hour; a bargain by jet airplane standards. Combined with the minimal staffing needed to conduct flight ops, and a relatively low acquisition cost, about $2.3 million for a good low-time specimen, it made for a very lean regime.[3]

No one involved in the quest started out knowing aircraft type, staffing, or even budget. As the business person responsible for the enterprise, and the only one in the company with any aviation experience, I can testify that the good outcome was 100 percent a standing on the shoulders of giants success.

It began with a casual conversation with my cousin, Rob Sands, at the time CEO of Constellation Brands, one of the largest family-managed beverage companies in the country. Constellation's flight department started with a Piper Aztec in Rob's dad's day, but quickly graduated to larger aircraft including a fleet of cabin-class, 4,000-nautical-mile-range Dassault Falcon 900s, and more recently, two Gulfstream G-550s.

Rob's advice was timely because it set the stage for a more disciplined, objective, and mission-oriented approach to setting up the corporate flight department. High on his list of recommendations was to recruit a client-focused expert with the credentials needed to facilitate a professional process. The unfortunate reality of many corporate flight departments is that they are steered by individuals out to serve their own interests, not the sponsoring enterprise. The usual suspects include the OEMs, fractionals, charter companies, brokers, and even the pilots under company employ. So, I hired Mickey Dalton, professional aviation consultant.

My cousin introduced me to Mickey almost twenty years before the jet project when I was searching for my first personal aircraft, a Beech V35 Bonanza. Although Mickey's specialty (and business model) was jets, Rob asked him to help me as a personal favor.

---

[3] Based on 2007 market conditions when the flight department was created.

Not understanding the benefit of a competent intermediary, I initially resisted. The additional cost was a concern, but mostly I saw his involvement as redundant. After all, I had 100 hours in type and was familiar with the history of the airplane. I knew model years and equipment needed to satisfy the search. How hard can buying an airplane be, anyway?

Mickey proved his worth, however, when about halfway through the search for a perfect Bonanza I let it be known I would be operating from a personal 1,700-foot grass airstrip with tall trees at one end. The Bonanza is an excellent short-field, soft-field airplane and it said in the airplane's manual that my field would work. Mickey pointed out that on hot days the actual required performance would be very close to the theoretical available performance—with little safety margin. Knowing that I sought maximum utility, he asked me to consider how I would feel needing to reduce payload and/or fuel on a regular basis to mitigate for the short field. The answer: not good! We turned our attention to finding the perfect short takeoff and landing (STOL) Cessna 180 Skywagon instead.

Mickey never charged me beyond his expenses for finding, vetting, and negotiating to buy N315AG, a great airplane and the newest Skywagon available—the last specimen Cessna produced before closing the line in 1981. I have added six more personal aircraft to the fleet over the years, but I still use the C-180 for much of my get-around-town flying. As for Mickey's compensation, he explained that someday I would buy a jet airplane, and when I did, I would no doubt hire him. It seemed a curious thing to say, given I barely had the money to buy the small single-engine Cessna.

Mickey's patience and enthusiasm for me as a prospect proved prophetic. We were working together again, only this time the project was to establish a new corporate flight department. A case of jet airplane delayed, but not denied.

Having somebody like Mickey on the team assured more than just the acquisition of a good aircraft. Like any good business, a flight department must be built to last. A good aviation consultant comes with a template for the enterprise, to be adjusted to meet the requirements of the company. Foremost among the tasks is reconciling the budget to the transportation needs of the company. All else follows from this, including determining aircraft type, model year, avionics and other equipment needed, maintenance strategies, staffing profiles, training requirements, basing and hangar/housing solutions, record keeping (especially for personal versus business use tax accounting), dispatch functions (passenger manifest, fuel, catering, ground transportation, selection of destination FBO), and, key to efficacy,

*Mickey Dalton, aviation consultant, flying copilot position in the G-44 Widgeon.*

control authority (the person or persons responsible for approving business/ personal use, the person or persons responsible for determining the mission is safe to conduct). Incidentally, the *safe conduct* person and *business/personal* use person ideally would not be the same person.

What was clever about what we did was not so much picking the right jet type or a great pilot. More germane to success, and accomplished with the help of our consultant, was identifying the functions necessary for managing and operating a professional flight department, and recruiting personnel to perform the various tasks. So while our little flight department was a department of only one in the beginning, multiple long-term tenured employees embraced the opportunity, stepping up to fill the necessary, critical positions. For example, my administrative assistant trained for and assumed the role of "dispatch." Our company tax person became an expert in standard industry fair level (SIFL) laws and rates. And, despite operating under the less formal Part 91 rules, we adopted a very formal flight operations manual and the "N1 form" authorization system for approving use of the airplane.[4] Voila, a crisp, well-run, small flight department. Benefits: expenses largely within budget, dispatch reliability approaching 100 percent.

The new department also operated with great attention to safety. In a situation with a controlling traveler directing the pilot to go, when stop is

---

[4] The N1 form is a proprietary form used to document passenger manifest, purpose of flight (business versus personal), origin/destination legs, crew assigned, FBO contact info, catering requirements, ground transportation requirements, and billing account details.

the right answer because of weather, mechanical problems, or other issues, the right answer would prevail: *stop.* The system as designed, and left to its own devices, simply won't permit an unsafe event.

But what if the owner of the company, and business manager of the flight department, is also a line pilot, perhaps captain qualified? Is there a systemic safety concern? The question is not just academic because small flight departments often have an owner-pilot advocate eager to do at least some of the flying. Cessna cleverly built much of its Citation business around appealing to owners wanting to fly their own jets. We faced this issue almost immediately, as the plan was to have me trained to type in the airplane and then, eventually, command company missions. Of greater worry perhaps, many of those flights were to be conducted single pilot (SP)—by me.[5]

Fortunately, there are simple safeguards to prevent an owner-pilot suffering from inexperience, cockiness, bad judgment, or just a strong need to go, from compromising safety. High on the list is for someone other than the owner to take on the chief pilot role. The chief pilot is the person with ultimate responsibility for the safety of the operation. All pilots including the owner report to the chief pilot, whose job would include crew qualification, assignment, and control over the dispatch of any flight. This doesn't preclude the owner running the flight department as a business unit, but for purposes of the actual flying, the flying owner-pilot has to agree that the chief pilot's word is final. A good chief pilot would never allow an owner, serving as a pilot or in any other capacity, to compromise safety even if it meant ultimately quitting the flight department to prove the point.

We were fortunate to recruit Karen "KK" Harvey to be our chief pilot. She came from a fractional company with experience flying Beechjets, and later did the same for a big local construction company. In her new role, she would fly our Citation Jet while also looking after all other aspects of the operation. Paramount was making sure my flying met the high standards outlined by Mickey and approved by me. So off to jet school we went; easy for her, a challenge for me as it turned out. Moving to jets takes flying and everything else up a notch.[6]

---

[5] Cessna certified the Citation Jet design to be flown as both a crew (two pilots) and single pilot (SP) airplane. Pilots flying the airplane alone must accomplish a special SP type rating.

[6] Instructors at Simuflite, the training provider we selected, rated KK's aptitude for flying in the top 5%. Their assessment was not only consistent with my own view of her abilities, it also confirmed a more general observation that women are on average better pilots. Although some genetic advantage could provide the explanation, my speculation is that those women choosing flying as a career need to be better to survive in what has always been a male-dominated industry. Only about 5% of US airline pilots are women according to the Airline Pilots Association.

The company flight department turned out to be a tremendous success. So much so that in three years we had outgrown our small Citation Jet and purchased a more capable CJ3. Three years after that, we added a CJ4, becoming a two-airplane flight department with a fulltime mechanic and second professional pilot.

The list of destinations expanded, too. In addition to North and Central America and the Caribbean, there were occasional flights to Europe, in support of business operations in the UK, France, Germany, and Switzerland.

There were many other unforeseen benefits. Recruiting key personnel for the company was easier because the specter of frequent unpredictable airline travel out of Burlington, a spoke airport, could be avoided. Before there was a flight department, there were trips that should have been taken but were skipped because of the whole airline experience. These now happened seamlessly, which contributed to the company's growth in revenue and profitability. The airplane also makes a spectacular conference room for a private meeting. When you have your own flight department, there is no danger of being overheard while en route to that trade show by some competitor sharing the same flight.

Perhaps most telling is that the flight department budget always sails through the annual process without question. What started as a frightening, possibly foolhardy expense is now seen as the minimum needed for a bright prosperous future. Even my fiscally-conservative brother has come to view the flight department as an indispensable resource.

Still, if ever there were a conceptual sell needed, jet airplanes and private corporate flight departments are the posterchild. Those who have them know the merit. Those who don't regard the enterprise as an extravagance, lacking any tangible return. The fear of sending the wrong message to shareholders, customers, and employees prevents even the largest companies from considering a private flight department. Companies located near large hub airports would be hard pressed to justify private flying unless their employees frequently fly to small, out of the way places. In the world of public and private companies, the private ones like ours are more likely to go for a flight department, especially if there is an enthusiastic owner.

A lot depends on how much value is placed on the people traveling. We believe our employees are the company's greatest asset. We don't want to see their time wasted in the airline system. So, private jets make sense whether or not we can justify them on a strict cost for service basis. What is true is that since the creation of the flight department the company's revenue has more than tripled and its profitability has quadrupled. Coincidence?

In business, stormy days go with the territory. For those focused on the pennies, nickels, and dimes on the ground, airlines are for you. If you've got an eye for the larger denominations, $100 bills for example, a flight department deserves consideration.

## Lessons learned:

**Lesson 1:** Involving a trained and experienced aviation consultant in the creation of a new flight department, acquisition of aircraft, and recruiting of personnel pays big dividends. At the very least, there should always be a professional insulating the client from the seller, or buyer as the case may be, in any transaction involving aircraft. During negotiation, the person with the authority to make the final decision should not be present.

**Lesson 2:** For those who expect to fly 200 hours or more on a private jet aircraft, a private flight department is likely more economical than the alternatives, such as on-demand charter, fractionals, or jet cards.

**Lesson 3:** When creating a flight department, seek advice from those who have already done it.

# 24 | Living the Dream and That New Jet Airplane Smell

You have been saving for years and finally the time has come. You have enough to buy one of those brand new shiny jet airplanes on display at your local airplane dealer. Much to consider. The smaller designs are more in line with the mission requirement and budget, but the larger ones with the fancy paint jobs, bigger engines, and luxurious interiors are just so sexy. While you're enjoying filet mignon and other five-star treats on the menu in the dealer's private dining room, the salesperson politely answers all your questions about the smaller aircraft. Before leaving the showroom facility he (or she) makes sure to provide you with all the glossy brochures extolling the virtues of that much more expensive design. He says something to the effect of "how good you would look piloting one of those," adding that with the end of the quarter near there could be incentives. "Let me talk with my manager," he says, and leaves briefly. Then something amazing happens. Returning, the salesperson confesses that the very nice demonstration aircraft, the one typical of the model under consideration, used to transport you and your team from Vermont to the dealer location in the Midwest, is unfortunately not available for the return. "Will a new, larger, more luxurious, aircraft be okay?" he says, adding that there just happened to be one around. "You'll love the handling," he says. It's then that the company captain assigned to the mission offers to let you fly the leg, from beginning to end. This despite your logbook showing absolutely no time in type.

The flight home is amazing—faster, more comfortable, far superior to the small jet experience characteristic of the trip out. While the salesperson, also on the flight, highlights the many fabulous interior features to your colleagues in the back such as broadband, swivel reclining seats, and fancy cup holders, the captain in right seat next to you elaborates on the capabilities of the bigger airplane's systems and avionics. What's not to like! By the time we arrive in Vermont—refreshed, enthusiastic—all are 100 percent convinced that bigger is better. The salesperson kindly offers to write up a "very attractive" offer, saying something about sealing the deal before the end of the quarter. The smaller, more modest jet option now a fading memory, budget busted, negotiations for purchase of the bigger aircraft underway, a typical day of jet shopping reaches its inevitable conclusion.

Buying new (or used) airplanes, especially jet airplanes, is a domain reserved for the privileged. A light jet like our CJ3, purchased new, costs around $7 million. Bigger business jet airplanes cost much more; the largest among them approach $55 million to $100 million. Few have access to this kind of capital. Even for those who do, an investment like this gives pause. Curiously, though, the sales process would be familiar to most of us. Satisfying the very utilitarian business purpose normally used to justify purchase of a jet airplane is only part of the appeal. OEM sales departments know that look, feel, and image also play an important role in the decision-making, and in this respect a jet dealer is not all that different from a car dealer. The jet salesperson wants you to imagine yourself behind the yoke, or as a pampered passenger in back, occupying the CEO's seat. Buy the right jet, and you will be younger, thinner, smarter, more handsome, more beautiful, and more virile in spades. You will have many friends—a truism that can be a downside for the new jet owner. Key to persuading the buyer to go forward is instilling a vision, that ownership equals a better quality of life. Buy this new jet airplane and you'll feel great. Sound familiar?

It's a compelling pitch, especially when the decision maker is only loosely connected to actual aircraft mission compatibility and such details as whether it's cost-effective. Independent of aspirations to maintain an analytical approach, defining the mission can be daunting. Yes, the airplane manufacturers are happy to help, but their bias is toward promoting the design, with an agreed target—the purchaser. There is a real risk that the airplane ends up defining the mission, for reasons that are more about superfluous criteria like striping colors or how the airplane looks on the ramp. Those delicious steak lunches are also a factor. Not ideal for rational decision-making. Consultants can help, but a good decision demands a renaissance approach, the goal to make mission, finance, operating cost, tax, and lifestyle harmonize perfectly. Mission, though, should drive the process. How does one define mission?

Adopting the 80/20 rule can be helpful. If, for example, 20 percent of the destinations account for 80 percent of the trips, convenient access to these places may define the mission. Identifying the destinations and then confirming which of the candidate airplane(s) can do the job, conveniently, robustly, and economically, advances the cause.

Our company wanted the flight department to support trips to Europe. A large aircraft like the Dassault Falcon 900 or 2000 series, with its nonstop transatlantic capability, certainly would have done the job. But given the low frequency of visits anticipated, we considered smaller, lower cost aircraft too, including Cessna's CJ3 and CJ4. Assuming passenger loads within reason (three or four passengers), and a stop in Newfoundland and Iceland, they would work. A longer day? Yes, but a fair exchange especially considering the cost of running the Falcons is three times the cost of the Cessnas. Once in Europe, destinations are close by, the Dassault and Cessna would be mostly the same, except when needing to pee standing up in the airplane's bathroom.

If, on the other hand, the mission is to transport travelers to major European or Asian cities quickly and on time, could a smaller business aircraft capable of reaching an international hub like New York, Boston, or Washington Dulles do the job? Employing an international carrier sans the notorious airline connection greatly improves the odds of reaching the foreign destination in a timely and predictable way. Even assuming a first class seat on the airline, the cost of a hybrid mission will always be less than the use of the company airplane.

Mission also means defining practical range, much different from the maximum range the manufacturers promote. Maximum range is the plane's range when it is flown in a controlled way under absolutely ideal conditions. Full fuel, a very rigid climb, cruise, descent flight profile, long-range cruise power settings, and still air are all part of making the distance work. More sobering, the manufacturer's distance claims assume National Business Aviation Association (NBAA) fuel reserves at the destination: fuel for go-around at destination airport plus climb to 5,000 feet and hold for 5 minutes plus fly to and land at alternate airport 200 NM away plus fuel to hold at 5,000 feet for 30 minutes. While more conservative than the Federal Aviation Regulation IFR requirement, for those flying jet airplanes the NBAA reserve can feel less than generous. Jet airplanes burn a lot of fuel closer to the ground. Imagining some kind of problem—weather, mechanical, or air traffic related—coincident with arriving at the destination airport, the 1 hour and 15 minutes of endurance typically available might not always be enough.

*Practical range* is the distance the airplane will go assuming typical passenger load, winds, origin and destination weather, and routing/air traffic related delays. For most destinations, practical range is about 25 percent less than maximum range, but actual performance can be worse, especially when larger payloads prevent flying with full tanks.

Our first jet airplane, the original Citation Jet, had a maximum range with NBAA reserves equal to 1,119 NM, allowing for nonstop travel to many destinations. Burlington, Vermont, to Wilmington, North Carolina, was always a nonstop flight. But Burlington to Palm Springs was always a two-stop flight, despite the great circle distance being only 2,089 NM. Knowing the airplane could do more than half the distance with reserves why was this necessary? Typical winds on a westbound flight in the summer average about 45 knots on the nose. (They can be much worse.) That equals a loss of about 200 NM in range for each leg. Even assuming direct routing, a perfectly centered mid-continent refueling airport, and perfect destination weather, there would be a real danger of fuel exhaustion prior to reaching the destination. At the very least, most of those NBAA reserves would be needed to complete the flight. Of course, two stops are not the end of the world. Flying 10 hours was still preferable to enduring the hassles of domestic airline travel.

Despite its allure, nonstop flying to faraway places does not provide the best mission definition. Assuming easy fuel stops en route, stopping is normally a minor inconvenience. A quick turn at Lincoln, Nebraska, one of our favorite Midwestern fueling stops on the way to California, can take as little as 20 minutes. The CJ4's central point refueling system can shave off even more time. In the context of total travel time, door to door, the penalty for stopping is usually very small.

Nonstop practical range is important if the plane will do a lot of flying over, or to, places with bad weather. If the only way to make the trip involves landing at a refueling airport with routinely terrible weather, there will be many days when the trip is cancelled. If travel involves frequent stops at airports notorious for storms or very low IFR, the airplane will need to have enough fuel to reach the destination, shoot an approach, miss, and then comfortably get to another airport where conditions are good, or at least not as bad.[1]

Once the flying involves crossing over large bodies of water, like oceans, nonstop capability ranks much higher on the list of desirable features. Stopping not an option? Amazingly, flying from New York to Paris can be accomplished without crossing a body of water longer than 467 NM—the

---

[1] Low IFR refers to weather that is very near the IFR minimums prescribed within the Federal Aviation Regulations; ceilings less than 500 feet, visibility less than 1 mile.

*Our CE-525 Citation Jet.*

leg from Iceland to the UK. Fuel stops in Canada, Greenland, Iceland, and the UK easily afford plenty of reserve fuel, even for the most range-limited business jet aircraft. Possible and practical are different things, however. Routine trips to Europe and certainly Asia using smaller jet aircraft requiring many fuel stops are probably not a good idea unless the end game is to do lots of local flying. Even then, it may make more sense just to rent a jet airplane from a local charter or fractional company, having arrived via commercial airline.

For anyone routinely needing to go to faraway places, selecting a design offering a big maximum range, the specification advertised by the manufacturer, is probably the right idea. If the goal is to routinely cross between North American and continental Europe, a maximum range of 3,600 NM is the minimum needed. Westbound transatlantic flights in particular often experience strong headwinds that dramatically lower the practical range. If US East Coast to Asia is part of the plan, 4,600 NM would be closer to the right answer. On most days the airplane could do the trip to Beijing, Seoul, or Tokyo with only two fuel stops westbound, one on the way back. There are many good lift options in this category, including aircraft manufactured by Gulfstream, Dassault, Bombardier, Embraer, and soon, Cessna. Boeing is also in the market with its large Business Jet based on the 737 airliner, but for most companies the space and range combination offered is overkill, especially given the vastly higher acquisition and operating costs. In some ways, the Boeing Business Jet is inferior to the others in terms of its maximum practical service ceiling, and generally slower cruise airspeed.

Mission payload capacity, passengers and luggage carried, is another important consideration. Although the range discussion, once settled, usually dictates the limits, some airplanes offer more than others while also covering the same distance. The CJ3 and CJ4 are excellent examples of this. Both claim a maximum range around 1,900 NM, but only the CJ4 can do this with six passengers in the back plus luggage. The CJ3 is limited to three passengers plus luggage max, assuming the goal is to go right to the end. Of course, the CJ4 costs more and is heavier, largely due to the slightly longer fuselage dimensions, bigger engines, externally serviceable lavatory, central point refueling and the additional 1,000 pounds of fuel needed to cover the distance.

But what if the typical mission distances were short, and the payload requirements big? Both the CJ3 and CJ4 are identical airplanes for all practical purposes.[2] The only difference is the CJ4's slightly faster cruising speed, largely immaterial because the cruise period is so short. And "short" is relative. Reduce the CJ3's fuel load by 700 pounds and max payloads become identical. That equals a CJ3 maximum range that is only about 300 NM less than what the CJ4 can do.

How high do you need to go? This doesn't sound like a mission-related question, except to be able to fly high enough to top most bad weather. But high is relative, and higher can be an advantage under some circumstances, such as flying westbound in the northern hemisphere. Headwinds are generally less in the stratosphere and traffic, airline traffic in particular, is almost non-existent.[3] Fuel burn is less, too. All good. Unfortunately, not all business jets can get there. Those that can aren't always as efficient up there.

Often, high altitude performance depends on weight. The Concorde, for example, would begin its cruise across the Atlantic Ocean at 50,000 feet and then slowly drift up to 60,000 feet as the fuel burned off and the fuel load decreased. Larger business jet airplanes like the Gulfstream G-550 departing at MGTOW start out lower and then step climb higher, and only

---

[2] The CJ4 comes with one additional side-facing seat, standard, and can optionally be configured to accommodate up to nine passengers in the back. The CJ3+ offers an optional side-facing seat, but is limited to eight in the back, total.

[3] Near the equator, the stratosphere starts at 59,000 feet, 11 miles; at mid-latitudes it starts at 33,000–43,000 feet, 6.2–8.1 miles; and ends at 160,000 feet, 31 miles; at the poles it starts at about 26,000 feet, 5.0 miles.

reach their final cruising altitude well down the road. A few designs, the CJ3 is one, can accomplish max altitude from sea level in one go, about 28 minutes elapse time, even when departing at maximum weight.[4]

Speaking as a pilot, I prefer having the higher flight level capability, 43,000 and 45,000 feet, where the airliners typically don't go. There are more options, including finding potentially smoother air. Assuming lower max altitudes and adherence to the odd/even rule—odd flight level altitudes east bound, even flight level altitude west bound—there are really only two or three efficient flight levels for business jets to go when mixing with airliners. These are in the high end of the range, FL360 to FL410. In flying one of our most common missions, Burlington to Boca Raton, conducted within the very busy northeast corridor, being assigned an altitude below 36,000 feet more often than not necessitates a stop somewhere because of the substantially higher fuel burn. The same mission flown at 43,000 or 45,000 feet, airliner free, could be completed nonstop and with plenty of reserve. Fortunately, for us, both the CJ3 and CJ4 can easily do the higher flight levels.

Naked performance is only one aspect of determining whether the plane is right for the mission. Many other functional characteristics serve to make the aircraft properly harmonized. These can range from avionics/system compliance with current and prospective regulations, to assuring there is adequate broadband in the cabin. There are many degrees of freedom.

WiFi and the internet didn't exist in the 1970s, when I learned how to fly. There were no emails, no texts. Now, both are entrenched in every aspect of our lives. Versions of the technology have worked their way into the cabin and cockpit, too.

Unlike ground-based systems, airplane internet and WiFi is very expensive—$3,000 to $5,000 per month for the service is typical. It's all satellite based and with practically no competition there is little incentive for the providers to reduce costs. In the airplane environment, care must be taken so there is no interference with other aircraft systems, especially the radios and navigation computers. Much effort goes into making these systems reliable and safe.

Having flown airplanes with internet and without, I would always opt for having it. The business advantage is clear, but internet is also useful to the pilot. It offers an array of weather products well beyond the traditional

---

[4] Max altitude from sea level in the CJ3 is 45,000 feet.

XM Radio weather[5] that has been the mainstay in the cockpit since the 1990s or even the newer ADS-B[6] weather offered to those with ADS-B In capability.

Then there is the cockpit itself, the front office, with the fancy buttons, dials, keyboards, and displays. Pilots have opinions about everything. While reasonable people might politely disagree about systems like electrical, hydraulics, propulsion, anti-ice/deice, and pressurization, nothing inspires more pilot passion than a discussion about the right (or wrong) avionics solution. The only topic more controversial is the pilot's seat, comfort being the priority. Manufacturers know that uncomfortable seats can kill the deal.

Most pilots would rather fly with avionics equipment and systems made by manufacturers they already know. The transition is just easier. But familiarity shouldn't really be high on the list of reasons to buy. What matters more is the airplane's capability of performing the mission, compliance with the regulations that govern access to the airspace one of the primary considerations.

Avionics systems regulatory compliance is important because it dictates where the airplane can go. If the altimetry system fails to meet reduced vertical separation minimums (RVSM), 28,000 feet is the maximum altitude ATC will assign. If the transponder is not at least Mode S capable, much of European airspace is off limits.[7] By 2020, airplanes not equipped with transponders with ADS-B will be grounded unless they have come from the manufacturer without any electrical system at all. Not many jets in this category. Controller-pilot data link communications (CPDLC), a system that allows the pilot to request and receive clearances and other information from ATC by text, is on the required equipment list item if the goal is to fit gracefully into the track system used by most airplanes crossing the Atlantic Ocean.

Compliance issues commonly arise when considering the purchase of a used airplane, but new airplanes are not immune. Sometimes the design

---

[5] XM Radio weather originates from the same satellite system used for music programming and includes TAFs, METARs, composite weather radar, and in some cases winds aloft.

[6] ADS-B is primarily an air traffic control management technology, but it also can be used to obtain weather information similar in content to XM weather. ADS-B and XM use different transmission/reception schemes and in the case of ADS-B weather some information originates from ground stations instead of satellites.

[7] Mode S transponders are backwards compatible with older designs; e.g., Mode A and C, but also offer a solution for compliance with ADS-B Out regulations. Mode S also carries a unique signature that identifies the individual aircraft while also transmitting certain flight parameters including indicated airspeed.

isn't finished, the plane coming with a kind of avionics IOU from the manufacturer following purchase. Very occasionally, there is no specification defining the needed functionality at all, a problem for both the manufacturer-seller and the buyer because the cost and timing of compliance is essentially unknown. The next generation of CPDLC is a good example of this.

Generational hierarchy can play a role in determining the right avionics solution. While all modern jet airplane panels are glass, LCDs or equivalent, with good autopilots, and highly automated flight management systems, some designs are more reminiscent of the days before point-and-click computers, when communication was often via DOS-style line editor. Collins and Honeywell systems operate much in this way. Although they are capable, there is much grammar and syntax to learn and typing required to communicate with the system. There are pages of functionality to remember. The Garmin system by contrast is visual, with touchscreen icons controlling most functions, not unlike the user interface in the iPhone. All these different designs work, they will do the job, but if flying the future is the priority, a system like Garmin's is probably the way to go.

Although a few OEMs offer different avionics solutions for a single model/type, most don't. The complexity and expense of integrating and supporting two or more designs is just too much. So it may be the perfect airplane does not come with perfect avionics, and vice versa. In the spirit that the perfect should not be the enemy of the good, all modern avionics designs are likely to deliver satisfactory results.

With the mission defined, candidate aircraft type(s) and installed equipment determined, the next step is to find the perfect specimen. Buying new is easier simply because, subjectively, *perfect* is mostly about deciding on options, and cutting a good deal. With used airplanes, the task is harder. Here an aviation consultant is vital because available specimens are likely to vary in quality, appearance, equipment, and history.

Used airplane shopping can be interesting, because of the larger than life characters that tend to be involved. While we were shopping for our CJ3, Harrison Ford's airplane came on the market. Our chief pilot really wanted to see that airplane, not at all motivated by the broker's promise that the actor would personally conduct the demo flight. Unfortunately, Ford's airplane was a little older than what we were looking for, so to her disappointment, we moved on.

Meeting celebrities can be fun, but buying new is more fun, a guilty pleasure. Beyond the five-course lunches, free fishing and skiing trips, and of course the customizing—customer striping and N-number—that goes with the deal, buying new allows for the acquisition of the nearly perfect airplane with everything in harmony: mission, finance, operating cost, tax, and lifestyle. Properly executed, the airplane looks, feels, and flies exactly right.

Some manufacturers will build white tails on speculation.[8] Even then, most will have secured a buyer before settling on the final option list. Specifying the details is not without its challenges. Options for interior appointments, exterior paint, colors, striping, even avionics, are many and varied. Just glancing through the list can be daunting. When it's a family business like ours buying, there can be controversy over aesthetics, selection of paint design, or fabrics, for example. After much discussion, my sister-in-law agreed to let my wife design the exterior striping and colors for our first new airplane, the CJ4, providing she could do the next. (Both are professional designers.) Happily, a family feud was averted.

For the owner-pilot or aspiring owner-pilot, buying a new jet can be an experience. Unlike used airplane sellers, the OEMs are more than willing (in fact, excited) to let their prospects fly the airplane under consideration. Cessna and Embraer's demo program has the buyer in the left seat, doing most of, if not all of, the flying while a company pilot assists. It doesn't seem to matter whether the customer is type rated or not, although I expect having no pilots license at all could be an issue. It's difficult to know. One sales representative told me there is some vetting of clients behind the scenes prior to letting them loose in the left seat. Recalling the many test flights I have done, though, I can't remember a time when someone asked me for my credentials.

Once the make and model have been determined, the specifications established, it is time to negotiate. Much like the new and used car buying experience, airplane manufacturers will negotiate, if properly engaged. The place to start is to learn the late-model used market, airplanes that are one or two years old, low time, with similar features and appointments, because in many respects this is the competition. A properly-equipped one-year-old airplane with, say, 300 hours logged is going to deliver identical performance to new. Yes, the warranty will be closer to term, but this is likely a minor consideration when the comparison is between new at list price and used at market.

---

[8] White tails are new airplanes built on speculation notably painted white, ready to accept customer specified exterior striping and colors.

Timing is also important, especially in the case of white tails. The combination of a new airplane sitting on the (ramp) and the end of the quarter is a wonderful thing, particularly for the business manager trying to make the period's target numbers. End of the year is even better.

One consideration is that, just as for cars, new airplane gross margins aren't that wide. Even assuming list price, 28 percent is likely the most any manufacturer is going to see.[9] So, the maximum theoretical discount will be something less than that. Up to about 14 percent is possible in my experience. A lot depends on general market conditions.

Discount incentives are painful for manufacturers because of the dollar-for-dollar relationship between the discounted amount and overall profitability. Salespersons will have a hard time obtaining approval for pricing below guidance, unless there are special circumstances, or a strategic reason, such as getting a branded specimen into a hangar full of competitor airplanes. Therefore, other approaches to extract value may work better. Free options? Some options are relatively inexpensive for the manufacturer to produce, but represent great value to the customer. In general, these are goods and services completed directly by the OEM, like multi-color paint striping schemes and extended airframe warranties. More free trainings beyond what comes with the airplane is also a possibility, because even with a third party supplier, the cost to the manufacturer is likely to be well below market rates. It doesn't hurt to ask.

Not all buyers are created equal. Airplane companies know this, so they routinely analyze customer profiles, to understand individual requirements, motivations, and most importantly, the nature and range of ability to pay. It's not sinister; mostly the OEM sales representatives want to assure a good match. Ability (and willingness) to pay, however, is interesting because some buyers have higher limits than others. It may be helpful to communicate the impression that the practical limit is closer to the cost of the aircraft at maximum discount, as opposed to something higher. Of course, at the end of the day, the buyer has to be willing to walk away from the deal to prove the point.

The most important piece of advice, however, is to negotiate every possible need up front. Forgetting something important can be expensive, especially provisional items like embedded wiring for avionics solutions not yet desired or available. Even small things left off the list can be outrageously

---

[9] The difference between the direct cost to manufacture and the selling price less commissions, discounts and other incentives.

expensive to address. I am still fuming about the $4,000 carpet runner we had to buy post-deal to protect the CJ4's relatively light-colored interior floor.

The truth is, new airplanes are a bad financial investment, however clever the buyer is at negotiating the deal. Real depreciation can be in the millions of dollars on an annual basis, especially during the first several years of ownership. So perfect also needs to include a fairly long ownership horizon for the purchase to make any sense economically. My cousin Rob says the answer is to buy the last airplane you are ever going to own first. New or used, fewer transactions reduce the overall cost of airplane ownership; there is less real depreciation, consultant, tax, and training expense. Of course, when forced to own up, Rob would admit somewhat sheepishly to having overseen the purchase of ten different airplanes for his beverage company before settling on the airliner-sized Gulfstream G-550s the company owns today.

The reality is that even accounting for great mission definition and a smooth acquisition process, the purchase of any jet airplane is going feel expensive. It is therefore wise to admit that the real benefits, including the business purpose, are related to lifestyle, the comfort and convenience afforded. For those owner-pilots living a dream to fly a new jet, economic justification is the means to an end, but the *end* is what really counts. *You fly your own jet. How cool is that!* And if you have shopping and decorating in your genes, there can be no better release than buying a new jet. What's more fun than creating a beautiful living room that flies at 500 mph?

No apologies here! It's your life, spend it well. There's nothing like that new jet smell.

### Lessons learned:

**Lesson 1:** Mission drives all. The more accurate and precise the mission definition, the better the results.

**Lesson 2:** Fewer jet purchases are better. Within mission parameters, buy the biggest, most capable jet aircraft you can afford.

**Lesson 3:** Negotiate all needed modifications, features, and accessories into the deal prior to signing. Expect post-deal requirements to be very expensive to satisfy.

**Lesson 4:** It's your life, spend it well!

# 25 The Theory of Everything: Our Global Aviation System

have often wondered what flying would be like if the world's dominant industrial power had been Russia or China in 1947, when the ICAO agreement which standardized aviation conventions, went into effect. Would altitude be represented in meters instead of feet, as it is in both China and Russia?[1] What about altimeter settings? When flying in Russia, the barometric pressure is given generally in QFE, the touchdown at zero altitude as displayed by the altimeter in the airplane.[2] (For most of the rest of the world barometric pressure is given using the QNH system, elevation above sea level.)[3] Barometric pressure most likely would be in millimeters of mercury, the standard not just in Russia and China, but UK, Europe, and a number of other countries. The big question is: would we be speaking Russian or Chinese instead of English when talking to air traffic control over the radio?

Dealing with meters or QFE would be manageable, but I thank my lucky stars that English won the day as the standard medium for flights conducted internationally. Understanding clearances is challenging enough. Getting it all down in Chinese, that would be game over. Happily for me, all charting, navigation, routing, and communications is, by the rules of the ICAO, in my native language.

The convention still allows for colorful moments when flying internationally, especially when communicating over the radio. English as a second language skills vary around the world, even in agencies that demand and test for one's proficiency with English. In many cases, it may take several attempts to understand what the ATC person on the ground is saying. Even assuming good language skills, strong accents can make comprehension

---

[1] Russia switched to feet for the flight levels in 2017. Altitudes below the transition level are still measured in meters.

[2] QFE is a Q code (Q-code field elevation) indicating the pressure at the station (or aerodrome) level.

[3] QNH is a Q code (Q-code nautical height) indicating the atmospheric pressure adjusted to sea level.

difficult. A lot depends on the individual, but in my experience, Mexican and French English speakers can be tough to understand. German speakers from Germany and Switzerland are better. Curiously, I find controllers in the UK the most difficult to understand—strange given their first language is English. And the challenge is not just limited to understanding thick accents. On occasion, the phraseology can be puzzling. Departing out of Midlands Airport on one occasion, I received an ATC clearance to "Line up and wait, immediately". Innocent enough, but the direction felt a bit like the *strictly no parking* signs sometimes displayed in front of many opportunistic parking spots in London and the surrounding area. Shouldn't *no parking* be enough?

Fortunately, pilots and controllers use mostly standardized phraseology when making requests and issuing clearances. With a little patience on both sides, the job gets done. Further, clearance information increasingly is transmitted to and from the airplane in digital form via systems like CPDLC, virtually eliminating any possible ambiguity.

The occasional communication challenges aside, much progress has been made wringing the last vestiges of provincialism out of the system. In the US, "position and hold" terminology was replaced with "line up and wait" in 2010, the last non-ICAO terminology to be addressed. Airport taxiway and runway markings, and lighting, are the same everywhere. Increasingly, weather information provided to the pilot also is standardized. Large international airports have been served by precision ILS for a long time, but with the proliferation of satellite systems (RNAV, LPV), many smaller airports that couldn't afford the expensive ground-based systems will be in a position to offer something closer to all-weather capability. This is all a direct result of global standards for instrumentation and procedures.

The global aviation system we use is amazing, and largely unprecedented. With the exception of the internet perhaps, no other standards are so universally accepted. The benefits are efficiency, convenience, and relatively affordable access to international travel for most. But, are there any downsides?

One concern is that the system, by virtue of its centralized nature, connectivity, and complexity, is somewhat fragile. In 2014, a fire at the Aurora, Illinois, radar facility caused more than 2,000 flight cancellations at Chicago's O'Hare and Midway airports. The fire was intentionally set by a contractor trying to commit suicide, but the FAA was still criticized for not having adequate back-up systems. Natural disasters also can affect travel. Many flights between Europe and the US were cancelled and millions of passengers delayed in 2010 due to the ash ejected by Iceland's Eyjafjalla-jökull volcano. Volcanic ash is volatile, and dangerous for jet engines. My colleagues traveling in Europe had their return home delayed for weeks. Then there are occasional labor actions, strikes. When French air traffic controllers walked off the job in 2013, ironically to protest further integration of European airspace, the Single European Sky 2+ (SES2+) package, large portions of European airspace suddenly were off-limits causing costly and time-consuming re-routings.[4] Common to these events was the negative impact on air system operations; many cancelled or delayed flights. The underlying cause was not the events themselves, but the rigid regulations, and the sometimes unreliable, ground-based infrastructure employed to manage and control the flights.

The problem presented by Iceland's volcano is interesting in that while the threat was real, the system's response had to be one size fits all. The ICAO guidelines at the time, with regard to the danger of volcanic ash, amounted to zero tolerance. All member countries had to close their airspace, independent of the actual risk, and despite there being no agreement as to what concentration of ash constituted a hazard to jet aircraft engines.

The decision to close the airspace over Europe stranded millions of passengers. Airlines lost hundreds of millions of dollars and the economies of Europe and its trading partners dipped as a direct result. No airplanes were lost due to volcanic ash, but some in the industry argued that a more flexible solution was needed. Unfortunately, the same ICAO standardization that has made modern air transportation practical and safe also has fostered a system that doesn't respond well to unforeseen external events like volcanic eruptions, or even the failure of small elements of infrastructure within the system (e.g., a single radar facility in the American Midwest going down).

Much effort has been devoted to reform, with the goal of increasing capacity, safety, efficiency, predictability, and resilience. SES2+ in Europe and Next Generation Air Transportation System (NextGen) in the US are part of this effort. Both programs reflect a move away from using ground-

---

[4] With SES2+, the EC proposed to update regulations that created the Single European Sky effort, which is comparable to NextGen in the US, and to amend rules governing the European Aviation Safety Agency (EASA). It builds on SES1, which entered force in 2004, and SES2, which became effective in 2009. Among changes, the SES2+ legislation calls for "full organizational and budgetary separation" of national authorities from the ATC organizations they oversee; opening ATC support services to competitive bidding; and strengthening air traffic management (ATM) performance targets. Companies will be able to form industrial partnerships with the regional ATC entities called functional airspace blocks (FABs). Bill Carey, "Parliament Approves Single European Sky '2+' Package," *AINonline*, March 12, 2014, https://www.ainonline.com/aviation-news/air-transport/2014-03-12/parliament-approves-single-european-sky-2-package.

based systems like radar for managing air traffic toward a satellite-based approach. The focus is on ADS-B capability in the aircraft. With most aircraft required to support ADS-B by 2020, ATC will no longer have to ping the traffic using radar to establish position, speed, altitude. The target aircraft will report all this information, along with many other parameters, to listening ground stations. There are big advantages to this system in the cockpit, too. For those with ADS-B In, a precise picture of the traffic environment is available. Eventually, there will be traffic alert and traffic resolution advisories similar to the present day TCAS system, only with ADS-B technology employed the guidance will be vastly more precise.

NextGen is a lot of things, including En Route Automation Modernization (ERAM), decision support systems (DSS), and National Airspace System Voice System (NVS). Together, the hope is that they will provide improved capacity and better general enroute traffic management, better flow control through the airspace, and more flexibility in allocating controlling related resources. DSS addresses the lack of resiliency demonstrated by the Aurora facility fire. Using a new internet-enabled digital voice conveyance system, designed to link multiple ATC TRACON and ARTCC facilities, it will be possible for the controller to manage aircraft flying in places far from the controller's physical location or normally assigned airspace. In theory, if one facility is saturated, or fails for some reason, another can take over via secure internet communication.

Given time, airspace traffic control will certainly improve. The improvements likely will be incremental in that the new system will look a lot like the old. It will still require enormous human resources to operate, and because the inputs to controlling originate via a centralized methodology, it will still be vulnerable to unpredictable events such as weather, infrastructure failure, and unexpected surges in traffic. It's the nature of central planning. Translation: aircraft will continue to wait on the ground, or circle in the air, as they do today, until there is enough room in the system.

More worrisome is the ATC system we're building today will only solve yesterday's air traffic control problems. Even if it all works, success may be fleeting. Pilots have been told what to do by controllers for as long as there have been pilots, but what if someday that's not the case? Welcome to the world of autonomous and semi-autonomous aircraft. First, it is important to point out that autonomous aircraft are not drones, in that the flying happens without a ground-based operator in control of the aircraft. Cruise missiles operate this way. Predator drone aircraft do not. There is almost always a human operator, however far away, telling the Predator what to do.

Driverless cars are the closest analogy in that the driving is performed by on-board systems plus, perhaps, some cloud-based enterprise software.

Despite the complexities, are driverless cars and aircraft fully capable of conducting themselves properly without a human pilot/driver in the loop? For cars, conventional wisdom plus money invested equals yes! Aircraft?

Actually, developing autonomous aircraft is technically easier because the natural governing rules are simpler. Conduct a smooth takeoff and landing, fly a prescribed course at determined altitude(s) from origin to destination. Don't crash into other aircraft along the way. Done! Autonomous cars face all kinds of problems, like other cars being driven erratically by humans and errant pedestrians jaywalking or crossing against the light. Autonomous cars have moral dilemmas, such as deciding whether to run over a child or hit a tree. There are not many wayward children or trees 10,000 feet above the ground.

Autonomous aircraft initially will be small, designed for short flights. This is largely to avoid conflict with legacy aircraft, as well as address availability of propulsion and energy storage systems (batteries). The concept advocated by Amazon founder Jeff Bezos, Amazon Prime Air, promises the most practical and socially acceptable next step.[5] Although electric motors are simple, light, powerful, responsive and relatively easy to control, and therefore ideal for VTOL designs like quadcopters, batteries are still heavy compared to jet fuel on a weight/unit energy basis, so endurance and range will be limited.

Hybrid versions leveraging gas turbine electric generator technology will be more capable. All technologies will improve, especially now that mainstream technology leaders like Bell, Boeing, and Airbus are committed to some kind of air taxi solution.[6]

The bigger, faster, higher service ceiling aircraft will have to interact with ATC in a very different way. Controllers telling pilots what to do won't work because there won't be anyone in the aircraft to direct. To the extent ATC interacts with autonomous airplane traffic, it's going to have to be via some kind of yet-to-be-invented telemetry directed at the ship's computer. That's something the old system can't do, not yet.

Irrespective of the availability of the technology, mimicking the commands normally directed at a human pilot in a way the aircraft's computer

---

[5] Amazon Prime Air, a drone-based package delivery system that promises thirty-minute-or-less delivery times.

[6] Daisuke Wakabayashi, "Flying Taxis May Be Years Away, but the Groundwork Is Accelerating," *New York Times*, February 27, 2018.

would understand may not be ideal. The whole idea that autonomous aircraft would be following directions from the ground may have to be revisited, especially given the likelihood of aircraft having the capability to chart all the surrounding traffic precisely, in real time. Consider traffic separation, ATC's primary responsibility when managing aircraft operating under instrument flight rules. Autonomous aircraft equipped with ADS-B In/Out and benefiting from some kind of block chain common ledger scheme may well do a better job, negotiating with each other directly to secure a safe path for both/all.[7] Dealing with airports, and the inevitable mix of human and non-human piloted traffic, will be more complicated. Here AI in the autonomous aircraft may be the answer, especially when human pilots are in the mix. The problem isn't insurmountable. Human pilots have been navigating their aircraft to thousands of uncontrolled airports safely and autonomously (without ATC involvement) using VFR, and often under very heavy traffic conditions. Autonomous aircraft will do the same, with the added benefit of knowing the position, altitude, and trajectory of every other aircraft in the area. And for the kind of point-to-point travel envisioned for electric VTOL aircraft, there will be few conflicts on the ground, anyway.

There will still be human controllers involved in traffic management at larger, busier airports, of course. They will enjoy final authority over access to airport resources (approaches, runways, taxiways, gates), the computer-controlled autonomous aircraft duty-bound to follow their instructions. But human controller involvement will be mostly supervisory in nature, leaving the actual controlling to the automation in the air and on the ground. Scary?

There are at least two categories of worry with modern, complex, dynamic enterprises like ATC and the aircraft under ATC control. The first category is systemic, a problem in the overall design that leads to unpredictable, perhaps dangerous events. Consider an ADS-B software bug in the ground-based software that, under certain circumstances, causes inaccurate but believable position reporting. If then used as an input for the control of autonomous and other aircraft, and assuming the defective software is widely shared, the error could affect all controlled traffic. The second category is non-systemic, at least relative to the ATC function. An example

---

[7] Blockchain holds records of digital transactions in such a way that makes them accessible and visible to multiple participants in a network, while keeping them secure. The digital shared ledger is updated and validated with each transaction, resulting in a secure, permanently recorded exchange. Treshock, Mark. "Blockchain for Healthcare & Life Sciences...Beyond the Hype." Analyitical, Life Science & Diagnostics Association, 2018 Senior Management Conference. October 1, 2018.

would be an individual autonomously-operated aircraft not complying with ATC guidance, or failing to negotiate in good faith with other autonomous aircraft, because of its own design flaw. The flaw may be systemic relative to the autonomous aircraft type and/or its specific avionics package, but limited beyond that. Other autonomous types/designs presumably would be unaffected, except that everyone is flying in the same airspace. *Note to file:* innocent aircraft, beware!

Systemic and non-systemic problems have always existed (and continue to exist) even in the current human-controlled and piloted system. The presumption, however, is that when something goes systemically or non-systemically wrong, there is a human in the loop, available to detect and correct the problem. That's why for those operating the aircraft in the air and those controlling them from ground there is so much emphasis on training to address those rare but potentially dangerous abnormal, emergency events.

One of the reasons operating ATC and aircraft manually or with low-to-medium levels of automation works well, is that the humans and the automation involved have evolved to be proficient at what they do. Viewed together, as a total enterprise, however, both have become increasingly susceptible to the kind of systemic and non-systemic problems being imagined for completely automated enterprises like autonomous aircraft. The reason? Dependency on automation is increasing. Automation itself is becoming more functionally capable, complex and, from the human operator's perspective, more mysterious, especially when something goes wrong.

Migrating to a satellite system by itself increases the chances of a systemic problem that may be difficult to detect. With the individual ground-based en route and radar systems gone, failures are more likely to have an impact on the whole system, instead of just one locality. While there will be redundant satellites in orbit and lots of backup servers on the ground, when things go wrong with common elements like the ADS-B software, it won't matter whether the aircraft flying are piloted by humans or not. The same is true for the automated text messaging systems like CLDPC, or their more advanced descendants that will be used in the future for communicating clearances directly to aircraft FMSs, with limited or no human intervention. There are many possibilities, including that a malicious actor might successfully hack the whole thing. And the worry is not an abstract one likely to materialize in some distant future. The systemic and non-systemic weaknesses that we nervously imagine for autonomous aircraft are to some degree with us now, inherent in the air traffic management enterprise that exists today.

Will autonomous aircraft in our future airspace bring additional risk? The answer depends on the reference point used for comparison. If the benchmark is human-piloted aircraft, the aggregate risk may be unchanged, because the two methodologies increasingly have so much in common. Most commercial flying is systematized, with less and less decision-making left to the pilot. Although the pilot always has the final say, a dispatch system normally handles routing, weather planning, fuel load and weight and balance calculation. Even when there is failure, the autonomous aircraft and human-piloted aircraft will address problems the same way. Improvisation, unique to humans so far, is less and less a part of flying; the vast majority of abnormal events, emergencies, and failures in general are addressed by training-enforced memorized responses and checklist items. The same is true for autonomous aircraft, except the machine's responses are likely to be faster and more precise due to the speed advantage, vast memory available, and deterministic nature of computer-based automation.

NASA and the FAA have been working for years on a blueprint for how autonomous aircraft might integrate into the current and future ATC system. The plan is to finish the research by 2019, and have a system implemented by 2025. Most likely the focus will be on smaller, low altitude flying autonomous aircraft, like those imagined by Jeff Bezos for delivering packages. It will be a while before people-carrying versions enter service, despite the efforts of Uber and other paradigm-shifting companies. What may appear earlier, however, is a hybrid solution, semi-autonomous aircraft with a human pilot in the loop, either on board or on the ground. The skill level required, and actual amount of piloting that the semi-piloting person performs, is unclear. By any standard, the flying itself would have to be a lot easier than it is today for the aircraft to be practical and safe. And more than likely, there will need to be special airspaces created to support truly autonomous variants. This is to insure separation from possibly conflicting legacy technology aircraft while providing mechanisms for both facilitating and regulating the technology required to fly safely without human intervention.

Automated elevators in buildings gradually replaced manually-operated elevators—and their human operators—around the middle of the twentieth century. The transition must have seemed terribly sad for the human operators (pilots of a sort), as they saw their numbers dwindle to nothing despite their union's best efforts. Recalling visits to my grandmother's apartment on Ninety-Fourth Street and Lexington, as a young boy in the early 1960s, there were few more dedicated employees in the apartment building than the elevator man, his passion a perfect landing on the right floor. Still, the change brought greater efficiency, perhaps a more pleasant ride for the passengers, the targeting of the floors—touch down—smoothly accomplished, automatically. It took fifty years, but automation won out in the elevator business, the smiling welcome of human operators replaced by scheduling algorithms, faster travel times, and precise floor landings. Much the same is happening in aviation. Like automated elevators, a modern day FMS and autopilot programmed correctly executes approaches to landing and other maneuvers more precisely, smoothly, and efficiently than any human pilots do. Many jets can't be flown safely without a working autopilot. Virtual copilots are likely next, as AI technology improves. Independent of whether there is a human pilot in the cockpit, it's not much of a leap to envision a fully-automated flight, whether managed in the air or on the ground.

Personally, I can't help feeling that deferring the captaincy to a machine is wrong. Computers are tools; efficient, precise, increasingly clever, and useful. Still, I prefer not to serve under them, even if the consequence is a more expensive and slightly less than perfect system. There are duties to fulfill, things men and women have to do to be men and women. Serving as captain of the ship, the final authority, responsible for the safety of all aboard, defines that role.

Caught on the wrong side of history, shall my romantic version of the captaincy eventually succumb to practicality and merit, delivered by the ever-superior machine? Will romance endure? Fifty years is a long time.

## Lessons learned:

**Lesson 1:** Centralized systems of control (e.g., ATC), are safe and mostly effective except in cases of unexpected events and/or singularly dependent or required equipment failure.

**Lesson 2:** Human- and autonomously-operated aircraft increasingly will follow the same rules. Systemic risks are similar.

**Lesson 3:** For those with practical horizons, romance is forever.

# 26
## Ten Excellent Mitigations to Make Flying Enjoyable, Useful, and Safe

Sometimes bad things happen to good people. Bad luck is not limited to the reckless and uncaring. (Ironically, it seems as if the reckless among us are the ones who defy the odds, to survive beyond what the actuarial tables might suggest.) Still, knowing that living a perfect life is not an option, the focus turns to devising strategies to survive the errors.

Flying is more unforgiving than many activities when it comes to managing bad luck, poor skillset, bad judgment, and inappropriate or poorly maintained equipment. A bad day in any one of these areas can lead to substantial losses, personal injury, and possibly death for those directly involved. *Kaboom!* But what to do?

I propose ten proactive mitigations. The operational assumption is that in the course of a typical flying career there occasionally will be threatening circumstances, some truly dire. The stories contained in this book are proof by example. But, rather than trying to teach the experience in advance using abstract methods, the idea here is to adopt and embrace mitigations that facilitate a predictable and successful mission, while also assuring a better outcome even in the event of something truly bad (scary) happening; hopefully learning a valuable lesson in the process.

For your consideration:

## Mitigation 1: Intimacy

Know all aircraft systems well, especially the automation!

Familiarize yourself with all of the automation installed in the aircraft. For aircraft flown IFR, with integrated navigator autopilot systems, determine the proper setup for every approach, published miss, and hold supported. A cheat sheet listing all possible scenarios, detailing all steps to be taken, can be exceedingly helpful. It is easy to misprogram these devices, and recovery in the heat of performing the actual procedure near to the ground can be daunting and potentially dangerous. Practice procedures using a PC-based (or other) simulator if available for your aircraft-specific system and configuration. Then fly the procedures in the actual aircraft on a nice day to reinforce both your old and newly learned skills. The more forgiving environment will afford you the opportunity to refine and perfect your techniques without any ATC yelling (or worse).

## Mitigation 2: Perfection

Ensure the aircraft is as close to perfect as possible.

Never fly an aircraft with failed equipment, unless there is a manufacturer certified MEL precisely specifying applicable limitations. Even assuming an MEL, the possibility of higher pilot workload and loss of redundancy demands considering other options. For example, to mitigate for the loss of a working autopilot, add a copilot (if flying single-pilot) or fly only in nice weather. In the case of the CJ3 and CJ4, the MEL explicitly requires a second crewmember if the autopilot is inoperative. Failure of one of the two radios in the airplane may require the addition of a battery powered portable radio or limiting the flight to VFR conditions. In general, flying an aircraft that is not 100 percent operational takes the flight a step closer to declaring an emergency. At the very least, should the unexpected or undesired happen, your workload will be heavier, and options fewer.

## Mitigation 3: Training

When it comes to recurrent training, more is more.

Avail yourself of recurrent training (more than just the FAA minimum), especially when it relates to something important in the aircraft breaking during instrument flight. In multi-engine aircraft, simulated single-engine approaches to minimums are typical, but it is more useful to practice failures that require flying by hand with reduced instrument functionality. In the jet airplane, a dual generator failure triggers a similar sequence of events because the energy stored in the ship's battery is only enough to run the normal complement of automation and instrumentation for about 10 minutes. Hand flying and partial panel scanning is the only way to make it to the runway before the power runs out.

It's also advisable to conduct some of the training in a simulator airplane. The simulator is very good for representing most instrument flying challenges, and is by far more efficient than the real thing. Safer, too.

# Mitigation 4: "Danger, Will Robinson!"

Take extra care when conducting training in the aircraft.

Airplane salvage yards are littered with the wreckage of simulated emergencies that turned into the real thing. Think twice before shutting off an engine to simulate an in-flight problem.

The twin-engine Beech Baron training flight crash briefly mentioned in Chapter 11 is a case in point. Amazingly enough the two instructors on board, one prepping the other for a multi-engine instructor rating test, concluded it would be a good idea to conduct a single-engine approach to landing with the totally operational left engine shut down. The result, a near-deadly crash landing at the threshold of the runway because the flight test candidate both lowered the flaps to "land" and failed to maintain airspeed above $V_{MC}$ (minimum controllable airspeed).[1] Even assuming the motivation for shutting down the engine was something different than saving money (e.g., single-engine approach training), would a left engine standing by, idling, have done a better or safer job of demonstrating single-engine performance while also addressing any student inadequacies? Yes! Thankfully, no one on board was injured.

The same risk applies when practicing emergency procedures in helicopters. Performing flawless autorotations in case of engine failures is often the mainstay focus of recurrent training. But the training itself can present its own dangers. *Never actually shut the engine down in the course of conducting this maneuver*, and be mindful of the risks in actually performing an autorotation all the way to the ground (full-down autos). Approximately 21 percent of helicopter accidents occur in the course of training gone wrong.[2]

Recalling Simuflite's simulator training policy—"We fail only one system, create one emergency, at a time. It's up to the student to create all the other emergencies."—sometimes in the heat of training, the trainee takes actions that make things much worse, like accidentally shutting down the one remaining good engine during a simulated engine fire scenario. In the simulator airplane, that's a "retraining needed" box checked in the pilot's training record. In the real airplane, well, that's perhaps game over. The possibility of induced and cascading problems occurring while training in

---

[1] Generally, single-engine approaches flown in twin engine airplanes are conducted with flaps set to "approach."

[2] Roskop, Lee. "U.S. Rotorcraft Acident Data and Statistics." FAA & Industry Avionics Forum. January 31, 2012.

the real aircraft suggests great reward for assuring an environment where there are more rather than fewer options, should things not work out as expected.

## Mitigation 5: Speak up

The Baron crash notwithstanding, in almost all cases flying with a trained flight instructor familiar with the equipment and training syllabus is the right answer. The training experience will be much more helpful and safe. But having an instructor on board does not mean the pilot receiving training should be any less vigilant or acquiescent, accepting a subordinate role in the face of impending doom. Don't let the training experience devolve into something scary. The same idea applies to serving as subordinate crewmember while flying an aircraft requiring two pilots. Yes, the captain is the captain, the final authority. It is also true that the first officer is the first officer, duty bound to assure a safe flight. Speak up if there is a concern.

## Mitigation 6: Improvising

There should be nothing done during the course of normal flying that has not been previously analyzed, rehearsed, and competently demonstrated under controlled conditions. Yes, very occasionally, the situation demands spontaneous invention to solve a problem. The United Airlines Flight 232 that crash-landed in Sioux City on July 19, 1989, is a case in point. When all three hydraulic systems failed due to an uncontained failure of the airplane's number two (tail-mounted) engine, the crew improvised a way to control the airplane using engine thrust only—the aerodynamic control surfaces completely dead. The idea worked, but not perfectly. Of the 269 people on board, 111 died during the landing attempt.

Most of the time, it is improvisation that causes the problem.

Helicopter pilots are notorious for succumbing to this, largely because of the amazing versatility of the machine, and the many shiny objects that serve as lures. What's more fun than a spontaneous landing on a high-elevation mountain-top pinnacle without any significant pinnacle and/or high-altitude ops training? Caution required? Helicopters perform very differently in thinner air and natural pinnacles can be uneven, slippery, and rough. That's not to mention the unpredictable winds around mountains.

Improvised airplane events follow a similar pattern. While airplanes can't land on pinnacles, they can takeoff overweight and out of CG. Welcome to test pilot school. Less typical, but equally dramatic, is some kind of off-field landing dalliance involving an unprepared surface. In the classic 1965 movie *Those Magnificent Men in their Flying Machines*, the French air race competitor lands repeatedly in appropriate places to enjoy a romp in the haystack.[3] Affairs are dangerous, but fields not properly surveyed can be fatal. What all have in common is a trial and error philosophy that, acknowledged or not, implies unpredictable results.

## Mitigation 7: Worry

Some worry during flying is a good thing, especially when preparing for and conducting the actual flight. This nagging friend can save your life.

Although most of us navigate with givens, certainties that serve us well, the resulting good outcomes that frequently result depend on luck to some extent, things going according to plan. We drive our car to work expecting to arrive safely, without accident or injury. Most of us walk the streets feeling safe, without risk of robbery, assault, or worse. But every so often a reckless driver or migrating moose crosses our path wreaking havoc. And, sadly, muggings still occur in some places. Would worrying a little more help? It depends. If it inspires vigilance, the answer is probably yes. If it degrades into paranoia and panic, the answer is probably no. More germane is determining whether the outcome of worry translates into useful action, something that can be done in real time to avoid the collision or attack.

In flying many factors, like weather, that affect the probability of success theoretically remain within the pilot's control. Random events sometimes characteristic of day-to-day living don't play a big role. No one can control the weather, but it is possible to understand, monitor, and, within limits, predict its behavior. There are excellent tools for this, many now accessible in the cockpit. Prior to and once underway, the pilot may worry that the weather may change, be worse than expected. They then regularly check the METARs and TAF information en route and at the destination and alternate airports. Should the new information be substantially different from what was expected, and in a bad way, action can be taken, including an early deviation to the alternate airport or somewhere else where the weather is better. Worry leads to updated information, leads to appropriate action.

The same idea applies to fuel reserves. Despite excellent planning, the pilot worries that fuel reserves may not be adequate. Checks of progress, actual winds against forecast, and other factors (e.g., changes in routing that

---

[3] Competitor Number 12: Pierre Dubois, flying "Santos-Dumont Domoiselle."

may be important to making the distance with adequate margins) are made. Reality check accomplished, the pilot may elect to continue the flight, or deviate from the original plan to preserve safety.

Mechanical anomalies that develop while en route also should prompt worry. Even relatively minor problems can portend trouble. We had a curious failure that affected the CJ3's FMS weight on wheels (WOW) clock. The only display affected was the progress page shown on the FMS. This page provides average speed and completed mileage information among other historical trip metrics. Much of the information on the page was wrong, including lower than expected logged average speeds. Most concerning, the WOW clock was showing an inaccurate takeoff time. But why worry? All other systems in the airplane were working perfectly.

The FMS WOW clock's malfunction suggested that one of the WOW squat switches in the landing gear assembly also may have failed. Knowing that the squat switches are used to trigger a number of airplane system functions including the progress page's WOW clock activation, prudence demanded identifying other systems possibly affected and the extent to which any of them were critical. Ticking down the list, we discovered that the antiskid system uses the squat switches as inputs to various antiskid functions. Conclusion: the airplane's antiskid function might not work properly. Action taken: determine if the destination airport's runway is sufficiently long to allow for a safe landing with antiskid failed. Prepare for possible erratic operation of the system. Outcome: happily, the sleuthing assured a safe landing well within the runway length limits. When the airplane pulled left at touchdown, we were ready to correct aggressively using right rudder.[4]

Unlike the CJ3 experience, most of the time the flying goes exactly as planned. This is one of the reasons going to simulator school is so valuable. For many pilots, school offers the only insight into the possible (improbable) problems that may need to be addressed in the course of flying. What school doesn't impart is that innate *yellow alert* feeling, usually hairs standing on the back of the neck, warning things might not be quite right. That's what developing a healthy dose of worry is all about.

---

[4] Although there was a defect in the FMS related to WOW, a bad brake accumulator component, not the squat switch, ultimately explained the braking problem manifest on landing. Sometimes the right answer results from an incorrect diagnosis.

## Mitigation 8: Curiosity

How do you make a truly *befarkeling* experience useful?[5] Be curious. In flying, puzzling things happen. The automation works differently than expected, weather doesn't play out as forecasted, the airplane itself flies differently on some days, the event is often benign, even beneficial; who wants to argue with success? Why not just declare victory and move on? On days when things don't go well, there is more incentive to find out why. Unfortunately, some pilots don't connect a lack of understanding with the bad outcome, making way for a repetition in the future.

Most of my puzzlements have occurred while managing the automation. The procedures ATC has us conduct are very complicated, the programming not always intuitive. The new satellite-based RNAV LPV approaches, for example, offer many *why did it do that* moments, especially when conducting the procedure from an initial approach fix that requires the automation to guide the altitude step down prior to intercepting the final approach course and glide path.

There are many other sources of confusion. I am embarrassed to report that it took me years of jet flying before learning (from a senior captain) that it was a good idea to keep some forward pressure on the yoke during the takeoff roll. This despite experiencing significant nose wandering during the early part of the takeoff. *Note to file:* jets and taildraggers demand a different technique. Makes sense, now. Just one of the many bemusements I have puzzled over in my flying.

Independent of the source of the confusion, researching the applicable explanation can pay big dividends. Even when things work out well, without truly understanding what happened, there's no guarantee that all endings will be so happy. Hope springs eternal, but knowing is the safer bet.

## Mitigation 9: Humility

Humility is the key to self-preservation. Be humble! There really is nothing more dangerous than a big ego in the cockpit. No amount of smarts, skills, or cleverness offsets this nemesis. Even stubbornness, a close cousin to big ego, is less menacing, largely because stubborn people tend to succumb to their belief system while egomaniacs succumb to their unwavering belief in themselves independent of merit. If ever there was one mitigation to embrace, keeping ego in check is it.

---

[5] Southern term I learned from my first wife to indicate some form of inexplicable occurrence.

Ego-related problems are more acute in flying because so much of the activity revolves around good judgment, evidence-based criteria, and a willingness to accept and internalize new information. Paramount to success is the ability to admit error and a lack of invincibility. The egomaniacs and narcissists among us aren't very good at this. Rigorous preflight planning, for example, can feel foreign to these types, because the high confidence levels that accompany egomania don't allow for conventional process. Too pedestrian! "I am good, I can wing it," represents this kind of thinking.

There is another aggravating factor that puts pilots with big egos at a big disadvantage. No one wants to help them! Who would? They're stereotypical know-it-alls. Perhaps the worst drag on safety is that, in the unlikely event the subject displays openness to advice, there are few who'd dare or want to provide it.

Fortunately, there are actually relatively few documented cases of totally unbridled ego in flying. I personally know of only one example, a pilot who flew competition gliders at Sugarbush. Outwardly bold, ambitious, fearless, a person that impressed the pretty girls, but behind the scenes he was surprisingly ignorant of the flying discipline in general and the potential dangers of the sport. Compounding the problem, the glider he used to compete, while very high performance, also was notoriously twitchy. Sadly, he died in a competition, bypassing multiple safe landing sites for a last desperate attempt to thermal away from the trees at low altitude.

We all share some of the characteristics of this glider pilot. What matters is that we try, naturally or by design, to keep our worst egomaniacal tendencies in check. Knowing that big egos in flying tend to self-select for extinction, matching confidence with training, knowledge, experience, and demonstrated proficiency is by far the more prudent course. In short, I'm sorry, but, it's not all about you.

## Mitigation 10: Fortitude

Never give up! Easier to say than do, especially in the heat of a serious problem. Yet, there is little argument that battling to the end is the right answer. So, how to prepare. One approach is to train, practice the correct responses to the most likely serious problems while at school. The crisis happens, training kicks in, proper actions are taken, a successful conclusion is assured. Helpful, especially in the context of increasing confidence, but not necessarily a predictor of success in the event of something serious befalling the flight. Most people don't really know how they will react in a crisis. Some degree of panic, an initial inability to take conscious useful action, will always be present, at first. But with panic, sometimes, comes a more sinister demon: helplessness. Bad problems are depressing, the temptation to give up, sometimes, perhaps, overwhelming.

At the risk of being lugubrious, I present my top five most depressing scenarios for consideration:

1) An uncontained fire on board while crossing the Atlantic Ocean.
2) Loss of all electrical power while flying cross-country at night in bad weather.
3) A dual-engine failure over mountainous terrain.
4) Structure failure in flight significantly limiting the controllability of the aircraft.
5) A loss of control event in bad weather.

All of these situations are bad, but they are not hopeless. In every case, there are many things a crew can do, must do, to increase the chances of survival. In the fire scenario, fight the fire if practical, it's also time to issue a distress call, emphasizing the airplane's coordinates and intentions. The ELT is next, activated to alert the authorities responsible for launching a rescue. Point the airplane in the direction of land, if that makes sense. And, prepare the passengers for ditching. For the loss of both engines over mountains, declaring an emergency, locating and performing the items on the dual-engine failure checklist, and establishing a glide path to the nearest airport, or at least more level terrain, seems like the right idea. Seeking radar vectors to aid in the search for a suitable landing site may also help improve the odds. The other scenarios have a similar list of actions that can make things better.

The common thread of each one of these hypothetical bad day events is that clear, definitive, and correct actions can improve the outcome. Why not try? Giving up is bound to make the situation worse.

Unfortunately, rising to the occasion can be very difficult for some if not most people. Despite the convincing intellectual argument in favor of survival, fatalism can win out over fighting the good fight. That's why it is helpful to mentally rehearse, and actively simulate, scenarios like those mentioned. So, make your own list. Contemplating how you will feel, and react, in a crisis can be a good predictor of a positive outcome. It's not that you will do exactly what you imagined you would do during the thought experiment. More valuable is that there will be a familiar benchmark for comparison should the real crisis occur, most likely in the form of a not so gentle reminder to stop feeling sorry for yourself and fight on. (Fight on.)

## Conclusion

This is certainly not an exclusive list. There are undoubtedly other equally good mitigations to aid in the cause of making flying safe and enjoyable. The common intent, however, is to facilitate a safe learning process by which, independent of skill level and experience, all who embrace it will get better. But, are we done?

I often tell my more fearful flyer friends not to worry, "We have a no crash policy." It has proven to be curiously effective. Some passengers, seemingly under the impression until then that crashing is socially acceptable in certain circles, visibly relax. Anxiety levels drop, the flight transformed from a grin and bear it endurance test to something more benign, even fun.

The calming effect shouldn't be taken lightly. Nor should the words themselves. A true no-crash policy implies that everything else takes a back seat. What is paramount is avoiding an accident risking death and injury. While the mitigations advance safe learning, commitment to a no crash policy demands more.

In my experience, the best, safest pilots and crews have in common a genuine respect for colleagues, passengers, and the aircraft they fly. All else seems to follow. Why? Could it be that that respect (and mutual respect) indicates other virtues, resulting in reflective, collegiate, caring, earnest, selfless, prudent, and, ultimately, safer behavior? I've noticed that reflective people welcome and embrace challenges to their prevailing beliefs and views. Those who are collegiate, seek advice from others. Caring means having empathy for those charges in custody. To be earnest requires investing whatever is necessary to develop a complete understanding of the challenges presented. Selflessness puts the interests of others ahead of yours. Prudence naturally follows the other virtues in play. Of all the indicators, including superior skillset and experience, there is no better predictor of a safe flight than the respect and mutual respect enjoyed among those involved.

# Acronyms

| | |
|---|---|
| ADS-B | automatic dependent surveillance-broadcast |
| ARTCC | air route traffic control center |
| ATC | air traffic control |
| ATIS | automatic terminal information service |
| CAT | clear air turbulence |
| CAT I | Category I approach minimums |
| CAT II | Category II approach minimums |
| CAT IIIb | Category IIIb approach minimums |
| CAVU | ceilings and visibilities unlimited |
| CG | center of gravity |
| CPDLC | controller-pilot data link communications |
| EFIS | electronic fight information system |
| FAA | Federal Aviation Administration |
| FAR | Federal Aviation Regulation |
| FD | flight director |
| FBO | fixed base operator |
| FMS | flight management system |
| FFS | full flight simulator |
| GPS | Global Positioning System |
| HSI | horizontal situation indicator |
| IAS | indicated airspeed |
| ICAO | international civil aviation administration |
| IFR | instrument flight rules |
| IMC | instrument meteorological conditions |
| JFK | John F. Kennedy International Airport |
| LIFR | low instrument flight rules |
| LAHSO | land and hold short operations |
| METAR | aviation routine weather report |
| MFD | multi-function display |

| NASA | National Aeronautics and Space Administration |
|------|------|
| NDB | non-directional beacon |
| NextGen | Next Generation Air Traffic System |
| NEXRAD | Next Generation Radar |
| NOTAM | notice to airmen |
| OAT | outside air temperature |
| PFD | primary flight display |
| RNAV | area navigation |
| RVR | runway visual range |
| RVSM | reduced vertical separation minimum |
| STAR | standard instrument arrival |
| SID | standard instrument departure |
| TAS | true airspeed |
| TCAS | traffic alert and collision avoidance system |
| TRACON | terminal radar approach control |
| UTC | Coordinated Universal Time (also known as Z-Time or Zulu) |
| VFR | visual flight rules |
| VMC | visual meteorological conditions |
| VNAV | vertical navigation |
| VOR | very high frequency omni-directional radio range |
| WAAS | wide area augmentation system |

# A Brief Glossary

**14 CFR Part 91:** Defines the operation of small non-commercial aircraft within the US (many other countries defer to these rules as well). These rules set conditions, such as weather, under which the aircraft may operate.

**14 CFR Part 121:** Part 121 applies to scheduled airline operators. Any commercial airline that you would fly on, as a passenger, is a "Part 121 airline." In general, the rules governing Part 121 operations are the strictest of all.

**14 CFR Part 135:** Part 135 applies to commuter and charter operations.

**Aerodynamic stall:** An aerodynamic condition in which the angle of attack, the angle at which the relative wind strikes the airfoil, becomes so steep the air can no longer flow smoothly over the airfoil. When an airfoil stalls, it stops producing lift.

**Air route traffic control center (ARTCC):** A facility established to provide air traffic control service to aircraft operating on IFR flight plans within controlled airspace and principally during the en route phase of flight. When equipment capabilities and controller workload permit, certain advisory/assistance services may also be provided to VFR aircraft.

**Angle of attack:** The acute angle formed between the chord line of an airfoil and the direction of the air that strikes the airfoil.

**Area navigation (RNAV):** A method of aircraft electronic navigation that permits aircraft operations on any desired flight path within the coverage of station-referenced navigation signals, or within the limits of a self-contained system's capability. These station-referenced navigation signals are referred to as *waypoints*; the RNAV flight path goes from one waypoint to the next.

**Automatic dependent surveillance-broadcast (ADS-B):** A surveillance technology in which an aircraft determines its position via satellite navigation and periodically broadcasts it, enabling it to be tracked.

**Aviation Routine Weather Report (METAR):** Observation of current surface weather reported in a standard international format.

**Cat I approach:** A precision instrument approach and landing with a decision height no lower than 200 feet and with either a visibility no less than 2,400 feet, or a RVR no less than 1,800 feet.

**Cat II approach:** A precision instrument approach and landing with a decision height lower than 200 feet but no lower than 100 feet and a RVR no less than 1,200 feet.

**Cat IIIb approach:** An ILS approach to an appropriately certified runway which has an alert of 50 feet and a minimum RVR of 600 feet.

**Ceiling:** The height above the earth's surface of the lowest layer of clouds or obscuring phenomena reported as *broken, overcast,* or *obscuration,* and not classified as *thin* or *partial* (per 14 CFR Part 1).

- **Clear:** No clouds below 12,000 feet; used mainly within North America, and indicates a station that is at least partly automated.

- **Scattered:** A cloud layer that covers between 3/8 and 1/2 of the sky.

- **Broken:** The height of the lowest layer of clouds, when the sky is broken. Clouds that cover between 6/10 and 9/10 of the sky.

- **Overcast:** The height of the lowest layer of clouds, when the sky is overcast. Clouds that cover 10/10 of the sky.

- **Sky clear:** No cloud/sky clear is used worldwide but in North America it is used to indicate a human generated report.

**Center of gravity (CG):** The point in an object at which all of the weight is considered to be concentrated. The algebraic sum of the moments about the center of gravity is zero. The center of gravity may be expressed in inches from the datum or in percent of the mean aerodynamic chord. Center of gravity may also be thought of as the point within an object about which all the moments trying to rotate the object are balanced.

**Class A airspace:** Generally, that airspace from 18,000 feet MSL up to and including FL 600, including the airspace overlying the waters within 12 nautical miles of the coast of the 48 contiguous States and Alaska; and designated international airspace beyond 12 nautical miles of the coast of the 48 contiguous States and Alaska within areas of domestic radio navigational signal or ATC radar coverage, and within which domestic procedures are applied.

**Class B airspace:** Generally, that airspace from the surface to 10,000 feet MSL surrounding the nation's busiest airports in terms of IFR operations or passenger enplanements. The configuration of each Class B airspace is individually tailored and consists of a surface area and two or more layers (some Class B airspace areas resemble upside down wedding cakes), and is designed to contain all published instrument procedures once an aircraft enters the airspace. An ATC clearance is required for all aircraft to operate in the area, and all aircraft so cleared receive separation services within the airspace. The cloud clearance requirement for VFR operations is "clear of clouds."

**Class C airspace:** Generally, that airspace from the surface to 4,000 feet above the airport elevation (charted in MSL) surrounding those airports that have an operational control tower, are serviced by radar approach control, and that have a certain number of IFR operations or passenger enplanements. Although the configuration of each Class C airspace area is individually tailored, the airspace usually consists of a 5 NM radius core surface area that extends from the surface up to 4,000 feet above the airport elevation, and a 10 NM radius shelf area that extends from 1,200 feet to 4,000 feet above the airport elevation.

**Class D airspace:** Generally, that airspace from the surface to 2,500 feet above the airport elevation (charted in MSL) surrounding those airports that have an operational control tower. The configuration of each Class D airspace area is individually tailored, and when instrument procedures are published, the airspace will normally be designed to contain the procedures.

**Class E airspace:** Generally, if the airspace is not Class A, Class B, Class C, or Class D, and it is controlled airspace, it is Class E airspace.

**Class G airspace:** Generally that airspace that is uncontrolled, and has not been designated as Class A, Class B, Class C, Class D, or Class E airspace.

**Controller-pilot data link communications (CPDLC):** A two-way digital VHF air/ground communications system that conveys textual air traffic control messages between controllers and pilots.

**Conventional landing gear:** Conventional landing gear, or tailwheel-type landing gear, is an aircraft undercarriage consisting of two main wheels forward of the center of gravity and a small wheel or skid to support the tail.

**Coordinated universal time (UTC):** Time corrected for the seasonal variations in the earth's rotation about the sun. Coordinated universal time is also known as universal time coordinated (thus UTC), Greenwich mean time (GMT), and Zulu time.

**Flight management system (FMS):** A computer system that uses a large database to allow routes to be preprogrammed and loaded. The system is constantly updated with respect to position accuracy by reference to conventional navigation aids. The sophisticated program and its associated database insures that the most appropriate aids are automatically selected during the information update cycle.

**Global Positioning System (GPS):** A navigation system using a constellation of between twenty-four and thirty-two satellites in orbit around the Earth. Each satellite transmits precise microwave signals that enable a GPS receiver to determine its location, speed, direction, and the current time.

**Instrument flight rules (IFR):** Rules and regulations established by the Federal Aviation Administration to govern flight under conditions in which flight by outside visual reference is not safe. Instrument flight rules govern the flight of aircraft along the federally-controlled airways and airports, and this flight is directed and controlled by operators on the ground. Flight according to instrument flight rules depends upon flying by reference to instruments in the cockpit, and navigation is done by reference to electronic signals.

**Instrument landing system (ILS):** A special type of electronic guidance system used to allow aircraft to land when the ceiling and visibility are too low for a safe visual approach to the runway. An ILS is made up of four basic parts: the localizer, glide slope, marker beacons, and approach lights. The localizer produces a narrow electronic path extending out along the center line of the instrument runway, to direct the pilot laterally as they approach the runway.

**Instrument meteorological conditions (IMC):** Meteorological conditions expressed in terms of visibility, distance from cloud, and ceiling less than the minimums specified for visual meteorological conditions.

**International Civil Aviation Organization (ICAO):** A specialized agency of the United Nations whose objective is to develop the principles and techniques of international air navigation and to foster planning and development of international civil air transport.

**Lift capacity:** The amount of lift available usually expressed as a coefficient relative to a maximum value.

**Minimum controllable airspeed ($V_{MC}$):** The lowest airspeed at which an airplane is controllable with one engine developing takeoff power and the propeller on the other engine windmilling. $V_{MC}$ is marked on an airspeed indicator with a red radial line.

**Multi-function display (MFD):** A supplementary display with the capability to depict all information provided by the PFD should the PFD malfunction. Normally, MFD information depicts routing, engine parameter, weather, traffic, and enroute waypoint/leg metrics relative to distance and estimated crossing time.

**Next Generation Radar (NEXRAD) system:** A network of Weather Surveillance Radar-1988 Doppler (WSR-88D) sites situated throughout the US as well as selected overseas sites. The NEXRAD system is a joint venture of U.S. government departments, and the agencies with control over it are the NWS, the Air Force Weather Agency (AFWA), and the FAA. Convection and precipitation data collected from WSR-88D returns are used to prepare weather radar products that can be supplied to the cockpit via a broadcast weather service.

**Nondirectional beacon (NDB):** The ADF/NDB navigation system is one of the oldest air navigation systems still in use today. It works from a simple radio navigation concept: a ground-based radio transmitter (the NDB) sends an omnidirectional signal that an aircraft loop antenna receives.

**Primary flight display (PFD):** A computer screen (LCD or CRT) that electronically displays flight information. The PFD replaces the round dial altimeter, airspeed indicator, attitude gyro, heading indicator, vertical speed indicator, and turn coordinator.

**Reference landing speed ($V_{REF}$):** The speed of the airplane, in a specified landing configuration, at the point where it descends through the 50-foot height in the determination of the landing distance.

**Sugarbush Airport:** A private 2,575-foot asphalt surface airport located in the Mad River Valley near Warren, Vermont. The airport is open to the public offering soaring rides and instruction (through Surgarbush Soaring) during the spring, summer and fall months.

**Terminal aerodrome forecast (TAF):** A report established for the 5 statute mile radius around an airport which uses the same descriptors and abbreviations as the METAR report.

**Terminal radar approach control (TRACON):** A facility that provides radar and nonradar services at major airports. The primary responsibility of each TRACON is to ensure safe separation of aircraft transitioning from departure to cruise flight or from cruise to a landing approach.

**Traffic Collision Avoidance System (TCAS):** or traffic alert and collision avoidance system designed to reduce the incidence of mid-air collisions between aircraft. The technology is largely based on a transponder radio transmission exchange of position, heading, and velocity information between aircraft in near proximity.

**Tricycle landing gear:** Tricycle gear is a type of aircraft undercarriage, or landing gear, arranged in a tricycle fashion. The tricycle arrangement has a single nose wheel in the front, and two or more main wheels slightly aft of the center of gravity. Tricycle gear aircraft are the easiest to take-off, land and taxi, and consequently the configuration is the most widely used on aircraft.

**VHF omni directional radio (VOR):** A type of short-range radio navigation system for aircraft, enabling aircraft with a receiving unit to determine their position and stay on course by receiving radio signals transmitted by a network of fixed ground radio beacons.

**Visual flight rules (VFR):** Flight rules adopted by the Federal Aviation Administration to govern aircraft flight when the pilot has visual reference to the ground at all times. VFR operations specify the amount of ceiling (the distance between the surface of the earth and the base of the clouds) and the visibility (the horizontal distance the pilot can see) that the pilot must have in order to operate according to these rules. When the weather conditions are not such that the pilot can operate according to VFR, he or she must use another set of rules, IFR.

**Visual meteorological conditions (VMC):** Meteorological conditions expressed in terms of visibility, distance from cloud, and ceiling meeting or exceeding the minimums specified for VFR.

## Aircraft

**Bell 206B JetRanger III:** The latest, most refined, member of a family of two-bladed, single-engine, light, turbine powered JetRanger branded helicopters, manufactured by Bell Helicopter in Mirabel, Quebec.

**Boeing-Stearman PT-17:** The PT-17 is a variant of the Stearman Model 75, a biplane used as a military trainer aircraft, of which at least 10,626 were built in the United States during the 1930s and 1940s. Stearman Aircraft became a subsidiary of Boeing in 1934.

**Cessna 150:** The Cessna 150 is a two-seat tricycle gear general aviation all metal airplane that was designed for flight training, touring and personal use.

**Cessna 182 Skylane:** A four-seat, single-engine light all metal airplane built by Cessna in Wichita, Kansas.

**Cessna 310:** A six-seat, low-wing, all-metal, twin-engine monoplane that was produced by Cessna between 1954 and 1980. It was the first twin-engine aircraft that Cessna put into production after World War II.

**Cessna CE-525 Citation Jet:** A series of light business jets designed and built by the Cessna Aircraft Company. Its variants are marketed under the CJ, CJ1, CJ1+, M2, CJ2, CJ2+, CJ3, CJ3+, and CJ4 names.

**Cessna L-19/O-1 Bird Dog:** The first all-metal fixed-wing aircraft ordered for and used by the United States Army. Originally used as liaison and observation aircraft during World War II.

**Cessna T-210:** The Cessna T-210 is a turbocharged variant of the Cessna 210 Centurion six-seat, high-performance, retractable-gear, single-engine, high-wing general aviation aircraft which was first flown in January 1957 and produced by Cessna until 1985.

**Grumman G-44 Widgeon:** A small, five-person, twin-engine amphibious aircraft produced from 1941 to 1955. It was designated "J4F" by the United States Navy and Coast Guard and "OA-14" by the United States Army Air Corps and United States Army Air Forces.

**Lockheed P-38 Lightning:** A World War II-era American twin piston-engine fighter aircraft. Developed to a United States Army Air Corps requirement, the P-38 had distinctive twin booms and a central nacelle containing the cockpit and armament.

**McDonnell Douglas MD-11:** An American three-engine, medium- to long-range wide-body jet airliner, manufactured by McDonnell Douglas and, later, by Boeing Commercial Airplanes. Based on the DC-10, it features a stretched fuselage, increased wingspan with winglets, refined airfoils on the wing and smaller tailplane, new engines, and increased use of composite materials.

**North American P-51 Mustang:** The North American Aviation P-51 Mustang is an American long-range, single-seat fighter and fighter-bomber used during World War II and the Korean War, among other conflicts.

**Piper PA-18 Super Cub:** A two-seat, single-engine, metal and fabric constructed monoplane.

**Piper PA-23 Aztec:** A four-to-six-seat, twin-engine, light all-metal retractable gear aircraft produced for the general aviation market but also saw service with the United States Navy and other countries' military forces in small numbers.

**Robinson R22:** The Robinson R22 is a two-bladed, single-engine, light utility helicopter manufactured by Robinson Helicopter Company. The two-seat R22 was designed in 1973 by Frank Robinson and has been in production since 1979.

**Robinson R44:** The Robinson R44 is a four-seat, light helicopter produced by Robinson Helicopter Company since 1992. Based on the company's two-seat Robinson R22, the R44 features hydraulically assisted flight controls. It was first flown on 31 March 1990 and received FAA certification in December 1992, with the first delivery in February 1993.

**Schweizer SGS 1-26:** A single-seat, mid-wing, metal and fabric glider that was built by Schweizer Aircraft in Elmira, New York.

**Schweizer SGS 1-34:** A single-seat, mid/high-wing, all-metal glider that was built by Schweizer Aircraft in Elmira, New York.

**Supermarine Spitfire:** A British single-seat fighter aircraft that was used by the Royal Air Force and many other Allied countries before, during, and after World War II.

# Bibliography

Carey, Bill. "Parliament Approves Single European Sky '2+' Package." *AINonline*, March 12, 2014. https://www.ainonline.com/aviation-news/air-transport/2014-03-12/parliament-approves-single-european-sky-2-package

Federal Aviation Administration. *Pilot's Handbook of Aeronautical Knowledge*. FAA-H-8083-25B. Newcastle, WA: Aviation Supplies & Academics, Inc., 2016.

German Aerospace Center (DLR). "DLR to Build Replica of the World's First Series-Produced Aircraft." February 11, 2019. https://www.dlr.de/dlr/en/desktopdefault.aspx/tabid-10280/385_read-16705/year-all/#/gallery/21944

Lukasch, Bernd. "From Lilienthal to the Wrights." Otto Lilienthal Museum. Accessed January 8, 2012. http://www.lilienthal-museum.de/olma/ewright.htm

Roskop, Lee. "U.S. Rotorcraft Accident Data and Statistics." Lecture, Lee's Summit, MO, FAA & Industry Avionics Rotorcraft Forum, January 31, 2012. https://www.aea.net/events/rotorcraft/files/us_rotorcraft_accident_data_and_statistics.pdf

Silke Forbes, Mara Lederman, and Zhe Yuan. "Do Airlines Pad Their Schedules?" Rotman School of Management Working Paper No. 3065986. Toronto: University of Toronto Rotman School of Management. https://papers.ssrn.com/sol3/papers.cfm?abstract_id=3065986

Van Dam, Andrew. "The Blimp Industry is Changing, Right Over Our Noses." *Washington Post*, June 9, 2018.

Wakabayashi, Daisuke. "Flying Taxis May Be Years Away, but the Groundwork Is Accelerating." *New York Times*, February 27, 2018.

# About the Author

Innovative aviation author Adam L. Alpert holds FAA commercial certifications in glider, single-engine airplane (land and sea), multi-engine airplane (land and sea), and helicopter. He also is type rated in all Cessna CE-525 Citation Jet aircraft.

His personal fleet includes a Boeing Stearman biplane, Cessna L-19 Bird Dog, Grumman G-44 Widgeon, Cessna 180 Skywagon, Cub Crafters X-Cub, Bell 206B JetRanger III helicopter—and he has experience flying over 40 other types.

Alpert served as vice president of BioTek Instruments, Inc., (www.biotek.com), a large multinational life science tools company, until his retirement in 2018, and holds B.S. degrees in computer science and mathematics from the University of Vermont, 1981.

He lives with his wife in Delray Beach, Florida.

# Index